T5-BAO-865

GLOBALIZATION
AND
HIGHER EDUCATION

GLOBALIZATION
AND
HIGHER EDUCATION

Jaishree K. Odin and Peter T. Manicas, Editors

UNIVERSITY OF HAWAI'I PRESS

Honolulu

© 2004 University of Hawai'i Press
All rights reserved
Printed in the United States of America

07 06 05 04 03 02   6 5 4 3 2 1

Library of Congress Cataloging-in-Publication Data

Globalization and higher education / Jaishree K. Odin and
Peter T. Manicas, editors.
    p. cm.
  Includes bibliographical references and index.
  ISBN 0-8248-2782-1 (cloth : alk. paper) —
  ISBN 0-8248-2826-7 (paper : alk. paper)
  1. Education, Higher. 2. Globalization.
  I. Odin, Jaishree Kak. II. Manicas, Peter T.
LB2322.2.G55 2004
378—dc22
                2003061621

University of Hawai'i Press books are printed on
acid-free paper and meet the guidelines for permanence
and durability of the Council on Library Resources

Designed by Trina Stahl

Printed by the Maple-Vail Book Manufacturing Group

Contents

Foreword
Deane Neubauer · vii

Acknowledgments · xi

Introduction
Peter T. Manicas and Jaishree K. Odin · xiii

Part I. The Larger Context
1. Higher Education in an Era of Globalization: What Is at Stake?
Peter Wagner · 7
2. The Withering of the Professoriate: Corporate Universities and the Internet
Michael Margolis · 24
3. The Neo-Liberal Paradigm and Higher Education: A Critique
Jan Currie · 42

Part II. A Closer Look
4. Globalization, Higher Education, and Markets
Charles W. Smith · 69
5. Lessons from the For-Profit Side
Richard S. Ruch · 82
6. Globalization, College Participation, and Socioeconomic Mobility
Scott L. Thomas · 104

Part III. Implications for Pedagogy
7. The Erosion of Face-to-Face Pedagogy: A Jeremiad
John J. McDermott · 131

8. The Used Car Dealership and the Church: On Resolving the Identity of the University
   Charles Karelis · 140

9. New Technologies and the Reconstitution of the University
   Jaishree K. Odin · 147

PART IV. SOME REGIONAL RESPONSES TO GLOBALIZATION

10. Interaction of Global Politics and Higher Education
    Su Hao · 167

11. Knowledge and Higher Education in Latin America: Incommodious Commodities?
    Leonardo Garnier · 181

12. Corporate, Technological, Epistemic, and Democratic Challenges: Mapping the Political Economy of University Futures
    Sohail Inayatullah · 202

PART V. THE FUTURE OF HIGHER EDUCATION

13. The Changing Craft Nature of Higher Education: A Story of the Self-Reorganizing University
    Tom P. Abeles · 223

14. Does the University Have a Future?
    Gerard Delanty · 241

Selected Bibliography · 255
List of Contributors · 259
Index · 261

FOREWORD

AT ITS FOUNDING in 2002, the Globalization Research Center (GRC) at the University of Hawai'i defined its mission as identifying the dynamics of globalization and analyzing its impacts. One vehicle toward doing so was the convening of various "dialogic" conferences organized around globalization and its many problematics. The conference that forms the basis for this volume focuses on higher education as one of these.

The "Globalization and Higher Education" conference was preceded by an initial conference oriented around the emerging discourses of public institutions in the policy space previously and familiarly occupied by market institutions and the state. Much like the participants in this higher education conference, the public institution group, convened by James Dator and Richard Pratt, discovered a healthy source of difference in how the multiple dimensions of globalization interact. However various groups come to accept and work with concepts of globalization, it is apparent that rapidity and unpredictability of change mark its course. This sense was present as well in the third conference of this series, conducted in December 2002, which was convened by Manfred Steger to examine the ideologies of globalization. As Odin and Manicas remark in the Introduction to this volume, it is "clear that 'globalization' is a real phenomenon and is not to be taken lightly" even as its complex and multidimensional character continues to challenge our analyses and understandings.

All three GRC conferences convened to date have found the state at the center of the dialogues they have created. Interestingly, all three were conceived prior to the events of September 11, 2001, when much of the momentum in public and market relations shifted strongly in the direction of privileging privatization relationships, a dynamic much in evidence during the U.S. presidential election of 2000. The volumes that emerge from this initial dialogic series will greet a world in which state relations—especially those of security and order—have been much strengthened by the perceived and real demands of a post-9/11 society. In the United States a government formed by the election of neo-liberals and organized around their commitments to further the transformation of governmental relations in the direction of market behaviors—in health care, education, housing, transportation, and welfare—and predicated on the fiscal principles that reducing budget deficits and taxes were the primary work of the administration, has come to promote a stronger state that necessarily embraces regulatory power as it seeks to meet the perceived demands of providing security from terrorist attack.

To some degree the events of the past two years appear superficially to be a retreat from the impetus toward globalization associated with developed capital, neo-liberal political ideology, and the policy dynamics of those nation-states most significantly under their sway. But, as the chapters of this volume attest, the dynamics of globalization available for review through this lens of higher education extends beyond the press of events that recouple neo-liberal states with familiar patterns of state control. The dynamics of globalized higher education now defines portions of the work and aspirational lives of scores and even hundreds of millions of people across the planet. Linked to technological innovations and developments that are themselves the core aspirations of many of the world's largest capital firms, the myriad practices and novel institutional structures associated with the complex of "higher education" range far beyond the deliberate or even consensual claims of any single state or set of states.

This volume steers us toward a navigation of these complexities, engaging the work of some fifteen exceptional scholars. When I first conceived this series and in particular this conference, I thought only of Peter Manicas as its organizer and convener. As a regular participant in an informal political economy seminar that has run at the University of Hawai'i at Mānoa for more than sixteen years, I knew Peter to be brilliantly capable of identifying the right people to conduct this dialogue, and passionately committed to the subject matter. It was Peter's great good fortune to have Jaishree Odin agree to be co-editor of this volume, for her work has provided insights into that interesting subspecies of activity we call distance education as a window on globalization and its impacts.

The thanks of the Globalization Research Center go to the two of them for their exceptional work and to all the conference participants for accepting the task of moving forward our understanding of this critical dimension of globalization.

DEANE NEUBAUER
March 2003

Acknowledgments

THE EDITORS WISH TO THANK Deane Neubauer, who was both the inspiration for the construction of the Globalization Research Center and its first director. Deane had the idea for the conference and was important both in helping to find just the right people to invite and in planning the structure of the conference. Although he had to take on a new and important position in the university, he was thoroughly supportive throughout. Of course, we thank the center for funding the conference and for the assistance given by his excellent staff, currently headed by Barry Gillis. Like Deane, Barry has been a terrific shoulder to lean on. Of his staff, we thank especially James White, Troy Knott, and Nicole Robinson. Perhaps the most vital person as regards the conference was Yvonne Yamashita, who had the onerous task of seeing to the arrangements for the conference site, travel, accommodations, and a host of other details. We thank you, Yvonne.

One essay in the present volume, by Richard Ruch, was based on his book, *Higher Ed. Inc.* It is reproduced here, in revised form, with the permission of Dr. Ruch and the Johns Hopkins Press.

JAISHREE K. ODIN AND PETER T. MANICAS

INTRODUCTION

Peter T. Manicas and Jaishree K. Odin

THE PRESENT VOLUME had its genesis in a conference entitled "Globalization and Higher Education," held in Honolulu in February 2002 and sponsored by the Globalization Research Center at the University of Hawai'i at Mānoa. There were a number of novelties to this conference that bear on the contents of the volume. We think that these novelties make this a very different and important book. Of course, readers will determine how different and how important.

First, there was a very deliberate effort to bring together for three intense days people who could offer very different perspectives on the nest of problems generated by joining the already complex ideas of globalization and higher education. The authors of the essays in the present volume do indeed come from very different places, both in terms of geographical location (Australia, Britain, China, Costa Rica, Germany, Hong Kong, Kashmir, Pakistan, and the United States) and in terms of their institutional positions in higher education, as either active players or as scholars or both. Thus, we invited not only academics from several disciplines, but entrepreneurs, those who had served as deans in several very different kinds of institutions of higher education, and a past president of a prominent eastern university. (See List of Contributors.) These many different voices give this volume an inclusiveness and comprehensiveness not attempted before.

The second novelty was that the conference would be "dialogic." With the particular angle of vision of each participant in mind, the organizer asked the participants to speak from their position to issues that had been the primary area of concern and expertise, but not to present a paper. Instead, they would offer the group their reflections on how they saw things. This would be followed by moderated conversation—a dialogue. This gave us ample opportunity to explore issues, to raise questions, to offer dissent, to learn. It was not long before we had congealed a kind of a community. Given the chance to understand one another, we were forced to rethink things, perhaps even to change our minds. This gives the volume an integrity that, given the very different orientations of the participants, would not otherwise have been possible.

There was also a danger in this process: it wasn't easy to stay on track. We knew at the outset that the problems were interconnected, but did not appreciate how profoundly interconnected they were. Indeed, not only are both the leading concepts, globalization and higher education, complex, but trying to identify the causes and connections between them was forbidding, contestable, and conjectural. The essays in this volume give ample evidence of this.

We also decided that after we had all dispersed across the globe to our home bases, we would keep the conversation going asynchronously. A web site was established for electronic conferencing. Not everyone was equally comfortable with this mode of conversation. That was to be expected. But even our Danforth Award teacher and powerful defender of face-to-face teaching and learning made his appearance!

Despite differing perspectives, we found a common discourse. Indeed, gradually, there emerged considerable consensus on a number of key ideas. To be sure, there were some very wide disagreements, especially as regards *explaining* what we could agree to, and partly as a consequence of these differing views, there were disagreements about alternative versions of the future of higher education.

For convenience, we offer some of the consensus ideas, beginning with some hard lessons learned during the course of our conversation (but not always noticed by standard accounts).

We had no trouble agreeing that postsecondary education is now a massive globalizing industry and it is perhaps impossible to overestimate its potential. Asia alone offers fantastic possibilities. It is projected that by 2010 there will be 100 million people in the world, all fully qualified to proceed from secondary to tertiary education, but there will be no room left on any campus. A recent study by Merrill Lynch reported that the higher education market outside the United States is worth $111 billion annually, with perhaps 32 million potential students (*Chronicle of Higher Education*, June 28, 2002). To be sure, this raises more questions than it answers, especially regarding the possible consequences for the future of higher education.

The presence of participants from so many different locations forced us to see that there is a huge risk of overgeneralization when we speak of higher education. First, even if one restricts one's sight to higher education in the United States, it is an error to think of higher education in terms of the University of Michigan or Ohio Wesleyan. This overlooks the huge differences in the character and goals of the institutions of higher education: public/private, research I universities/liberal arts colleges, four-year colleges/community colleges, nonprofit/for-profit, proprietary schools (which offer training in trades and regulated industries, e.g., auto-mechanics, tourism), online universities, corporate universities (e.g., Sun Microsystems University, the University of Toyota) and finally, "diploma mills," digital and otherwise (see Ruch, Thomas, Delanty, Wagner).

Worse, it is easy to slip into the assumption—not always noticed, even by participants in a conference on globalization—that arrangements in higher education globally are largely the same as arrangements found in the United States. This is anything but the case. Differences in the histories and political economies of the nations of the world have resulted in differences in the situation of higher education across the globe. (See especially essays by Wagner, Currie, Inayatullah, Su Hao, Garnier, and Delanty.) This regards not only questions of access, funding, organization, programs, and institutional variety, but questions of needs and goals as well.

To take but one important example, globally there are remarkable disparities in the sources of funding for institutions of higher education. Although the situation is made especially complex by differences in institutions and recent figures are difficult to come by, European institutions of higher education still get the majority of support, as much as 90 percent, from public funds (Slaughter and Leslie, 1997). In the United States, state support peaked in 1979 at 62 percent and has declined steadily ever since. At the beginning of its most recent spiral, in 1991, it was 40 percent. "We used to be state-supported, then we became state-assisted, and now we are state-located." Other chief executive officers talk about leading "privately financed public universities." Currently, in the United States, both private and public institutions draw the majority of their support from nonstate sources, including tuitions, research grants, and gifts (Duderstadt, 2000). On the other hand, there is evidence that the trends clearly visible in the United

States toward privatization are visible elsewhere as well. Thus Garnier (below) argues that in 1930, private universities accounted for only 3 percent of enrollment in Latin America; today, they might account for almost half. As he notes, this is particularly troubling given the explosion of "garage universities," charging high tariffs and offering very low-quality programs.

But given differences in the situations of American, European, Latin American, Australian, and Asian colleges and universities (with differences among these as well), the public university is currently the dominant form of higher education globally. With nearly one-quarter of its institutions of higher education private, the United States is nearly unique. (Only Japan compares.) Nonetheless, in the United States, public institutions enroll some two-thirds of all college students, or some 5.8 million, in four-year institutions. Two-year public colleges add 11.1 million students, or taken together with the four-year institutions, over 80 percent of the total (Duderstadt, 2000). But of course all this could easily change.

Similarly, while it is clear that globalization is a real phenomenon and is not to be taken lightly, it is easy to fail to acknowledge its complex and multidimensional character (Wagner, Currie, Delanty, and Inayatullah). Accordingly, globalization will have different consequences for different institutions of higher education within a nation. And because of differences in the histories and political economies of the nations of the world, the consequences of globalization will likely be very different between the world's nations. This is brought out quite forcefully by comparing, for example, the accounts of Currie, Su Hao, and Garnier.

Although the evidence comes mainly from students in American institutions of higher education, student attitudes toward and expectations of postsecondary education are increasingly oriented toward career advancement and economic return. (See especially Ruch, Thomas.) This observation joins with another. While there is no doubt that higher education is changing rapidly, there is an unfortunate tendency to think nostalgically in terms of the "ideal" university as a place where students and faculty collaborate in face-to-face teaching/learning and where the goal is the emancipation of the human spirit. But not only was it the case that this ideal was rarely realized, but historically, it was the condition of only a privileged few. Moreover, there were always alternatives to the traditional college and university, sustained, as seems likely, by responding to needs unmet by this model. Of course, this raises questions regarding the uses and relation of markets to institutions of higher education (Ruch, Karelis, Smith).

For reasons that are not entirely clear, perhaps an aspect of globalization and perhaps not, there has been the rapid and surprising growth in recent years of degree-granting, for-profit colleges and universities, not only but perhaps especially in the United States. In 1991, there was one for-profit, degree-granting, accredited institution listed on U.S. stock exchanges, DeVry, Inc. By 1999, there were forty (Ruch). Generating some $16.5 billion in revenues, growth of for-profit revenues increased by 20 percent in 2001 over the previous year. (As Ruch points out, the essential difference between private nonprofits and for-profits is not that nonprofits do not seek "profit," but that their tax liability differs both as a source of revenue and as a form of expenditure.) More generally, institutions of higher education are increasingly engaged in what Max Weber termed "rationalization"—"privatizing," adopting business-like strategies, "managerialism" (Currie), with an eye toward cost-saving, for example, replacing retiring tenured faculty with adjuncts (who now comprise some 42 percent of teaching faculty), and marketing in a competitive search for students who are "consumers." (See Margolis.)

Finally, with the use of Internet technologies, distance education has taken on new meaning as "the virtual university." Thus, as of November 2002, Phoenix University Online had a staff of some 1,700 with some 7,000 faculty—mostly part-time, teaching some 49,400 students. Phoenix reported a net income of $64.3 million for the year 2001 (*Chronicle of Higher Education*, November 1, 2002). Universitas 21, an international consortium of seventeen universities from Asia, Australia, Europe, and North America, will offer wholly online degrees, beginning with an MBA to be offered in Asia in 2003. Nevertheless, at least the majority of our participants would agree that the traditional university is not going to disappear even if it changes its character and/or becomes increasingly less important.

But the hard questions remain. What does it all mean? While not all of the following essays address all the hard questions, most have a view, be it implicit or explicit.

1. First is the question of capitalism, globally considered. Given differences in the understanding of global capitalism, all would grant

that it is a critical "mechanism" (or complex of mechanisms), but disagree as to what it explains. Do the processes of global capitalism fundamentally challenge the inherited forms of the university? Scholars fiercely debate the challenge of neo-liberalism, and whether the traditional university will become marginalized. (For some different views, see especially Currie, Margolis, Garnier, and Delanty.) Second, as part of this, there is disagreement regarding the role of the state, in terms of both its fiscal capacities and its direct and indirect roles in shaping the institutions of higher education, including its role in defining the tasks of higher education (Currie, Garnier, Hao, Wagner).

2. Related to the foregoing are questions of the use and nature of markets as regards higher education. While our participants would agree that the market/state polarity is at best an often misleading oversimplification, how should they be conceived and how are they related (Wagner, Smith, Ruch)? In what sense are students *not* consumers? In what sense, alternatively, can the university be transformer of value systems (Karelis, Thomas, Garnier, Delanty)?

3. The role of technology is unclear. Our contributors reject a technological determinism, but differ, sometimes subtly, regarding how technology figures, or should figure, in these outcomes. Odin notes that faculty are anything but enthusiastic about the use of the new technologies, even as supplements to their teaching, and our group acknowledged that a very solid case can be made for their appropriate use and that their capacities are by no means fully explored. But if it be granted that not all uses of the technologies are pedagogically sound, what is the appropriate pedagogy for the new technologies and what are its limits? For example, are there technological solutions to increasing access? How do we involve faculty in their use (Odin, Margolis, Delanty)?

4. A series of questions concerns the mission and goals of higher education, from an inherited ideal of *Bildung*, to the search for and dissemination of knowledge, to a concept emphasizing instrumental values, to its role in national and economic development, to a future-oriented idea of providing "institutional spaces where cognitive models for society to learn can emerge," to a view that holds that higher education is and should be all of these. But if so, how is

this to be accomplished? Who should determine this (Karelis, Abeles, Bowen-James, Inayatullah, Smith, Delanty)?

5. The foregoing raises deeper questions regarding the very idea of knowledge, including the provocative contrast between what Bowen-James and Abeles call "just-in-time" versus "just-in-case" knowledge, the distinction—increasingly difficult to draw— between "teaching" and "training," the differences, overlapping with these, between knowing in the theoretical mode, knowing in the practical mode, and knowing as an essentially reflective process, and, finally, the view that there are alternative ways of knowing (Odin, Abeles, Delanty, Garnier, Inayatullah).

6. Another series of problems regards questions of justice, including questions of access and inequality. Thus, if widening participation is an over-riding good, should this be conceived in terms of the realization of human capacities, of attaining employment skills, including credentials for personal success, or in terms of efficiently realizing national goals, including the development of managerial, scientific, and technical knowledge? Or perhaps these are not disconnected? What changes in our current institutional arrangements are necessary (Karelis, McDermott, Thomas, Su Hao, Bowen-James, Abeles, Garnier, Delanty)?

This volume aims to energize readers to rethink higher education. In what was the third main novelty of this book, the authors have tried to be provocative and plain-spoken—not an easy thing for persons socialized in the university. And consistent with our efforts to communicate, they have foregone the usual academic apparatus of footnoting references. A bibliography of works drawn on by our participants is appended following each essay, along with an end-of-book annotated bibliography of works pertinent to the themes of our volume.

REFERENCES

Duderstadt, James J. (2000). *A University for the 21st Century*. Ann Arbor: University of Michigan Press.

Slaughter, Sheila, and Larry L. Leslie. (1997). *Academic Capitalism: Politics, Policies and the Entrepreneurial University*. Baltimore: Johns Hopkins University Press.

PART I

THE LARGER CONTEXT

INTRODUCTION

PETER WAGNER begins this volume with a sensitive and wide-ranging look at globalization. He notes that "there are conjoined economic, cultural, and political processes that we may describe as 'globalization,' and they do have an impact on research and higher education, the two core functions of the universities." But he sees many reasons why we should not jump to conclusions about the future of the institutions of higher education. Globalization is a multidimensional process—and not, for example, merely a process of "marketization." Second, not only are there countertendencies in all these processes, but also it is an error to ignore very large differences in institutions of higher education, both nationally and regionally. To examine this, Wagner develops some analytical tools and concludes that the outcomes will "depend upon the strength of the belief in substantive academic autonomy and the willingness of political actors, including university administrators who implement internal hierarchy, to permit both community and market principles to work." For him, "historical and cultural differences" will be "decisive in these comparative outcomes."

Alan Bowen-James had led off our conference with an enthusiastic endorsement of what he saw to be the future of higher education in the new context of globalization. His position is essentially what is usually termed *neo-liberal*. Accordingly, he was an essential contributor to our conference. Unfortunately, for a variety of reasons, he was unable to offer a final version of his presentation. Fortunately, we have a synopsis of his contribution taken at the time of his presentation. We think that it captures the main threads of his presentation, which we summarize here.

Bowen-James examined the role of technology in global and higher education from the perspective of transnationalism rather than nationalism or internationalism, and argued that "there will soon be a disaggregation of traditional customs and an unshackling of competitive advantage" in higher education, concluding finally that "in short, everything will be commodified." For Bowen-James,

> Higher education is an anachronism, as it is not necessarily universal nor higher. We are now threatened with deinstitutionalization and a twilight zone—neither what is thought nor what it aspires to be. There are in fact two models of learning: just-in-case learning and just-in-time learning. The commanders of the former dominate current higher education; the latter is cutting edge and overlaps. In this time of the diminishing of higher education, the difficulty is to appease conflicting masters.

Accordingly,

> the higher education industry must change or become marginalized. Currently, it is protected by laws, restrictive trade practices, and self-governance. It may have to link with trade associations and the like to become an international growth industry. For instance, education is considered an industry in China and it has already begun to partner with commercial companies. Increasingly, brand, flexible work practices, price elasticity, and perceived career value are more essential. The industry can offer child care, a social life, an influence network, jobs, the convenience of access, and an education. International forces in the industry are leading to value chain contestability, deflationary forces, and a consumer orientation. This increases the international tradability of the industry. Protectionism will fail, and education will fail in the globalized economy.
>
> Productivity in higher education should lessen cost; students will choose where to go, and it will be cheaper in China. In the United States, the public higher education system must consider who owns international property as well as remuneration policies, and out of state tuition is uncompetitive. Although this is fine art, not McDonald's customization, there are fixed marginal costs. It is not scaleable, not replicable to multiple sites, does not generate cash flow, inventory cannot be replicated, and the industry is unwilling to disaggregate. Competition for market share will happen, and already distance education is far advanced in Asia (and the United Kingdom). India currently has several hundred thousand online students. In Harbin, China, all dorms are wired. China is advanced in the areas of online education, the Internet, and outsourcing/insourcing. Because of the price elasticity of demand, the product

cannot be delivered. With international competition, the university must stay local or go global, and may come to be seen as a node.

At some distance from the perspective of Bowen-James are the views of both Michael Margolis and Jan Currie. Margolis paints a rather gloomy picture. But from Bowen-James's point of view, Margolis will seem nostalgic. In Margolis's picture of the preglobalized past, "colleges of arts and sciences within the universities provided places where students and faculty could learn together, mature intellectually, and reflect upon how their knowledge ought to affect the conduct of private and civic affairs of the broader society." And perhaps there was but a small price to be paid for this, for example, in limitations on access. But whether or not Margolis's background assumptions can be sustained, it would be hard to deny that we need a radically different picture of the current academic scene. Margolis offers a penetrating analysis of the current situation in large public universities and of the causes of the changes that such institutions are undergoing. He concludes with an assessment of what he sees to be the consequences.

Jan Currie offers a full-blown critique of neo-liberal thinking, and depending on a number of variables, sees potential benefits as well as costs for higher education. Critical for her are the responses by state agencies, which she notes "appear to differ according to the type of market economy, the strength of the economy, and the willingness of a country's citizenry to pay enough taxes to fund public institutions." It is in these terms that one needs to examine the challenge of neo-liberal globalization. Her account, accordingly, would seem to be along lines suggested by Wagner.

CHAPTER I

Higher Education in an Era of Globalization: What Is at Stake?

Peter Wagner

The term *globalization* has become a short-hand for the condition of our time. Since the closing decade of the twentieth century, it suggests, some worldwide processes have begun to shape each and every walk of our lives. Almost invariably, this new condition is discussed with some skepticism. Few people wholeheartedly embrace globalization—understandably so, since the term refers to rapid change with not quite foreseeable consequences. Most writers about globalization, though, also see it as inevitable, as something that we cannot escape or would not want to reject, because it also brings considerable advantages.

If globalization is such an encompassing change in our condition, then there is good reason to assume that universities and higher education will also be affected by it. If the consequences of globalization, furthermore, are marked by considerable ambivalence, then there is also some urgency in addressing its likely impact on universities. To do so, however, we first have to see what precisely is referred to when one talks about globalization.

Three Dimensions of Globalization

Usually, three dimensions of globalization are distinguished. *Economically* speaking, most centrally, it refers to the effective creation of a world market. Every economic actor—companies, workers, consumers—now enters directly, knowingly or not, into relations with other actors potentially anywhere in the world. This is certainly true for financial markets, as we witness daily, and it is also true for communication flows in general. Electronic technology is the major factor behind these developments. But despite the fact that the networks of economic exchange have grown considerably since the end of the Second World War, and then again since the end of the Cold War, much production and consumption still takes place in settings that, even though they should not be called "local," are much smaller than the globe.

In *cultural* terms, globalization may mean two quite different things, or even both at the same time. On the one hand, the term is used to talk about the alleged emergence of a homogeneous world culture and the extinction of cultural difference and specificity. Sometimes this homogenization is associated with a general rise of mass culture, or some may want to say middle-class culture. Sometimes it is related to cultural hegemony. In both cases, cultural globalization may also be referred to as *Americanization*, seeing the United States as the typical middle-class society and as hegemonic at the same time. On the other hand, the cultural effect of globalization is seen as the precise opposite of homogenization. In this view, societies historically used to be culturally homogeneous, but increasing migration has led to mixed cultures in many societies, and thus to the rise of multiculturalism. Given that the United States, as the largest settler society with a long history of immigration from different regions of the world, can be seen as having pioneered this trend, the emergence of multicultural situations elsewhere in the world, notably in Europe, can also be called *Americanization*.

Although the two meanings of cultural globalization appear to be opposed to one another, they are not mutually exclusive. Certain cultural artifacts and cultural orientations may now be ubiquitous—or almost so—in the world; thus elements of a world culture have come into existence. But most social settings may now no longer be describable by a single, predominant set of cultural values—if indeed they ever were. Thus, cultural diversity may now be more pronounced in many places of the world, certainly in all metropolitan settings.

In *political* terms, the meaning of globalization changes entirely. Politically, globalization refers in the first instance to the alleged decline of the sovereign nation-state. And it is precisely the effect of economic and cultural globalization that is seen as undermining the capacity of national political actors to steer and manage the economy and to express and support the cultural values of their own society. Some observers claim to witness elements of political globalization, such as global economic coordination through the World Trade Organization, first steps to the institutionalization of global legal arrangements with the establishment of the International Court of Criminal Justice, and an increasingly global commitment to human rights and democracy. But most analysts agree that the real problem of globalization is here: politics, to speak loosely, is not able to catch up with economic and cultural global developments. And since it is difficult to argue that those developments are exclusively benign—though to some extent they of course are—and do not generate problems, there is a need for communication and coordination. Under conditions of globalization, in other words, there is an absence, or at least weakness, of politics despite a considerable need for politics.

GLOBALIZATION AND HIGHER EDUCATION: A FIRST ASSESSMENT

If these are the broad, general contours of what we mean when we talk about globalization, what does it mean for universities or, more cautiously, what could it mean for universities? Assuming economic globalization affects higher education institutions, it will have an impact on the two "markets" in which universities operate. First, as regards their teaching function, universities may see themselves as operating in a global higher education market and competing worldwide to capture a share of the demand for education. Second, with regard to research, rather than entertaining special relations to government offices and to firms based in their own national economy, universities may need to compete worldwide for business funding of research. They may be less able than before to count on public funds in support of national economic growth or other policy objectives. Both of these trends are clearly identifiable, although their significance and impact on university organization is much less clear.

In cultural terms, globalization would mean that universities are catering to a multicultural studentship and may gradually abandon—or at least relativize—their old role of educating national elites and transmitting specific cultural values. This raises questions of the canon as well as of affirmative action, which are well known in debates on U.S.

campuses, though at this point much less elsewhere. At the same time, there may be something like intellectual globalization, which would spell the end to national traditions of knowledge, as they are known in the humanities and the social sciences, but to some extent even in the natural sciences. Some may argue that such a development is plainly to be welcomed, since those national traditions only existed because of unjustifiable boundaries to scholarly communication and exchange. Globalization would then fulfill the time-honored promise of universal knowledge. While there is some validity in such a view, one should nevertheless not underestimate the value of diversity in approaches to knowledge and the contextual nature of knowledge and knowledge production. (See Inayatullah, below.)

Political globalization again provides the mirror image to the other two trends. For universities, a weaker and less autonomous state may mean that they can count less on what used to be in many countries the most reliable and steady source of funding for research. In turn, greater emphasis is laid on the evaluation of publicly funded research, applying a value-for-money conception that is close to business behavior. At the same time, policy actors may show a decreasing commitment to educating their "own" population. Higher education has been at the margins of policy interest in many countries for at least two decades—although there are some signs of insight into the consequences of such neglect, even if the remorse may mostly be about what is nowadays called deficits in employability of the potential workforce.

It is easy to see that both of the trends we have briefly discussed do exist: there are conjoined economic, cultural, and political processes that we may describe as "globalization," and they do have an impact on research and higher education, the two core functions of the universities. However, the conclusions to be drawn from these observations for the future of universities are nevertheless not straightforward. This is so for mainly two reasons. First, globalization clearly is a multidimensional process. But those who draw quick conclusions often see it as a one-dimensional one, mostly as a process of "marketization" driven by new technology. However, some of the cultural features of globalization may well give different shapes to the economic ones in different settings. Second, globalization is sometimes seen as leading toward a situation in which global networks regulate themselves and in which all other institutional structures are erased. But we can observe some countertendencies, and in some cases even the opposite is true: the dynamics of globalization often creates the demand for stability and the request for regulation, and this often at a smaller level than the global one. Thus, we need to think about globalization not merely as a multidimensional process, but even as one that may create new economic, cultural, and political forms, and does not only destroy such existing forms.

MARKET, HIERARCHY, COMMUNITY: THREE WAYS OF REGULATING HIGHER EDUCATION

To widen the discussion, let us use market, hierarchy, and community as three dimensions of globalization. These are not only empirical economic, cultural, and political tendencies, but are conceptual tools, ideas that provide means to think about ways in which social life can be organized. Indeed, in economic sociology and in organizational analysis they have been used to conceptualize the firm. Here we can use them to reflect upon higher education institutions in an era of globalization.

Higher education can be thought of as being regulated by *market* rules. In such an economic view, there is a demand for training and expertise, and universities and other higher education institutions are suppliers in the market in which this demand is voiced. They fund themselves by asking a price for the commodity they offer, and they cater to those who cherish the commodity and are able to pay the price. The observable trend in our time is for this market orientation to grow more important. There is pressure on higher education institutions to gain at least some of their earnings through selling their product. The relation of such trends to globalization is clear: this is a case of economic globalization driven by market imperatives.

Alternatively, higher education can be thought of as being ruled by *hierarchy*. There are two senses of this regulating idea. First, public universities are subject to external orders, namely, by the state that funds them and that, in some cases, may even have the final say in the appointment of key personnel, namely, the professors. Second, higher education institutions can be hierarchically organized internally. The actual core activities of universities, research and higher education, may be subject to decisions of a strong university president or governing board. In the current period, we observe by and large opposed trends with regard to the two meanings of hierarchy. External hierarchy is reduced insofar as states withdraw from their commitment to universities, in the overall context of the so-called decline of the nation-state. Such withdrawal of regulation by hierarchy is mostly to the benefit of regulation by markets. On the other hand, internal hierarchy is often strengthened as higher education institutions are seen in need of increasing their capacity to act and react in an ever more fluid and mobile environment. Such rising importance of hierarchical features is mostly to the detriment of what we can call regulation by community.

Third, higher education can also be thought of as being regulated by *community* values. In such a cultural view, universities appear as guilds in which the teachers are the masters and the students are the apprentices. Between them there is an interaction of a personal kind, and in substance, the interaction is guided by time-honored guild rules and the idea of knowledge and skills being preserved in persons and in the communities they form. The idea of the university as a community does not contain any rule as to who funds it. Endowments, of course, provide a firm ground to stand on even in the long run. Otherwise, the idea is materially speaking not self-sustainable, and it needs to enter into a compromise with another regulating idea, either market or external hierarchy or a combination of both. But it is ideationally the strongest idea, since it is the one in which the commitment to academic freedom and the pursuit of knowledge resides. The core of the university is here, in its self-commitment to this value.

This regulatory ideal should not be idealized, though. The strength of the whole argument hinges on an enormous confidence in the academic community, viewed idyllically as a free community of scholars disinterestedly engaged in open-ended, domination-free communication and search for knowledge. In his sociology of science, Robert Merton provided a systematic account of such an ideal, which he took to be governing much of the actual science institutions at the time of his writing. But Wilhelm von Humboldt already knew better when he wrote, in 1810, that it is not only the state that threatens the freedom of scholarship, but also "the institutions themselves which, as they begin, acquire a certain spirit and like to suffocate the emergence of a different one." Cultural communities can be very closed affairs, and the scientific community is not necessarily different from other ones.

GOVERNANCE OF UNIVERSITIES AND THE SELF-IMAGE OF MODERN SOCIETY: A SHORT HISTORICAL DETOUR

The idea of community-based self-regulation may be most under threat in the current era. While the idea of self-organization of higher education is almost a thousand years old, it found full acceptance by the powers-that-be since the university reforms in Europe in the late eighteenth and early nineteenth centuries—the time when Humboldt was writing. This was also the period of the "market revolution" and the "democratic revolution," that is, the era in which the ideas of regulation by market mechanisms and by an accountable form of hierarchy became fully accepted. No doubt, European and American societies were conflict-ridden throughout all of the two centuries since then, and several attempts at profoundly changing or reinterpreting their institutional structures were made, sometimes successfully. Nevertheless we may say that most of them, most of the time, were based on the acceptance of the following basic ideas: there is a plurality of different modes of organizing social life; these modes are equally legitimate, although they ground their legitimacy in different ways; a good and viable form of social organization should try to identify which principles of regulation are adequate for which social activity; criteria of adequacy are mostly combinations of forms of freedom and of efficacy.

More concretely, this consensus was often interpreted in the following way: for the production and distribution of most goods, market exchange between large numbers of producers and consumers is the adequate mode of regulation. But as regards rules for the life in common, two criteria need to be fulfilled: everybody concerned by the application of those rules needs to have a say in determining them; and there needs to be a clear and unequivocal way of arriving at those rules and implementing them. Together, these criteria form a combined principle of democracy and hierarchy. Third, and in our context most important, the search for knowledge and its diffusion should not be restricted or guided by principles foreign to it. Research and higher education, thus, should not be institutionally directed by criteria of usefulness in other areas of social life.

This principle was probably most clearly formulated in 1798 by Immanuel Kant in his *The Dispute of the Faculties*. Kant well recognized that education in professional schools—theology, law, and medicine—

needed to be geared to the application of knowledge in professional practice. However, such professional training in higher education institutions needed to be grounded in the complete freedom and the exclusive commitment to knowledge and understanding in what was then called the "lower faculty," the faculty of philosophy. Across the nineteenth century, the philosophy faculty grew in two directions. On the one hand, it became the home for the scientific disciplines that gradually splintered off from philosophy to form the natural sciences, the social sciences, and the humanities. On the other hand, its original mission was transformed into the ideal of liberal education that, depending on institutional context, either kept informing all university life or became the first phase of higher education before students moved on to professional schools. At the beginning of the twenty-first century, those principles for the pursuit of research and higher education are still recognizable. They have not disappeared and they keep being revived in recurrent debates about "the idea of the university," as Gerard Delanty points out in his contribution to this volume. However, they have become weakened, maybe less as ideas and principles, but in the ways in which they are institutionally entrenched.

In our current era of globalization, the risk is that we may lose these principles altogether. The view, as briefly described above, that social life could be harmoniously compartmentalized into different activities governed by different criteria of adequacy has always been overly optimistic. There is no Western society in which the delimitation of those realms—the economy, politics, and knowledge production and diffusion—has not been fiercely contested at various times. Both the interpretations put forward on how they were to be understood and the institutional solutions found have indeed often diverged across countries and over time. There have been very few situations, however, in which any one of those criteria of regulation has been completely abandoned and another one made predominant over all walks of life—the case of Soviet socialism being the most striking of such instances. In a quite different form, such a proposal for unbalancing the plurality of justifications for institutional arrangements is again on the agenda today. This proposal is the economic interpretation of globalization, and if it gains in force it will transform higher education institutions beyond recognition.

Up to this point, I have tried to develop some conceptual tools to understand the situation of higher education in an era of globalization.

I conclude with three more steps. First, I briefly show that there has always been a variety of quite different ways of combining regulation by market, hierarchy, and community in the governance of higher education institutions. In other words, there has always been a viable and legitimate diversity in institutional arrangements in higher education. Currently, however, one strand in the debate on globalization and higher education suggests that market regulation should reign supreme. Second, I propose that a more subtle interpretation of the present period suggests that the ongoing transformation is better understood as the search for a new compromise—or several compromises in different settings—between the three regulatory principles. Third, I offer reasons for concluding that the "product" of higher education is inadequately treated if the search for market efficiency guides these institutions.

VARIETIES OF HIGHER EDUCATION REGIMES

The self-image of modern society, to which I briefly alluded, suggests that everything has its appropriate place. This, however, is by far not the case. If we look at the contemporary situation, we easily recognize that higher education in the United States is to a considerable extent regulated by market mechanisms. Students pay fees the level of which is assumed to correspond to the quality of the product they buy. Professors, as employed producers of this product, are paid wages that again are supposed to relate to the quality of their work. Even doubts about this connection, which are widespread, point only to another explanation that also refers to a market mechanism: professors may be paid according to the effective demand their product creates and, thus, to the revenue they earn for their employer. Universities, playing the role of the firm in this market, compete with one another for both students and staff. Their competition, as every market model will predict, can raise salaries for certain categories of employees, and it can create "special offers," in term of scholarships, for instance, for certain kinds of students, as buyers of the product. In short, a market model goes quite far in describing the workings of U.S. higher education institutions.

In continental Europe, in contrast, students do not pay fees, or at least not fees that come close to anything resembling the cost of the education they receive. Staff, in turn, is paid according to general salary schemes, often the same nationwide, which leave little leeway for individual discretion. The funding for higher education institutions comes almost exclusively out of the public budget, be it the nation-state as in France or the states in the German federation. European societies show a political commitment to higher education that is not much different from their commitment to primary and secondary education, almost all of which is publicly organized and free of charge. Such institutional arrangement certainly entails that regulation of higher education proceeds to a considerable degree by external hierarchy. Governments and lawmakers set the framework terms for the organization of higher education. This feature, though, does not make European institutions necessarily less self-organized in substantive terms than North American ones. While there are more cases of substantive interference by the state than one would like to see, there is nevertheless a general commitment, more or less clearly pronounced and practiced, that academia should internally—that is, substantively—be self-ruled. Distribution of public funding for research in peer review processes, for instance, is common.

A normative comparison between the two arrangements—here presented in a somewhat stylized, almost ideal-typical form—would need to show the difference between an articulation of community regulation with market mechanisms and an articulation of the former with external hierarchy. While space does not permit such a comparison here in any detail, it is easy to see that its result cannot be predicted on the basis of the logic of regulatory principles. The actual outcomes depend upon the strength of the belief in substantive academic autonomy and the willingness of political actors, including university administrators who implement internal hierarchy, to permit both community and market principles to work. Historical and cultural differences, of course, are decisive in these comparative outcomes.

TRENDS TOWARD CONVERGENCE UNDER CONDITIONS OF GLOBALIZATION?

These observations suggest that the basic model of the place of higher education in a modern society is subject to considerable interpretation. In our time, however, these interpretations are open to one strong objection: they are said to provide nothing but a snapshot of the present, or at best an extrapolation from the past, and completely ignore powerful current trends. These trends—globalizing trends—are then said to be strong trends toward convergence to a single institutional model, a model that closely resembles that of the United States.

There are two core components of this assertion. First, there is said to be a strong movement toward strengthening the market elements in higher education. The evidence provided is multiple. (See Currie, Margolis.) Some universities, predominantly in the United States and in the United Kingdom, see themselves as operating in a global higher education market. They try to channel effective purchasing power to their institutions by advertising their products in demand-intensive societies, most clearly in East Asia. Private "providers" of higher education have increasingly entered the market, and they often do not show any particular attachment to one society at all, but operate wherever profits are likely. And even in Europe, there is an opening—slow, but perceivable—of the university system toward private institutions.

Sometimes these observations are connected to normative arguments. Market arrangements in higher education are said to be more efficient, because they will bring the supply to where the demand is. National boundaries no longer play an unduly restrictive role. Market arrangements are also said to be fairer, because the consumer will pay a price for the product she or he consumes that roughly corresponds to the cost of the fabrication of the product. Free-access public higher education systems, in turn, are considered to be inherently unfair, because they require that all taxpayers pay for a service made use of only by the children of a part of them. Furthermore, empirical evidence shows that this asymmetry often leads to a redistribution from the bottom to the top of society, since middle- and upper-middle-class families are more likely to send their children to university than working-class or lower-middle-class families. (See Thomas.)

Before taking up these arguments in more detail, the second allegedly globalizing trend needs to be briefly discussed. While the trend toward the market is immediately consonant with the declining role of external hierarchy, the same trend is often seen as increasing the importance of internal hierarchy. (See Smith.) As actors in markets, universities need to be able to develop strategies and products, they need to adapt to changing environments and to be able to perceive and to grasp new market opportunities. Thus, their organization needs to be more streamlined to act more quickly and more coherently. A university model in which the collegial interaction in discipline-based institutes and faculties predominates is seen as too inert and incapable of decisive action. (See Ruch.) Such a form of interaction has to be reined in and subjected to the command of the organization's executive.

From these two trend observations, a model of the university as a firm is emerging. The product of this firm is higher education and research. All of the internal orientation of the organization is directed to producing these products swiftly and efficiently, and all of its external orientation is directed to selling them at a profit margin in competition with other providers of these products. This scenario is sometimes praised as opening up new opportunities, but sometimes it is employed in a discourse of decline of the old university, one in which values and commitments were still important. It is significant, though, that both these versions agree on a future of the university that is marked by the full imposition of market rationality and organizational efficiency on higher education institutions.

THE SEARCH FOR A NEW COMPROMISE OF REGULATORY ARRANGEMENTS

This vision, however, has only some superficial plausibility. At a closer look, it is deeply flawed. As a first step, it is useful for a moment to accept the market analogy, and to show that, even in its terms, the future of the university will look different from the image just presented. In a second step, then, one can show that the appropriateness of the market analogy in general is—and is likely to remain—quite limited.

The idea of a coming globalized higher education market normally assumes—and quite plausibly so—that there will be a global expansion of the demand for higher education. While some of the Western societies may have reached saturation levels, this is certainly not true for the rest of the world. (See Garnier, Su Hao.) And since non-Western students, if their families can afford it, are often willing and eager to spend their university years in the West, there is even growth potential on the campuses in North America and Europe. If this is so, then one needs to underline that, as I think economists will confirm, growing markets do not have strong tendencies to foster rationalization moves and to impose efficiency requirements. Growing markets offer spaces for "less efficient" producers, which will tend to be "crowded out" only when markets contract. While it may thus be true that we are currently witnessing a certain increased emphasis on rationality and efficiency in some institutions of higher education, this is not likely to occur at the expense of other institutions that do not transform themselves in such a direction.

More constructively speaking, every product market of a certain size—and this holds both for markets that are stable and for those that are growing—will provide a range of products of variable features, price, and quality. (See Ruch, Smith.) Not all providers in such a market will compete with each other; market segmentation will protect groups of suppliers from other groups. In periods of growth, there is likely to be increasing segmentation and even stratification in markets. This seems to me to be clearly visible in higher education. At the bottom end of the market, some—often new—providers offer products produced with all rationalizing means of information technology and offer them at relatively low cost to a wide audience of potential consumers. This includes, for example, long-distance learning programs in certain vocational and professional fields. At the top end, elite universities face relatively little cost pressure, since they can offer their product at higher prices without facing slacking demand by the small audience of both affluent and quality-conscious consumers they cater to. In between, there are all kinds of suppliers of specialties, often with a very specific demand and little competition. Furthermore, since few students are—in the literal sense—globetrotters, much of the demand will remain territorially circumscribed.

Research in comparative political economy has long shown that there are highly different production and marketing conditions for standardized mass production compared to what is termed "diversified quality production." Furthermore, researchers have also shown that politico-institutional and socio-cultural features may be more conducive to the one or the other type of product, so that highly different "varieties of capitalism" (Peter Hall and David Soskice) or "worlds of production" (Robert Salais and Michael Storper) coexist and persist. There is no reason at all to assume that what is true for other commodities should not be true for higher education.

But let us also gradually move beyond the market analogy. There are some markets for which even economists admit that price-quality relations cannot explain buyers' behavior. (See Smith, Garnier.) The art market is the prime example for such explanatory problems, but we can just as well look at, for instance, the less exotic realm of fashion goods. While there are certainly price and quality differences between fashion items, the demand for some such goods is unrelated to those differences. It is instead guided by considerations of prestige, reputation, rarity, and similar "cultural" rather than "economic" features. The same is true for higher education, and there we can even observe a particular phenomenon of, so to say, cultural upgrading. In higher education, a tendency of academic drift has long been noticed; it refers to the inclination of institutions that are located at the bottom end of academic prestige and reputation, such as technical universities, polytechnics, and vocational schools, to relocate themselves, whenever given the chance, toward higher ends on that spectrum. This institutional tendency is by and large mirrored by students' orientations. To speak again in economic terms: many students would "buy" the same course from a prestigious university rather than from a less known, maybe new, higher education provider, even if the former charges a higher fee. Such behavior may not even be economically "irrational," since job chances may be increased by the "brand name" on their certificate. (See Thomas.) In any case, though, this parallel example of both organizational and personal behavior shows the significance of broader criteria in higher education than those of instrumental rationality and organizational efficiency. Those criteria, in turn, provide an important background for the assumption that a wide plurality of different forms of higher education can viably coexist on the globalized higher education market. Universities err if they think market-cum-technology is the only name of the game under conditions of globalization.

Finally, then, we also need to note that there is considerable resistance to the widespread use of the market model for higher education. In most European societies, but also in many other societies worldwide, there is a persistent commitment to higher education as a public good that should not be provided on the basis of an individual exchange agreement between a producer and a consumer. (See Garnier.) This is not to say that there is necessarily no concern about cost-efficiency and the rationality of existing arrangements in those societies. Virtually all observers of higher education and research in Europe, for instance, agree that there is considerable need for reform, and that such reforms are not really forthcoming because of institutional inertia and lack of political will and insight. However, very rarely can one hear a voice that calls for abandoning this public commitment. In the self-understanding of many societies, universities are a part of the cultural infrastructure that needs to be maintained by collective effort rather than by sum of individuals' will to buy their product.

THE SPECIFICITY OF HIGHER EDUCATION AS A "PRODUCT"

Should one then, in those contexts, think of higher education as a public good in the same sense in which clean air is a public good, something that we are dependent on, but that we cannot individually provide ourselves? There is some truth in the analogy in the sense that our institutions of higher education are a historical accomplishment that can easily be destroyed by mere inattentiveness to its preconditions. But unlike clean air, higher education is precisely never just "there"; it needs to be "produced." Thus, we need to ask ourselves more explicitly about the specificity of this "product." (See Garnier.)

When companies speak about their products, they think in terms of fabrication, that is, in terms of an orderly, routine process the outcome of which is conceived and planned in advance. Every deviation of the product from the expectation is considered to be a failure or a fault. From Aristotle to Hannah Arendt, however, philosophy has made a distinction between action and fabrication as two different modes of human activity. In contrast to the latter, the former is about the creation of something that was not—at least not entirely—known before, and the production of which cannot be planned.

The "product" of universities seems to fit this description, with regard to both of their major activities. Scholarly research is about novelty and innovation, by definition about creating something that was not known before. And higher education is about the formation of a personality in the interaction between teacher and student. And again, a personality is something that by definition cannot be fabricated according to a plan. Arguably, thus, the criteria of adequacy for settings of knowledge generation and diffusion remain quite different from those for other "production sites."

Such reflections provide strong reasons why the market mode of regulation should not predominate in the realm of higher education, not even in an era of globalization. Furthermore, they also suggest that none of the three regulatory modes—market efficiency, hierarchical command, or community rules—can guarantee a proper functioning of higher education institutions. What safeguards the quality of this specific "product" is the people who populate those institutions and use the action-space that it provides. This space, in turn, may best be secured by a multiple, movable reference to all three modes of regulation. It makes little sense either to just try to defend community values against the inroads of the market. The former, as Wilhelm von Humboldt knew, can be more stifling than anything else.

In an era of globalization, the challenge of market and technology is rightly in the center of attention. (See Odin, Abeles.) But globalization is a multidimensional process. It may mostly be driven by the use of new technological possibilities with a view to their profitability. But it has a cultural component as well, which furthers the reconfiguration of cultural communities and, with this, generates new needs for knowledge and understanding that only a plural constellation of higher education institutions can offer. And even though the combined effect of economic and cultural globalization has undermined the control of a territory and a population by the sovereign state, politics is not bound to disappear. Rather, it is stimulated to take up the challenge of supporting knowledge forms that are adequate to a particular polity and its members.

The technological and economic forces in globalization are not on their own likely to destroy the diversity of the institutional space that higher education institutions provide. These forces are part of a major societal transformation, which will include a transformation of higher education as well. The challenge is to understand this transformation in its complexity and, in particular, in its specificity in diverse settings. This transformation as such would not destroy the creativity and diversity of higher education, as we know it. What would destroy it is something else: the failure to grasp the meaning and consequences of this transformation and, in its course, the disappearance, among practitioners and policymakers in higher education, of the knowledge about and the belief in the specificity and the value of the activity they are engaged in.

REFERENCES

Arendt, Hannah. (1958). *The Human Condition*. Chicago: University of Chicago Press.

Hall, Peter, and David Soskice. (2001). *Varieties of Capitalism.* Oxford: Oxford University Press.

Humboldt, Wilhelm von. (1990). "Über die innere und äußere Organisation der höheren wissenschaftlichen Anstalten in Berlin." In *Gelegentliche Gedanken über Universitäten*, ed. Ernst Müller, 273–283. Leipzig: Reclam.

Kant, Immanuel. (1997). "Der Streit der Fakultäten." In *Werkausgabe*, ed. Wilhelm Weischedel, vol. XI, 265–347. Frankfurt/M: Suhrkamp.

Merton, Robert K. (1973). *The Sociology of Science: Theoretical and Empirical Investigation.* Chicago: University of Chicago Press.

Salais, Robert, and Michael Storper. (1993). *Les mondes du production.* Paris: Éditions de l'EHESS (1997 Engl. trans., *Worlds of Production*, Cambridge, Mass.: Harvard University Press).

CHAPTER 2

THE WITHERING OF THE PROFESSORIATE: CORPORATE UNIVERSITIES AND THE INTERNET

Michael Margolis

For anyone who grew up in a small town, the term "Main Street" must evoke memories of warm community gatherings, neighbors who have the time to "pass the time," and friends coming together.

Whether from small town or big city, UC's incoming students will be able to savor the best of these traditions. Our Master Plan calls for the development of a living campus MainStreet that will serve not only as a social center with shopping, restaurants and recreation but will also provide vital commercial and academic services. Look for a bigger and better bookstore, banking, visitor assistance, counseling and advising centers, and a brightly renovated student union. It's a legacy, designed by award-winning landscape architects and planners Hargreaves Associates and local partners Glaser Associates, to enhance and extend the quality of life beyond current boundaries. . . . The total cost of MainStreet is about $200 million, and construction will be completed in stages over several years.

    —Retrieved November 6, 2002, from
        <http://www.uc.edu/ucinfo/webstree.htm>

BRAVE NEW UNIVERSITIES

For most of the twentieth century, communities of scholars thought the American academy provided some refuge from the vicissitudes of the market economy. Scholars at universities and liberal arts colleges typically immersed themselves in study and in teaching. They occasionally turned out a scholarly article, book, or review, but a small minority produced the bulk of these publications. For most, the primary mission of a university remained "the diffusion and extension of knowledge rather than the advancement" (Newman, 1996). Rhetorically, scholars in the liberal arts and sciences generally embraced the idea that their institutions valued education for its own sake, not necessarily for its immediate utility. Colleges of arts and sciences within the universities provided places where students and faculty could learn together, mature intellectually, and reflect upon how their knowledge ought to affect the conduct of private and civic affairs of the broader society. More lucrative employment might be found outside academia, but it usually offered a less congenial environment for learning (Sperber, 2000).

Of course, higher education had a practical side. Specialized programs, schools, or colleges found within and without the universities provided training for various occupations and professions from farming and business through engineering, law, and medicine. Patrons and clients of these institutions—governments, businesses, churches, and philanthropies—expected that graduates would combine the virtues of educated citizens with the practical skills or knowledge necessary to secure desirable livelihoods. And from the final decades of the nineteenth century, American universities progressively leavened Anglo/American ideas that emphasized teaching, learning, and citizenship with continental European ideas of academic research that emphasized the advancement of knowledge (Sullivan, 1999).

To be sure, higher education that emphasized training skilled professional and nurturing civic leadership was hardly for the masses. The United States's official commitment to public education was first articulated in the Northwest Ordinance of 1787, but prior to World War II only about a quarter of adults over twenty-five had completed high school and only one in twenty had completed four years of higher education. Nevertheless, the United States generally devoted larger proportions of governmental resources to public education than did its democratic counterparts. Consequently, even before the GI Bill initiated a significant increase in higher education enrollment, the proportion of Americans who were high school or higher education graduates exceeded those of most economically advanced nations not only in 1940 but also throughout the twentieth century. Higher education received a second boost when the Soviet Union launched *Sputnik*, its first orbiting satellite, in 1957. By the mid-1960s institutions of higher learning grew as programs were developed or expanded to meet both the Soviet Cold War challenge and to accommodate the influx of postwar baby boomers. By 1970, 55 percent of adults over twenty-five had completed high school and 11 percent had completed four or more years of higher education.

Much of this has changed in recent decades. In the aftermath of a great expansion in the 1960s and early 1970s to accommodate the influx of postwar baby boomers, universities and other higher educational institutions found themselves facing increased costs. They had new facilities and infrastructure to maintain, and they had bid up salaries in order to staff courses for their larger student population or to recruit scholars and researchers of great repute. When the American economy entered a long period of "stagflation" in the mid-1970s, therefore, higher education faced new financial problems. Increases in public appropriations lagged behind economic inflation, as did profits and asset values of corporate and philanthropic donors. Moreover, the baby boomer population bulge was moving beyond the traditional college age. In order to support their expanded programs and operations, universities had to seek additional sources of revenue. Their efforts included recruiting and retaining new and nontraditional students, increasing alumni financial support, and promoting revenue-generating activities such as basketball and football teams or nondegree programs such as alumni travel or education in retirement. They also implemented businesslike evaluations of the revenue streams that stemmed from enrollments in particular academic programs, research projects, clinical income, or other contracts for services. Lastly, encouraged by federal policy embodied in the Bayh-Dole Act of 1980, they entered into public-private partnerships to market inventions developed from federally funded research projects.

The upshot of these developments gradually transformed higher education from a collegial to a corporate enterprise. As institutional life became more complex, a separate class of career academic administrators was needed to oversee the educational enterprise. Even though higher education had always had a central role in preparing a skilled and adaptable workforce, educational administrators came to stress its economic benefits, both personal and societal, as the main justification for its receiving public and private subsidies. Functionally, faculties began to adopt the role of corporate employees and students the role of full-fledged customers (Yudoff, 2002).

Still faculties remained an unusual class of employees, for most of their members, after a six-year trial period, had been granted career-long tenure in their positions. Tenure was established to protect and encourage free inquiry in scholarly endeavors, especially teaching and research. As the need for new revenue became more pressing, however, the criteria for granting tenure tended to favor published scholarship and research supported by external funding more than factors like the quality of instruction or the impact of scholarly activities on communities outside the university. Nowadays, the rewards for producing good research often include a diminution of responsibilities for teaching regularly scheduled classes (Bok, 1993).

This development makes sense fiscally: having teaching assistants, adjunct faculty, and other untenured faculty substitute for higher paid professors saves money. Today, over 40 percent of faculty are part-time. Ironically, therefore, the surest way to gain tenure at institutions of higher learning is to demonstrate that one's research not only merits publication but that it also satisfies the priorities of external funders. Whether or not the prodigious output of research demonstrates intellectual independence, or whether or not it increases the total value or overall quality of scholarship, tends to take second place to whether or not the monetary considerations associated with it—grants, contracts, or potential profit—are sufficiently lucrative.

By the mid-1990s, the conservative turn in American politics had penetrated the academy itself. Once the putative bastion of "liberalism," signs of a corporate culture pervaded most American universities. The ratio of full-time administrators to full-time faculty had risen. Faculty who retired were replaced by part-timers and graduate students, especially in those disciplines that brought in fewer research dollars from external sources. Universities not only encouraged faculty to seek research dollars and contracts from external sources, but they also actively lobbied state legislatures and Congress to receive funds earmarked for their specific institutions. In fiscal year 2002, earmarked appropriations from Congress alone exceeded $1.66 billion (Brainard and Southwick, 2001). Administrators commonly likened students to "customers" whose patronage—notwithstanding rising tuition—their institutions needed to attract and retain. Pressures increased to raise the teaching load of scholars who failed to bring in research dollars, and politically conservative academics attacked the professoriate in general and the institution of tenure in particular.

Faculty members themselves were by no means entirely innocent in this matter. By making "grantsmanship" a key element of the tenure process, they lost sight of the hard-won principles of tenure that most universities had formally ratified only in 1940. They effectively acquiesced to new standards that tended to divide the professoriate into a well-compensated, tenured class of researchers who tend to teach or work with advanced undergraduate or graduate students and an under-compensated, untenured class of teachers who deal mostly with freshmen and sophomores. Perhaps in belated recognition of the situation, efforts of faculties to unionize have increased.

When popularly accessible computer-mediated communication through the World Wide Web and multimedia browsers like Netscape Communicator and Microsoft Internet Explorer arose in the mid-1990s, the corporate culture was the catalyst for profound changes in higher education. Higher education had always been a labor-intensive task, but heretofore there had been no fully acceptable way to cut labor costs by eliminating lectures and classroom discussions. The new technology had the potential to overcome this limitation and perhaps, at long last, to break the professorial guild. Indeed, the very manner in which the educational product had been marketed provided the justification for such changes. The anticipated savings, combined with high-tech delivery of the product, would certainly please their financially strapped customers; and if the product still resulted in a sufficiently trained workforce, those savings alone would also please their patrons and clients (Bromwell, 2002; Taylor, 1999).

In sum, the stage has been set for the adoption of Internet technologies to bring about profound changes in the conduct of teaching and research in higher education. The next section examines the likely changes. The final section assesses their likely consequences.

THE INTERNET AND HIGHER EDUCATION

The Internet and related media provide the opportunity to alter, enhance, and otherwise improve traditional forms of instruction and research. Uses include placing syllabi and assignments online; developing web sites and courseware for teaching and for facilitating students' research; computerizing classroom presentations to enhance or replace lectures and face-to-face discussions; using e-mail and online discussions (synchronous and asynchronous) to improve communication with (and among) traditional students on campus and to reach new students at a distance. Beyond this, remote access to digitized libraries and databases can enhance or replace on-campus resources, both for coursework and for original research.

In a perfect world incorporating these media would be largely unobjectionable. We can imagine idyllic campuses where mentors guide students through the fundamentals of their academic disciplines, where rigorous study builds good character, and where students and mentors use the knowledge gained to contemplate questions of philosophic import. Combining this setting with access to the Internet's vast stores of information could lead to an enlightened civic-minded public whose good works, according to liberal democratic theory, would result in a better life for all.

The most obvious problem with this scenario is its cost. No modern society has offered so rich an education to any but its elite, and arguably, none could do so without diverting substantial resources from other public and private commitments. In the United States an intimate association of students and teachers "without the distractions of . . . outside work or other competitive involvements" can be found only at leading private liberal arts colleges or at select undergraduate colleges of major public and private research universities (Trow, 1997). The cost of acquiring new information technology is unlikely to become a primary concern at these institutions. Notwithstanding the premium tuition they usually charge, most have large waiting lists of qualified students who desire to matriculate. They can use the technology largely to enhance the value of the education that results from the close student-teacher relationships already in place, and if necessary, they can charge an additional premium for this enhancement.

Higher education for the masses takes place mostly at public institutions and generally focuses upon the transmission of knowledge. It has less concern for building character or shaping society's leaders through personal interaction between students and mentors. Studies are less intense than at elite institutions, student to faculty ratios are larger, and in the United States most students combine their studies with substantial outside employment during the school year in order to meet educational and other expenses. Outside employment may enrich their studies, but that usually is not a requirement. The key concern is for students to gain skills and knowledge necessary to certify them as trainable employees in their chosen fields. While adopting information technology can enrich the curricula at these institutions, it costs money to do so. Adoption tends to be justified, therefore, as providing wider access to courses and, inevitably, as cutting the per capita cost of delivering the educational product.

The second problem is that the great majority of undergraduates, the customers so to speak, are interested mostly in securing employment and a good income directly upon graduation or in gaining entry to graduate or professional programs to increase their skills, prestige, and potential income. They are far less concerned about honing their critical thinking, developing philosophies of life, improving social and political values, becoming community leaders, participating in civic or cultural affairs, or realizing other benefits of a rigorous education. To gain a general education and appreciation of cultural ideas will suffice. The way in which the majority of undergraduates view education as personal economic investments comports with the corporate marketing of education as an investment product.

This brings us to the third problem. Where traditional institutions may view new information technologies as an enrichment of the established curricula, private-sector companies view the technologies as entrepreneurial opportunities to penetrate the near monopoly of the $250 billion higher education market that traditional institutions have enjoyed in the United States. Whereas most degree programs still require students to attend class at a physical campus, for-profit enterprises believe that delivering instructional programs via the Internet can eliminate this requirement. By delivering degree programs online, virtual institutions can maintain scanty physical plants devoid of expensive laboratories, classrooms, libraries, dormitories, or offices. By employing only a few full-time (let alone tenured) faculty or librarians, they can drastically reduce the customary labor costs of instruction. At the same time they can hold out the promise of flexible access to higher education, complete with virtual tutors online, for everyone who can log on to the Internet.

So far most of the new institutions have confined themselves to niche markets, such as mid-career adult learners who seek to upgrade their current capacities or to acquire additional skills in new or related fields, usually while maintaining their present (often full-time) employment. Increasingly, however, they are introducing more traditional two-year associate and four-year baccalaureate programs that compete both in substance and in price with those of the campus-based "bricks-and-mortar" educational institutions. While the good will and prestige that accrue to graduates of traditional programs at established nonelite institutions justify some premium for their tuition, accrediting boards and systematic studies have concluded that their for-profit competitors offer course content and instruction that is sufficient to merit accreditation of numerous degree programs. In short, those that provide Internet-based distance education cannot be summarily dismissed as "digital diploma mills."

The presumption that for-profit distance education providers can extend their reach from niche markets that tend to emphasize specialized professional training into mass education that includes the core disciplines of the liberal arts and sciences, however, remains questionable. For most students effective K–12 education involves interpersonal relationships with teachers and fellow students, not merely digitized interaction via a networked communication device. Is postsecondary education so different or are the students so changed that such interpersonal relationships are no longer important? Critics argue that quality education at any level involves labor-intensive personal interaction. Most students need to spend some quality time with their instructors and with one another. Indeed, the dropout rate among distance learning students has been a perennial problem, regardless of the medium of instruction.

Distance educators insist that they can offer individualized instruction via the Internet that matches or exceeds the personal attention students usually experience on the crowded campuses of typical nonelite institutions. This argument is not new: the "edupreneurs" who ran for-profit correspondence schools during the "roaring '20s" made the same points. As it happened, however, correspondence school instructors found that responding to students via the post required large amounts of time. And as anyone who has employed the Internet to enhance a campus-based course or has used it to teach distance learning courses has found, preparing such courses and responding to student communications usually demand more time than do traditional classroom-based courses. Indeed, after reviewing the correspondence school boomlet during the 1920s, historian David Noble (1999) observed that in order to make a profit in higher education, most private-sector institutions were "compelled to reduce their instructional costs to a minimum, thereby undermining their pedagogical promise. The invariable result has been not only a degraded labor force but a degraded product as well. The history of correspondence education provides a cautionary tale in this regard, a lesson of a debacle hardly heeded by those today so frantically engaged in repeating it."

Over and above labor costs, distance learning via the Internet requires the same institutional investment in communications hardware and software, and the same access fees to proprietary courseware and databases that traditional institutions must make. Moreover, unless Internet education providers are willing to foot the bill, their students must purchase and maintain their own communications access as well as computer hardware and software. In short, the economic viability of postsecondary education in the liberal arts and sciences via the Internet, as opposed to more specialized professional training, remains unproven.

Nevertheless, adopting information technologies for instruction via the Internet allows university administrators to respond to pressures from politicians, taxpayers, and students-cum-customers to decrease the cost of delivering higher education. These technologies appear to provide opportunities for new types of higher learning enterprises—private and public, for-profit and not-for-profit—to emerge. Most of these enterprises claim to deliver higher educational products comparable to those of traditional university programs of mass education, but with greater efficiency and at less cost. The claim remains plausible; the evidence is inconclusive.

In the United States today, only 27 percent of undergraduates in the United States are "traditional" full-time students who enrolled directly after high school and who depend upon their parents for a substantial portion of their financial support. The arguments for enrollment for the "nontraditional" student commonly focus upon economic advantages: (1) The U.S. Department of Labor (or some other authority) predicts that the great majority—perhaps as many as 80 percent—of new positions in a rapidly changing job market will involve information technology. (2) In order to stay competitive, today's workers will have to keep acquiring new skills and knowledge. (3) Distance learning via the Internet can match traditional rates of tuition and can save students time and money by decreasing indirect costs—transportation, home help, wardrobe, room, board, and the like. (4) Online courses offer flexible hours and self-paced learning that cater to the needs of people who must work for a living. (5) Students who successfully complete courses online acquire marketable skills and learn as much as or more than students who complete similar courses in traditional college settings.

The idea that a college or university should be a place where learning extends beyond formal coursework receives short shrift. There is little concern for developing leadership and character, examining the nature of society, or pondering deeper philosophical questions. Nor is there much concern for the modern university's role in the research to expand our knowledge. The appeal, after all, is to "people whose geographic location, work demands, physical or social conditions, personal circumstances, or family and community responsibilities impede their access to traditional university-level education" (Atieh, 1998). Distance learning via the Internet is presented as the quintessential means of achieving success by fitting oneself to the job requirements set by corporate America.

An online education may be found lacking in comparison to the traditional programs at elite colleges or universities, but it looks more competitive when compared to standard programs for mass education. While a few studies cast doubt on claims that students learn as much or more online as in standard programs, such instruction is relatively new, and as Odin argues (below), there is good reason to believe that the pedagogy will improve. Similarly, claims that instruction online really costs less than standard instruction also remain unproven. Indeed, a number of start-ups have failed, including nonprofits like the California Virtual University and the American branch of Britain's Open University—but we have not yet completed the stage of venture capital investment and its attendant market shakeout. Once this is past the efficiencies of competition and economies of scale make entrepreneurs confident that the costs of hardware and software will shrink.

If nonelite institutions of higher education find online learning competitors making significant inroads into their traditional student base, faculty as well as administrators must share in the blame. Having marketed a college degree as an investment designed to produce a profitable return, they have helped to destroy the idea of a university as a gathering place where scholars and students engage in a mutual enterprise of learning and research, regardless of the immediate economic benefits. Forget the lofty ideals of Newman and Dewey. The idea of a university has begun to resemble that of an education factory designed to produce and disseminate knowledge with maximum efficiency.

ASSESSING THE CONSEQUENCES

Mindful that their patrons and clientele desire more bang for their educational buck, yet faced with increased costs, institutions of higher learning have adopted more businesslike practices. Differential markets for higher education are openly acknowledged. The best students clamor to gain admission to the most prestigious—and often most expensive—undergraduate programs. Although some scholarships are available, those students with both the skills to qualify and the money to pay have the best chances of gaining admission.

Institutions that offer programs primarily for the mass of traditional students are harder pressed to make ends meet. Increasingly, they evaluate the quality of courses or programs by the number of students enrolled and retained. Productivity involves achieving higher ratios of students to full-time faculty, often using low-paid teaching assistants to break large classes into smaller discussion sections. Threatened by the potential loss of many traditional students to less expensive two-year community colleges or to virtual educational institutions, they have sometimes ignored or lowered their standards for admission in order to maintain enrollments. Alternatively, they have begun to offer distance-learning courses of their own or in partnership with other educational providers.

Stuck with maintaining both their physical plants and a semipermanent labor force, however, campus-based educational institutions with traditional four-year bachelor degree programs fear they cannot match the prices that putatively efficient competitors—well-managed two-year community colleges and online educational providers—can offer.

In order to survive—perchance to thrive—in the new environment, traditional institutions have two general strategies. The first is to emphasize the cultural values rather than the direct economic benefits that higher education ideally fosters in its graduates and in the nation: democracy, equality, diversity, social mobility, scientific progress, moral enlightenment, enriched quality of life, and the like. These hark back to Newman's and Dewey's ideas, and they form part of the attraction of elite institutions. The second strategy is to model institutional practices more closely on the operations of profitable private corporations. This involves de-emphasizing noneconomic values and adopting hard-nosed businesslike criteria to measure performance.

Nonelite institutions might have succeeded with the former strategy if they had adopted it when faculty still played decisive roles in university administration. The strategy still might succeed for specific schools or subject areas, where nonelite institutions can establish programs of excellence for niche markets. As an overall strategy, however, it stands the proverbial snowball's chance in hell of success. Most faculties have never made the case successfully that new information technologies should be used primarily to enhance teaching and research, not to eliminate classrooms, undergraduate laboratories, libraries, and personnel. They often treat teaching as interfering with rather than complementing research, and they rarely object to marketing higher education as an economic investment. As we have noted, most students have now accepted this view.

Even though lip service is still paid to the idea of a university as a special place for study and thought, most educational institutions have already adopted aspects of the second strategy. They have revamped criteria for evaluating research, teaching, and community service to reflect their impact on university budgets. They have downsized full-time faculty through attrition and relied increasingly upon low-paid, part-time instructors and graduate students to teach undergraduate courses. They have begun replacing classroom lectures with interactive sessions on the Internet. They have cut research costs through use of digital libraries and networked computers, reduced support for nonlucrative scholarship, and begun to charge a fair price for services they formerly provided for free, such as computer setup and maintenance or access to special databases.

To differentiate themselves from online competitors some urban institutions, such as the University of Cincinnati, have begun to invest heavily in value-added features of campus life. Even though UC students are mostly commuters, and about half work twenty or more hours per week to pay for their education, UC envisions its campus of the future as a "MainStreet" where students will gather to spend significant portions of their day. Such value-added projects normally increase a university's bonded debt.

In order to generate more revenue over the long term, therefore, UC has also invested in conference centers on campus and community redevelopment corporations in neighborhoods surrounding campus. These are in addition to established alumni programs, university paraphernalia, varsity athletic enterprises, and exclusive contracts for on-campus sales with food, beverage, and clothing vendors. As a university president is expected to be an effective fund-raiser, the board of trustees has established rules that two representatives from the university's fund-raising arm, the UC Foundation, serve on the fifteen-member Presidential Search Committee. Faced with revenue shortfalls, public colleges and universities throughout the United States are taking similar action (Breneman, 2002).

The aim of reducing instructional costs comports with the economic values held by most students, public officials, and conservatively inclined corporate and philanthropic donors. The second strategy, therefore, is easier to adopt than the first. It stands a better chance of winning the university plaudits for good management and gaining it capital investment for technological development.

The next stage in the evolution of higher education for the general public will most likely entail full adoption of the corporate model of education as an investment product. We already have for-profit institutions like the University of Phoenix, Jones International University, and Knowledge Universe using information technologies online for degree programs or implementing such online programs for other institutions. As underclass courses of traditional universities adopt more and more of the characteristics of those offered by online institutions, we can expect greater standardization. Why spend money for faculties at separate institutions to develop and teach introductory courses, which have the same essential content? Wouldn't it be cheaper to develop online courses that not only could be accessed at the students' convenience but also could be taught by the world's best teachers? Nonelite institutions no longer would need to limit their course instruction to their own—and let's face it—mostly undistinguished faculty. Eventually, many of their under-graduate programs—perhaps even entire schools or colleges—could be marketed as franchises of greater, more distinguished institutions. Indeed, these prospects have led an increasing number of American universities to assert ownership and control over the intellectual output of their faculty (Twigg, 2000; Woody, 1998).

Some analysts argue that universities can use corporate-like man-agement to balance short-term objectives demanded by the new educa-tional market with established long-term objectives of cultural enrich-ment. Inexorably, however, the logic of corporate management of the higher education market leads to ending professorial tenure as we know it. Traditional institutions must spend more money just to recruit and retain their most profitable undergraduate customers. Must they also be obliged to carry their workers through lean times as well as fat? Academic freedom needs to be protected, but in the new competitive market of higher education tenure must be balanced against economic exigency. When a department or program cannot produce sufficient income to cover its costs, its payroll must be downsized. This could be accomplished in a flexible decentralized fashion that perhaps would not compromise academic freedom. The faculty members affected by the order to downsize could decide for themselves how to meet the cuts: whether to lay off colleagues, retain everyone at reduced salary, or implement some other creative solution.

Barring an unexpected resurgence of support for cultural strategies to preserve the traditional campus-based university model, the lines between most traditional higher educational institutions and the upstart educational enterprises that rely upon information technology seem likely to disappear. While the particular mix of partnerships, mergers, buyouts, consolidations, spin-offs, and the like cannot be specified as yet, established institutions will restructure their delivery of higher edu-cation in a businesslike manner that maximizes efficient use of informa-tion technologies for instruction and minimizes the need for personal instruction by highly paid professors. As basic courses in most disci-plines will be available in a limited number of standardized forms, fac-tors like ease of access and convenience of information delivery will be stressed. Institutions will strive to become the students' portal to higher education, the only connection they will ever need, at least for their undergraduate training. A good local or branch campus will stress advantages like the availability of personal consultation, meeting rooms, laboratory facilities, entertainment centers, low-priced health clubs, and similar services and facilities, much like stressing the advantages offered by a good local or branch bank. Nontraditional students will find that the restructured institutions also offer plenty of programs that employ information technologies suited to part-time study. All of this will be advertised at a suitably affordable price.

Outstanding professors and researchers will still be found in the best undergraduate colleges and universities and in the best graduate programs. Gifted students will still be able to attend select undergraduate institutions on scholarship or for a higher price, but the public will be spared most of the burden of supporting a tenured professoriate. That intellectual class will no longer be allowed to draw pay to support its inclination to study and to think. Its costly travel to attend professional meetings will be reduced by holding such meetings online. Graduate and professional studies, which offer increased economic benefits to those who earn advanced degrees, will be supported by tuition and by grants or contracts for research. Students, politicians, donors, and taxpayers will be happy. The campus of the future will be hailed as a triumph of the free market. Other than faculty, hardly anyone seems likely to object.

REFERENCES

Atieh, Sam. (1998). *How to Get a College Degree Via the Internet: The Complete Guide to Getting Your Undergraduate or Graduate Degree from the Comfort of Your Home.* Rocklin, Calif.: Prima.

Baldwin, Roger, and Jay Chronister. (2001). *Teaching Without Tenure: Policies and Practices for a New Era.* Baltimore: Johns Hopkins University Press.

Blumenstyk, Goldie. (1998, October 2). "An Entrepreneur Sees Profits in the Future of his 'Power Campus.'" *Chronicle of Higher Education.*

———. (1999a, July 23). "Banking on Its Reputation, the Open University Starts an Operation in the U.S." *Chronicle of Higher Education.*

———. (1999b, June 18). "A Company Pays Top Universities to Use Their Names and Their Professors." *Chronicle of Higher Education.*

Bok, Derek. (1993). *The Cost of Talent: How Executives and Professionals Are Paid and How It Affects America.* New York: The Free Press.

Brainard, Jeffrey, and Ron Southwick. (2001, August 10). "A Record Year at the Federal Trough: Colleges Feast on $1.67-Billion in Earmarks." *Chronicle of Higher Education.*

Braun, Dietmar, and François-Xavier Merrien (eds.). (1999). *Towards a New Model of Governance for Universities: A Comparative View.* London: Jessica Kingsly.

Breneman, David. (2002, June 14). "For Colleges, This Is Not Just Another Recession." *Chronicle of Higher Education,* B7.

Bromell, Nick. (2002, February). "Summa Cum Avaritia: Plucking a Profit from the Groves of Academe." *Harper's Magazine,* 71–76.

Carnevale, Dan. (2000, August 4). "Turning Traditional Courses into Distance Education." *Chronicle of Higher Education.* Retrieved August 3, 2003, from <http://chronicle.com/free/v46/i48/48a03701.htm>.

Cole, Robert A. (ed.). (2000). *Issues in Web Based Pedagogy: A Critical Primer.* Westport, Conn.: Greenwood.

Dewey, John. (1916). *Democracy and Education.* New York: Macmillan.

Evelyn, Jamilah. (2002, June 4). "Nontraditional Students Dominate Undergraduate Enrollments, U.S. Study Finds." *Chronicle of Higher Education.*

Fogg, Piper. (2001, November 2). "Colleges Have Cut Proportion of Full-Time Faculty Members, Study Finds." *Chronicle of Higher Education.*

Gladieux, Lawrence E., and Watson Scott Swail. (1999). *The Virtual University and Educational Opportunity: Issues of Equity and Access for the Next Generation.* Washington, D.C.: The College Board.

Grimes, Ann. (2000, July 17). "A Matter of Degree." *Wall Street Journal,* B29.

Huber, Richard M. (1992). *How Professors Play the Cat Guarding the Cream: Why We're Paying More and Getting Less in Higher Education.* Fairfax, Va.: George Mason University Press.

Katz, Richard N. and Associates. (1999). *Dancing with the Devil: Information Technology and the New Competition in Higher Education.* San Francisco: Jossey-Bass.

Lazerson, Marvin, Ursula Wagener, and Larry Moneta. (2000, July 28). "Like the Cities They Resemble, Colleges Must Train and Retain Competent Managers." *Chronicle of Higher Education.*

Lewis, Brian, Christine Massey, and Richard Smith. (2001). *The Tower Under Siege: Technology, Power and Education.* Montreal: McGill-Queens University Press.

Marginson, Simon, and Mark Considine. (2000). *The Enterprise University: Power Governance and Reinvention in Australia.* Cambridge: Cambridge University Press.

Margolis, Michael. (1998, May 4). "Brave New Universities." *First Monday,* 3(5). Retrieved August 3, 2003, from <http://www.firstmonday.dk/issues/issue3_5/index.html>.

NASULGC Universities Connecting to the Future: How Do They Do IT? How Do They Pay for IT. (1999). NASULGC [National Association of State Universities and Land-Grant Colleges]. Washington, D.C.: Office of Public Affairs, NASULGC.

National Center for Education Statistics. (1997). *Distance Education in Higher Education Institutions, NCES 98-062.* Prepared by Laurie Lewis, Debbie Alexander, and Elizabeth Farris. Washington, D.C.: U.S. Department of Education.

———. (2001). *Institutional Policies and Practices: Findings from the 1999 National Study of Postsecondary Faculty, Institution Survey.* Prepared by Andrea Berger, Rita Kirshstein, and Elizabeth Rowe. Washington, D.C.: U.S. Department of Education.

Newman, John Henry. (1996 [1899]). *The Idea of a University.* New Haven: Yale University Press.

Noble, David F. (1999). "Digital Diploma Mills, Part IV: Rehearsal for the Revolution." Retrieved August 13, 2003, from <http://communication.ucsd.edu/dl/ddm4.html>.

Olsen, Florence. (1999). "'Virtual' Institutions Challenge Accreditors to Devise New Ways of Measuring Quality." Retrieved August 3, 2003, from <http://chronicle.com/free/v45/i48/48a02901.htm>.

Resnick, David. (2000, August). "The Virtual University and College Life: Some Unintended Consequences for Democratic Citizenship." *First Monday, 5*(8). Retrieved August 3, 2003, from <http://firstmonday.org/issues/issue5_8/resnick/index.html>.

Russell, Thomas. (2002). "The 'No Significant Difference Phenomenon.'" Retrieved August 13, 2003, from http://teleeducation.nb.ca/nosignificantdifference/index.cfm and companion site http://teleeducation.nb.ca/significantdifference/.

Shea, Christopher. (1998, July 3). "Visionary or 'Operator'? Jorge Klor de Alva and His Unusual Intellectual Journey: Controversial Anthropologist Gives Up a Chair at Berkeley to Lead the U. of Phoenix." *Chronicle of Higher Education.*

Sperber, Murray. (2000, October 20). "End the Mediocrity of Our Public Universities." *Chronicle of Higher Education.*

Sullivan, William M. (1999). *Institutional Identity and Social Responsibility.* Washington, D.C.: Council on Educational Policy.

Sykes, Charles J. (1988). *ProfScam: Professors and the Demise of Higher Education.* New York: St. Martin's.

Taylor, Kit Sims. (1999, September 7). "Higher Education: From Craft-Production to Capitalist Enterprise?" *First Monday, 3*(9). Retrieved August 3, 2003, from <http://www.firstmonday.dk/issues/issue3_9/taylor/index.html>.

"The Bayh-Dole Act: A Guide to the Law and Implementing Regulations." (1999). *Council of Governmental Relations.* Retrieved November 2, 2002, from <http://www.cogr.edu/bayh-dole.htm>.

Trow, Martin. (1997). "The Development of Information Technology in American Higher Education." *Daedalus, 126,* 297–314.

Twigg, Carol A. (2000). *Who Owns Online Courses and Course Materials? Intellectual Property Policies for a New Learning Environment.* Troy, N.Y.: Center for Academic Transformation, Rensselaer Polytechnic Institute (Pew Learning and Technology Program 2000). Retrieved August 3, 2003, from <http://www.center.rpi.edu/pewsym/mono2.html>.

What's the Difference? A Review of Contemporary Research on the Effectiveness of Distance Learning in Higher Education. (1999). Institute for Higher Education. Prepared by Ronald Phipps and Jamie Merisotis for the American Federation of Teachers and the National Education Association. Washington, D.C.: The Institute for Higher Education Policy.

White, Frank. (1999, July 5). "Digital Diploma Mills: A Dissenting Voice." *First Monday, 4*(7). Retrieved August 3, 2003, from <http://www.firstmonday.dk/issues/issue4_7/white/index.html>.

Wilson, Robin. (1999, June 2). "Georgia State U. to Replace Part-Timers With Full-Time, Untenured Professors." *Chronicle of Higher Education* (online edition). Retrieved August 3, 2003, from <http://chronicle.com/weekly/v45/i40/40a01801 .htm>.

Woody, Todd. (1998). "Higher Earning: The Fight to Control The Academy's Intellectual Capital: Universities Are Facing a Revolution over Intellectual Property as Technology Blurs the Lines between Good Business and Good Education." *The Industry Standard*. Retrieved August 3, 2003, from <http://www.thestandard.com/ article/0,1902,874,00.html> (June 28).

Young, Jeffrey R. (1999). "Research Universities Team Up to Create a 'Portal' to Online Education." *Chronicle of Higher Education: Daily News*. Retrieved August 3, 2003, from <http://chronicle.com/free/99/06/99061001t.htm>.

Yudof, Mark G. (2002, January 11). "Is the Public Research University Dead?" *Chronicle of Higher Education*.

CHAPTER 3

THE NEO-LIBERAL PARADIGM AND HIGHER EDUCATION: A CRITIQUE

Jan Currie

THE CONCEPT OF GLOBALIZATION is contradictory and contested. However, it is generally agreed that the world's economy is integrated in a way that is different from that of the past. One of the differences is that there are no longer any substantial economic systems competing with capitalism. Proponents of neo-liberal globalization believe that through competition and market forces a more perfect world will develop. At the same time, critics of neo-liberal globalization believe that global economic forces tend to segment and divide societies and the world into different types of players: those who initiate globalization, those who are affected by it, and those who are left out of it.

Some see globalization as a politically neutral approach, defining it as an empirical reality in terms of the compression of time and space, particularly associated with instantaneous communications technology. The political-economy approach identifies globalization as an economic discourse actively promulgating a market ideology. Most writers on globalization agree that it creates tensions between pressures toward homogeneity (increasing similarities) and heterogeneity (increasing differences) in policies across nation-states and institutions.

The fall of the Berlin Wall in 1989 is a significant date, marking the triumph of capitalism over communism and an intensification of neo-liberal globalization. It is also significant that the Internet, although in existence prior to the 1990s, began to be used increasingly after that date as a tool by academics, bureaucrats, businesspeople, and private citizens. Its use sparked the recognition that we are living in an expanding information age. The thickening networks of instantaneous communication have created a mental schema of a world that is increasingly smaller in our minds. We conceptualize a different image of our world when we view the earth from space rather than in an atlas. We grasp the globe in its entirety. Space travel is not the only form of travel that opened people's minds to different images of the world. Air travel gave people new ideas about distant lands and foreign values. The movement of people around the world created a more pluralistic view of cultures. As people migrated to new lands, hybrid identities were developed, overlapping new values on old and deploying different values for varying situations.

With greater tolerance for different value systems, freedom of expression has created a more liberal attitude toward different lifestyles. Globalization brings new ideas and new opportunities. At the same time it raises issues of asymmetry. It is apparent in the political and economic dimensions, and asymmetry exists in the cultural dimension as well. This is well expressed by Appadurai (2000), who describes globalization as the world of things in motion, a world of flows. There are flows of ideas and ideologies, people and goods, images and messages, technologies and techniques. But, he says, these various flows are not coeval or spatially consistent; rather, they are in relations of disjuncture. An example he gives is of media flowing across national boundaries, producing images of well-being that cannot be satisfied by national standards of living and consumer capabilities. So, he concludes, globalization "produces problems that manifest themselves in intensely local forms but have contexts that are anything but local."

The foregoing suggests that globalization affects all countries in the same way. However, a number of writers are beginning to see patterns of difference emerging in the responses of countries to global forces. Hall and Soskice demonstrate that market economies differ and that their reactions to globalization have not produced the same policies. They identified at least three different patterns but wrote at length about two types: liberal market economies mainly in Anglo-Saxon countries (United Kingdom, United States, Australia, Canada, Ireland, and New Zealand) and coordinated market economies mainly in European countries (Germany, Switzerland, Belgium, The Netherlands, Finland, Denmark, Norway, and Sweden) and also in Japan. Hall and Soskice found that firms operate differently in these two market economies. Firms, for example, react differently to similar challenges, depending on the political economic culture in which they are situated. For example, firms in liberal market economies are more inclined to move off-shore to secure cheaper labor than those in coordinated market economies. Also, trade unions have not been as weakened by globalization in coordinated market economies, with their shorter working hours, more equal incomes, and lower unemployment rates. In contrast, liberal market economies have allowed higher income inequality to develop, probably due to the weakening role of trade unions, longer work hours, and reduced unemployment benefits. Both Pierson and Brown concur with these findings and point out how the neo-liberal agenda has created greater inequality in Anglo-Saxon countries. Furthermore, there is no clear evidence that those states that have more extensive welfare policies have actually fared any worse economically.

A flow-on effect of particular economic policies for universities exists in these different economies. Due to reduced taxes and lower public-sector funding in liberal market economies, universities are increasingly becoming corporatized and are forced to become more entrepreneurial. To survive in an increasingly competitive environment, universities are developing closer ties with industries, forming spin-off companies and private business arms, and moving toward a user-pays philosophy for most services. Universities in coordinated market economies are more heavily funded by government and still believe to a degree in free education for students or at least in keeping fees low enough to guarantee access to those students who pass the entrance examinations.

GLOBALIZATION AND UNIVERSITIES

Neo-liberal globalization is a significant challenge facing universities in this millennium. It is important to note, moreover, that responses of universities appear to differ according to the type of market economy, the strength of the economy, and the willingness of a country's citizenry to pay enough taxes to fund public institutions. What is this challenge of neo-liberal globalization for universities, and how does it vary by market types?

Most governments want universities to serve their national interests in the global marketplace and there is an increasing tendency to emphasize the practical and technical value of higher education. Students now look upon universities in an instrumental way to serve their individual, economic goals. One key economic element is to recognize that educational products can flow very easily across borders, creating a borderless higher education system. To take advantage of the fluidity of boundaries, universities, like transnational companies, are forming alliances to deliver education on a global scale, using Internet technology.

Governments in liberal market economies are also beginning the move to privatize universities, essentially by reducing public funding. However, privatization of higher education takes many forms. It includes allowing more private universities to be developed in a country, creating spin-off companies as part of public universities, establishing for-profit universities, and developing for-profit arms of public universities. It may mean a movement to a user-pays system, where students pay increasing amounts for their university education when previously it was an entitlement with no fees or very small tuition costs. This has increasingly led to the corporatization of universities, or treating universities like businesses.

Are there benefits in this move to privatize and corporatize universities? And does neo-liberal globalization create new opportunities as well as potential disadvantages for universities? How are the tools of globalization, such as the Internet and e-mail, transforming universities?

POTENTIAL BENEFITS

SPREAD OF ACCESS AND OPPORTUNITY

Online education and the development of borderless universities offer increased opportunities to spread higher education to every corner of the world. A global trend toward the massification of higher education is evident in the Organization for Economic Cooperation and Development (OECD) countries. Most countries now are attempting to have over 50 percent of their age cohort in some form of higher education. Third World countries have not increased their proportion to anywhere near that percentage; however, they are also attempting to increase their proportion of enrollments in higher education with limited resources. For this reason a call has been sounded for the gap between the North and the South in economic terms and the "digital divide" to be closed so that all those who are qualified to have a tertiary education can receive one. It is projected that by 2010 100 million people will be living in the world, fully qualified to proceed from secondary to tertiary education but there will be no room left on any campus. For this reason, writers are foreseeing the development of online education as a solution to this burgeoning demand.

INTERNATIONALIZATION AND INCREASING TOLERANCE

The increase in the number of students studying abroad and the overseas students moving to study in other countries is one form of internationalization of universities. This exchange of students and exposure to other cultures will purportedly lead to greater tolerance and an acceptance of the plurality of cultures in the world. This may occur if there is a mingling of students and if academics make an effort to internationalize the curriculum in universities.

INCREASING LINKS WITH INDUSTRY AND CREATING GREATER ECONOMIC GROWTH

Countries are increasingly relying on higher education institutions as key instruments for wealth creation in the belief that the knowledge economy needs more highly educated workers and universities are relied upon to train and educate these workers. Industries are also looking to universities to create new knowledge; by developing links with universities, this type of collaboration can lead to new discoveries and their more rapid transformation into commercial products.

MORE EFFICIENT OPERATION

Operating like a business allows universities to make decisions quickly and to find new market niches to tap into to meet the needs of their clients. Universities may benefit from developing more streamlined decision making in this new competitive environment. However, within these benefits lurk potential dangers, which are beginning to distort the traditional sense of the universities. The question arises: can the university, as we know it, survive in the marketplace?

POTENTIAL DANGERS

INCREASING INEQUALITY

People are growing increasingly skeptical about globalization as an economic process and whether the world is headed in the "right" direction. Many are critiquing globalization as an economic process. George

Soros, a well-known financier, writes about the instability of global capitalism and calls for greater regulation of a number of economic processes and for the democratization of transnational organizations. In a similar vein, Paul Krugman warns other nations not to listen to Washington policy makers and New York bankers because "they often prescribed for other countries the kind of root canal economics that they would never tolerate in the USA." Further, in a recent study Henderson reports that privatization in Australia had delivered little improvement to the financial performance of most government businesses. After the September 11 attacks, U.S. politicians and journalists raised questions about the efficacy of private providers operating the airport security systems. Immediately, the U.S. federal government was seen as a positive force for restoring national security. Previous to that, questions were raised about the privatization of electricity in California when there was not enough power available to consumers due to the deregulation of the system.

Kofi Annan, secretary-general of the United Nations, does not see globalization as an enemy of development. He sees the main losers in today's very unequal world as those who have been left out, not those who are too exposed to globalization. Annan calls for embedding the new global economy into a broad framework of shared values and institutionalized practices at the national and global levels, protecting human rights, labor standards, and the environment as well as we have protected intellectual property.

For universities, this means protecting traditional values that are currently being threatened by opening up universities to market forces. The market, however, is not a neutral force. It is socially constructed and comes embedded in different ideologies. Depending upon the particular ideology of the market, it will penetrate universities in different forms. The Anglo-Saxon neo-liberal paradigm of the market brings with it heightened competition, increased managerialism, commodification of knowledge, and instrumentalism in the curriculum.

SKEWING EDUCATION TOWARD THE MARKET AND VOCATIONALISM

Some vice-chancellors argue that the commercialization of universities is beneficial because it allows managers to shake up academics and make them look outside of the university. Others have argued against this direction because a shift toward the neo-liberal market and vocational-ism is not just an add-on to the university but fundamentally changes its essence.

WIDENING OF INEQUALITIES

Historically, access to higher education in developing nations has been extremely limited and beyond the means of most individuals. Failing to address the vast disparity between information rich and information poor countries may lead to a *digital divide* that could further exacerbate existing educational disadvantages faced by developing countries and further hinder their development. Allport (2000) estimates that the Internet's reach is to less than 2 percent of the world's population.

Although online learning may have the potential to broaden options and opportunities for teachers and learners in developing countries, technology by itself does not improve learning or cause change in educational programs. The basic conditions for effective learning remain centered on well-designed instruction, coupled with utilization of the new Information and Communication Technologies (ICT) opportunities presented to teachers and learners. Indeed, using the Internet to deliver education to developing countries presents many challenges and controversies to both the providers of online education and the recipients. Thus, in any form of distance education mediated by ICT, careful attention is required in areas such as cultural and pedagogical appropriateness, linguistic barriers, content relevance, and the functions and roles of the providers and recipients. ICT is not all the same, nor is it the case that teachers, without training, will use it appropriately.

Another important question raised by online education and its delivery by for-profit institutions is the nature of employment contracts for academics and the overall purpose of these institutions. If their main aim is to make profit and reduce the costs of providing an education, then this will probably result in few full-time faculty members and little expectation that they will be doing research. If there is a move toward greater privatization of public universities and an increase in the number of for-profit institutions, where will research be done? What responsibility will these universities have to contribute to scholarship and research? If they are competing with other universities for students, then their costs will be much reduced. They are likely to enter into fields that are less costly to run, such as business, law, and management.

Therefore, they are not as likely to contribute to the creation of knowledge and the development of the arts and humanities.

LOWERING STANDARDS AND QUALITY

Regarding some of the micro-processes of globalization, such as the accountability movement, there are questions raised about its consequences as well. Birnbaum (2000) analyzes a number of management fads in higher education and why most fail to endure in universities. He quotes a number of studies that show that management fads usually do not deliver what they promise. Most are adopted from the business or government sector and then are diffused into higher education as quick-fix solutions. The quality assurance movement, including total quality management (TQM), benchmarking, performance-based budgeting, responsibility centered budgeting (RCB), performance-based appropriations (PBA), balanced scorecards (BSC), and management for results (MFR), were fads that started in the business sector, then were applied to education and seem to follow the cycle of "early enthusiasm, widespread dissemination, subsequent disappointment, and eventual decline."

University managers seek out these business practices to try to increase the efficiency of their organizations. Yet, many studies conclude that what is good for the world of business is not what is good for higher education institutions. Applying the practice of quality assurance from the business world to universities may lead universities to adopt market rather than intellectual standards. Generally, academics do not see how quality audits will improve teaching and learning. Many assert that the reduction in funding has reduced quality and that quality procedures just add another layer of administration to their workloads without increasing quality. A former Australian vice-chancellor (O'Kane, 2001), writing before her resignation, concluded that quality in Australian universities had declined, citing these reasons:

- Staff are considerably busier, more stressed, and older than they were, on average fifteen or so years ago, and therefore have less time for informal contact with students.
- Class sizes are bigger and contact hours are sometimes lower. Students tend not to get the detailed guidance they got from tutors when groups were smaller.

- Many students are working part-time now, so that they have less time to devote to their studies.
- Staff have fewer opportunities to travel overseas, meaning that international contacts are in some ways weaker than they once were, increasing the isolation of the Australian system.
- Facilities are poorer.
- Fewer technical staff mean that laboratories are not maintained at the levels they were in the past.

O'Kane pointed to a widespread demoralization of staff leading to a decline in quality, which may not be a direct result of massification of the system. However, all of these factors together indicate that quality exercises are not likely to cure these ills.

Increased Managerialism and Secrecy of Decision Making

At a managerial level, universities are experiencing changes in the style, structure, and nomenclature of management directed toward more streamlined administration, greater control over spending, and more flexible staffing practices. In line with this, there are explicit attempts to move universities from collegial to executive decision making. The question may be posed whether globalization propelled this move toward managerialism or whether it would have occurred without the development of a global economy and its accompanying global practices. What is clear is that an increase in managerialism occurred simultaneously in a number of universities around the globe, leading to borrowing of practices from the world of business, seen as "best practices" and mainly derived from American businesses.

A number of commentators in Australia, the United States, and Canada observed this shift in power from academic departments to central administration. This change was accompanied by a new kind of fundamentalism suggesting that managers have all the answers and that answers to managerial issues are to be found in imitating business practices. Corporate managerialism assumes that managers should make the most important decisions and make them quickly, leading to restructured institutions whose streamlined operations give only a few people the information on which to base decisions. But of course this stands in direct opposition to assumptions regarding procedures of hiring and firing faculty, including tenure, and assumptions regarding the faculty control of curriculum, including programs.

In making these changes, management delineates which aspects of decision making academics can be involved in and which aspects the administration should control. Academics have never been central in allocating resources in the United States or Australia. Nevertheless, they sometimes have had a voice in various aspects of budget allocation and more control over academic policy, but even that role is declining. In Australian universities in the past decade, there has been a tendency to silence academics and other whistleblowers and to change the style of decision making to smaller groups making more secretive decisions. One of the reasons Australian university councils deliberate in secret is to enable them to discuss commercially sensitive information. They often exclude academic staff from their inner circles for fear of criticism of the commercial decisions taken.

CHANGING NATURE OF ACADEMIC WORK

A number of writers have discussed the changing nature of academic work around the world. A Carnegie Foundation study on the academic profession in fourteen countries found a professoriate under strain, with expansion of higher education occurring at a time of diminishing resources. Academics in many of these countries reported pressures to be more entrepreneurial, to teach larger classes, to be evaluated more often by students, to survive on fewer research dollars and relatively lower salaries, and to be generally more productive. Also, many of the respondents were concerned about the more hierarchical, more rigid governance structure and expressed dissatisfaction with governance arrangements. Scholars around the world felt alienated from central administration, and fewer than 10 percent felt that they played a key role in governance at the institutional level. The present author interviewed 253 academics in Australia and the United States in the 1993–1995 period and found a high level of concern among academics that the enhanced accountability requirement associated with increasing managerialism and the restructuring of universities had produced a greater emphasis on entrepreneurialism that impinged on institutional autonomy and individual academic freedom. Several studies also found staff to be demoralized and dissatisfied with the increasing intensification of work.

INTENSIFICATION OF WORK

Intensification of work is evident in most occupations as managers reduce staff and demand higher productivity. As in other professions, multiskilling is now the order of the day as most knowledge workers have to extend their skills to learn new software programs and become computer literate at a fairly sophisticated level. For academics, this includes the skills to deliver and teach courses online. Brabazon (2001) concludes that Internet-based teaching actually increases academic workloads because "*somebody* needs to design the content and layout. *Somebody* needs to write the Web pages. *Somebody* needs to ensure that hypertext links are up-to-date. *Somebody* needs to create evaluative criteria. *Somebody* needs to administer the students' results." Moreover, she suggests that current Internet teaching is not relieving academic staff of face-to-face teaching but it is a time-consuming addition to very full working days. And e-mail messages add yet more work. "Hour-long blocks must be set aside to read and reply to an ever-increasing stream of professional, academic, research and teaching inquiries" (Brabazon, 2001).

The cost of online and distance education is another concern because it takes money away from face-to-face teaching. Even though universities may have generated more revenue due to fees from overseas students, industry grants, and consultancies, the increased revenue has not gone toward teaching but toward other costs, including higher salaries for managers, offshore recruitment, and marketing. Therefore, student-staff ratios continue to climb and teaching becomes more stressful as academics have to teach more students, in more modes, be available 24/7 due to e-mail, fax, and phone access, and do more of their own secretarial work and marketing of their courses.

FRAGMENTATION AND LOSS OF COLLEGIALITY

A number of factors have contributed to the fragmentation of academic staff. The increased use of e-mail to communicate has meant that staff in offices right next to each other send e-mails rather than talk face to face about an issue. Of course, this is more efficient, yet the loss of human contact takes its toll. Another major factor contributing to the fragmentation of the notion of a community of scholars is the ideology of competition. The competitive neutrality principle has exacted its toll by making academics compete with one another as though they are on a level playing field. However, this level playing field never exists in reality. Universities are differentiated by history, age, reputation, location, size, types of courses offered, and so on. Departments are equally differentiated by similar factors. And academics by their very location in certain departments, in certain universities, are almost never on an equal playing field. Yet, the notions that the market knows best and that competition brings greater efficiency and that the competition must be based on a neutral stage has meant that formulas that do not differentiate among various types of institutions, departments, or academics are used to set performance indicators and distribute resources. This competitive ethos pits one academic against another, one department against another, and one university against another. This leads to a game of individuals in the survival of the fittest that fragments the university.

Loss of Traditional Values

What are some of the traditional values lost in the new enterprise universities? How have market forces changed our conception of a university? Four key traditional values of universities may be lost in the rush to privatize, commercialize, and create enterprise universities: the public interest value of universities, critical dissent and academic freedom, professional autonomy and scholarly integrity, and democratic collegiality. All of these overlap in some way to help produce students who will become the educated citizens of tomorrow with a social conscience and a desire to see a more just and democratic world.

Singh (2001) identifies a range of social purposes that can yield public benefits, including the facilitation of social justice and the ability of higher education to function as "critic and conscience of society." As Singh points out, "the social purposes of higher education are losing their resonance in the rush to make universities accountable within the logic of the market."

Commercialization, as noted above, is having an impact on academic freedom, often seen as a key legitimating function of the university. When this principle is in good health, academics are given the freedom to teach with passion and introduce controversial ideas that will challenge students to be more critically thinking citizens. Collier (2001) asks: "If the market is the measure of all things, and if only the 'fittest' institutions *and individuals* are likely to survive, where does such an economic rationalist discourse leave the 'inquiring soul' of the academic?"

An established principle, in fact a truism, is that the integrity of a university depends on the integrity of its scholars. This integrity, in its turn, depends upon honesty in scholarship and developing consistently high standards in assessing one another's work. It is important for academics to exercise independent judgment where there is no self-interest involved. Scholarly inquiry should be open-minded, and not influenced by any particular interests that are served by the results. Without the integrity of researchers and a certain amount of objectivity, what becomes of scholarship and a university's service to the public in producing knowledge based on the public interest?

Lastly, to produce both educated and active citizens, universities need to develop and maintain a culture of democratic collegiality. Managerialism, however, leads to just the opposite, as noted above.

Are any of the values still visible within Australian and North American universities? To what extent has the transformation of universities into enterprise universities crushed these traditional values and what kinds of universities have been created? With the acceleration of work and its intensification, along with the pressures to garner funds from industry and wealthy individuals, enterprise universities are making it very difficult for academics to hold on to these traditional values.

TRANSFORMATION OF AUSTRALIAN UNIVERSITIES

Australia's higher education system became a deregulated and commercially oriented system within a decade of major reforms. A number of initiatives came into play from the mid-1980s through the 1990s, all working to privatize the costs of education.

In 1985 the Labor government ended the Overseas Student Program that provided aid to Third World students, and it permitted universities to charge full-cost fees to overseas students. This resulted in one of the largest increases in the proportion of international students studying in any country in the world. For example, in 1986 there were 20,000 aid students and 200 trade students from overseas. By 1991 there were 6,000 aid students and 48,000 trade students. From 1989 to 2000 the number of overseas fee-paying students quadrupled from 21,112 to 95,540.

In 1989 certain postgraduate courses were made liable to fees; in

1994 the restrictions surrounding these courses were almost entirely removed, effectively leaving postgraduate coursework a fee-paying domain. Then from 1998 the Coalition (Liberal Party and National Party) government permitted universities to enroll a proportion of private Australian undergraduate students. Crucially, these measures were accompanied by falling levels of government support for individual students, with the amounts payable reduced and income tests tightened. Between 1984 and 1996 the proportion of students unable to obtain government support almost doubled, increasing from 35.1 percent to 61.9 percent.

According to Marginson (1997), as a result of such measures, the proportion of higher education income contributed by students (through fees and other charges) rose "from 3 percent to over 24 percent in the decade following the Dawkins (Minister responsible for higher education) reforms, while the proportion coming from government sources fell from 91 percent to 62 percent." Allied to this, public funding declined relative to the increase of student enrollments. Between 1988 and 1998, Marginson notes, "student enrollments increased by over 45 percent while the real value of operating funds per full-time student fell by around 15 percent." In the three years since 1998, government funding continued to fall so that it now represents approximately 50 percent of all funding for universities.

Marginson and Considine (2000) suggest that, due to these reforms, universities in Australia changed "more in the 1990s than in the previous 40 years." They also argue that "neo-liberal policies have been enforced with greater rigor in Australia than in the USA. Fiscal constraints have been tighter and competition reform has been harder." In line with this, many academics believe that intellectual traditions are being forcibly displaced by market directives. Tony Coady (1996), professor of philosophy at Melbourne, writes about the threat that the new practices pose to "intellectual virtues such as honesty, intellectual courtesy, indifference to the mere fashion in ideas, and a dedication to the regulative ideal of truth." Not only is there a loss of the humanities and the critical role of professors, there is also a change in the working lives of academics. An Australian study, *Unhealthy Places of Learning*, found that the majority of staff worked above a forty-hour week and the average for full-time academic staff was 52.8 hours per week. Some 83 percent of all academics and 77 percent of general staff reported increases in workload since 1996, with a majority working in departments that have lost staff. In another national study of Australian academics, McInnis reports that the great majority of academics talked about loss of morale and the deterioration of overall quality and working conditions.

Perhaps the most marked characteristic of the corporatized university is its downgrading of collegiality. As a result, success is individualized and highly tailored to the needs of the entrepreneurial institution. Another potential casualty of the corporatized university is academic freedom. It appears that cases restricting academic freedom are on the increase in Anglo-American universities and are taking different forms than half a century ago when loyalty oaths and one's political ideology were more often questioned. The commercialization of research and partnerships with industry are limiting the public sharing of research findings. When academics try to publicize results unfavorable to industry sponsors or criticize the university itself, university managers do not always support the academics but act to silence them. In extreme cases, they have dismissed or suspended faculty from the university. Industry sponsors try to obtain confidentiality agreements in their contracts with universities, delay publication of research findings until patents are obtained, or secure other rights over the intellectual property.

An Australian report (Kayrooz et al., 2001) discusses the threat to academic freedom of the increasingly commercial environment in which universities work. This study asked if academics saw a deterioration of academic freedom due to commercialization. Ninety-two percent of respondents reported a degree of concern about the state of academic freedom in their university. Seventy-three percent of the sample thought that there had been deterioration in the state of academic freedom. Respondents sounded the warning that both industry and the university can interfere with academic freedom, industry on political and commercial grounds and the academy on ideological grounds. The study found some direct interference; for example, 17 percent said they were prevented from publishing contentious results. Also, almost half of the sample reported a reluctance to criticize institutions that provided them with large research grants. However, most respondents were concerned about the indirect impact of commercialization, which has produced substantial systemic effects on their experience of academic freedom, such as the intensification of work, the pressure to attract research funding from industry, the emphasis on fee-based courses, and the shift to more corporate management structures.

More specifically, academics commented on how the emphasis on fee-based courses was affecting academic standards, the shift in orientation to more business-oriented courses, and concerns over intellectual property. Marginson notes a number of tensions within the current system.

In this context, the creation of a globalized international sector has led to fundamental tensions—tensions between the globalization of education and the fulfillment of local-national needs; tensions between international education and domestic education; tensions between commercial and noncommercial operations and objectives; and tensions between the private interests of universities, now redefined as self-managing corporations, and public goods. There has been a zero-sum trade-off between resources for teaching and for corporate development, and since 1995, a zero-sum trade-off between the increased participation of domestic undergraduates and the growth of foreign students.

This is just one instance of how the push toward the market can lead to a contortion of public universities. As governments ask universities to reduce their financial burden on society through privatization measures, individuals working in universities increasingly are being asked to "pay" for themselves and to account for how they spend taxpayers' money, whether on research, teaching, or other activities. The present writer investigated this process in three American and three Australian universities and found that legislators were interfering more in the lives of academics in both countries. Since 1991, the proportion of Australian government funding based on performance indicators has continued to rise for university research. Within institutions, parallel systems of distributing resources based on research are usually enforced and teaching performance indices are developed for internal university allocations. From the sample interviewed, it is evident that the respondents are experiencing increased accountability. The vast majority, slightly more than 85 percent in both Australian and American universities, said that accountability had increased, and no respondent reported that accountability had declined over the past five years.

In addition to the way academic activities are scrutinized, there is a perception that information is gathered without any clear vision of how it will be used. The emphasis on performance indicators and the increasing corporatization of universities have taken their toll on the service component of academics' work. Performance indicators are based on quantifiable measures and they usually measure what is easiest to count. This reduces the wide range of activities to a more narrow focus on publications of a certain type—international, refereed journal articles and books published by "respectable" academic publishers—and grants of a certain type, usually national competitive grants. Teaching and service to the community are generally dropped from these calculations as too difficult to assess.

Marginson and Considine (2000) identify five principal trends, which characterized Australian universities across the board in the mid-1990s, and summarize the managerialism implemented in many Anglo-American universities in the 1990s:

- A new kind of executive power, including a will to manage and to manage according to "good practice."
- Structural changes, including the replacement of collegial forms of governance with senior executive groups, moving from more formal to semiformal types of power.
- A move to produce flexibility of personnel and resources, through industrial deregulation and the use of soft money and commercial companies outside of the main legislative rules of the university.
- A decline in the role of academic disciplines, as a result of new super deans or executive deans who control several disciplines and are often drawn from outside of academic disciplines.
- A pattern of devolution supporting centralized control and increased line management authority.

In the end, as Marginson (2001b) notes, there are limitations to the enterprise university. It has short-term goals and is little concerned with community interests. In sum,

> It is not viable to use corporate self-interest to drive higher education's contribution to democratic culture, equality of social opportunity, or cultural diversity and cultural maintenance. Rather than maximizing all economic outputs, it maximizes short-term utilitarian outputs and private goods but weakens longer-term capacity and public goods.

CONCLUSION

Despite all the potential dangers of enterprise universities, many still defend the move to privatize universities in Australia. Clive Hamilton (2001) identifies three vice-chancellors who have all contributed to the right-wing think tank of the Centre for Independent Studies and are the most forceful advocates of globalizing universities: Vice-Chancellors Lauchlan Chipman of Central Queensland University, Alan Gilbert of the University of Melbourne, and Steven Schwartz, formerly of Murdoch University. Hamilton states:

> These Visionaries argue that cuts in public funding and greater reliance on private finance have been good for universities as they have compelled them to become more internationally competitive. More deregulation and greater market-orientation are required, as this will put more power in the hands of education consumers where it properly resides.

He notes that "the most striking feature of the world of the Visionaries is the absence of any discussion of the contribution that universities can make to the cultural and social richness of a nation." Neo-liberal globalization enshrines the market as a source of freedom. Not all vice-chancellors in Australia agree that competing in a free market environment is beneficial for universities. In a recent statement, even the generally conservative Australian Vice-Chancellors' Committee (AVCC) argued against the market approach to higher education:

> There is no example where the application of assumed pure market forces has brought a higher quality, more effective university system. A fully deregulated system exists nowhere. Local, national and international influences together with government intervention affect any market. There is no guarantee that a distorted market will produce the outcomes that are required in the national interest. The market is prone to failure.

Privatization is not always the answer to increasing freedom or creating a society based on the public good. If citizens are going to create healthier and wiser societies, there is a need to shore up public funding for universities and ensure that they continue to have the right to freedom of inquiry and persist in their role as "critic and conscience" of the nation. Also, if universities are going to be models of institutions for the general society, there is a need to shore up democratic collegiality against the rush to managerialize all aspects of decision making. Examples of faculty involvement in governance in the United States suggest that managerialism can be tempered with collegial government. Finally, adopting business practices may be prudent in some aspects of university management; however, there is a need for caution against picking up the latest fad and applying it in the university culture. The need to maintain scholarly integrity, peer review, and professional autonomy is central to the legitimacy of universities and a move toward managerial accountability can be an attack on all three.

REFERENCES

Allport, C. (2000). "Educating and Organizing across a Global World: A Perspective on the Internet and Higher Education Stakes and Challenges." Paper presented at the Conference on Globalisation, New Technologies, Academic Freedom and Intellectual Property. Paris.

Altbach, P. G., and L. S. Lewis. (1996). "The Academic Profession in International Perspective." In *The International Academic Profession: Portraits of 14 Countries*, ed. P. G. Altbach, 3–48. San Francisco: Carnegie Foundation for the Advancement of Teaching and Jossey-Bass.

Annan, K. (2001). "Laying the Foundations of a Fair and Free World Trade System." In *The Role of the World Trade Organization in Global Governance*, ed. G. P. Sampson, 19–27. Tokyo: United Nations University Press.

Appadurai, A. (2000). "Grassroots Globalisation and the Research Imagination." In *Globalisation*, ed. A. Appadurai. Special Edition of *Public Culture, 12*(1), 1–19.

Australian Vice-Chancellors Committee (AVCC). (2001). *Our Universities: Our Future*. An AVCC Discussion Paper. Canberra: AVCC.

Birnbaum, R. (2000). *Management Fads in Higher Education: Where They Come From, What They Do, Why They Fail*. San Francisco: Jossey-Bass.

Brabazon, T. (2001). "Internet Teaching and the Administration of Knowledge." *First Monday, 6*, 1–10. Retrieved November 28, 2001, from <http://www.firstmonday.org/issues6_6/brabazon>.

Brown, P. (2000). "The Globalisation of Positional Competition." *Sociology, 44*(4), 633–653.

Burgess, J., and G. Strachan. (1996). "Academic Employment: Current Pressures, Future Trends, and Possible Responses." *Australian Universities' Review, 39*(2), 28–32.

Coady, T. (1996). "The Very Idea of a University." *Australian Quarterly, 68*(4), 49–62.

Collier, R. (2001). "Gender, the Academic Career and Work Balance: Women,

Men and the 'Private Life' of the Law School." Paper presented to the Legal Studies Association Conference, Budapest, July 4–7.

Currie, J. (1998, February). "Globalization and the Professoriate." *Comparative Education Review, 42*(1), 15–29.

Gilbert, A. D. (2001, July 26). "Change, Continuity and the Idea of a University." In *The Idea of a University: Enterprise or Academy?* ed. P. Kinnear, 1–8. Proceedings of a Conference organized by Manning Clark House and The Australia Institute, Australian National University, Canberra.

Gray, J. (1998). *False Dawn: The Delusions of Global Capitalism.* New York: The New Press.

Hall, P. A., and D. Soskice. (2001). *Varieties of Capitalism.* Oxford: Oxford University Press.

Hamilton, C. (2001, July 26). "The University and the Marketplace." In *The Idea of a University: Enterprise or Academy?* ed. P. Kinnear, 9–15. Proceedings of a Conference organized by Manning Clark House and The Australia Institute, Australian National University, Canberra.

Hecht, J. (1994, November). "Today's College Teachers: Cheap and Temporary." *Labor Notes, 188,* 6.

Henderson, I. (2001, June 12). "Little to Show for Reforms." *The Australian,* 10.

Hollinger, D. (2001, May–June). "Faculty Governance, the University of California, and the Future of Academe." *Academe,* 30–33.

Kayrooz, C., P. Kinnear, and P. Preston. (2001, March). *Academic Freedom and Commercialisation of Australian Universities: Perceptions and Experiences of Social Scientists.* Discussion Paper 37. Canberra: The Australian Institute.

Krugman, P. (2001, July 20). "Do as We Do, and Not as We Say." *International Herald Tribune,* 8.

Marginson, S. (1997). *Educating Australia: Government, Economy and Citizen since 1960.* Cambridge: Cambridge University Press.

———. (2001a, March 27–29). "Australian Higher Education and the International Student Market: Commercial Affluence and Public Squalor." Paper presented to the Conference on Globalisation and Higher Education—Views from the South. Cape Town, South Africa.

———. (2001b, July 26). "Governance: It's Time for a New Paradigm." In *The Idea of a University: Enterprise or Academy?* ed. P. Kinnear, 58–70. Proceedings of a Conference organized by Manning Clark House and The Australia Institute, Australian National University. Discussion Paper 39. Canberra: The Australia Institute.

Marginson, S., and M. Considine. (2000). *The Enterprise University: Power, Governance and Reinvention in Australia.* Cambridge: Cambridge University Press.

McInnis, C. (1999). *The Work Roles of Academics in Australian Universities.* Canberra: Department of Education Training and Youth Affairs (DETYA), Evaluations and Investigations Programme, Higher Education Division.

National Tertiary Education Union (NTEU). (2000). *Unhealthy Places of Learning: Working in Australian Universities.* South Melbourne: The National Tertiary Education Union.

Newson, J. (1998). "Conclusion: Repositioning the Local through Alternative

Responses to Globalization." In *Universities and Globalization: Critical Perspectives*, ed. J. Currie and J. Newson, 295–313. Thousand Oaks, Calif.: Sage.

O'Kane, M. (2001, July 26). "Quality in Australian Universities: Decline and Change." In *The Idea of a University: Enterprise or Academy?* ed. P. Kinnear, 16–23. Proceedings of a Conference organized by Manning Clark House and The Australia Institute, Australian National University. Discussion Paper 39. Canberra: The Australia Institute.

Pierson, C. (2001). "Globalisation and the End of Social Democracy." *Australian Journal of Politics and History*, 47(4), 459–474.

Shirouzu, N. (2001, July 12). "Ford Rating System Flunks Out: Low Morale Worries Company as It Abandons Parts of Its Employee-Evaluation Plan." *Asian Wall Street Journal*, 7.

Singh, M. (2001, March 27–29). "Re-inserting the 'Public Good' into Higher Education Transformation." Paper presented to the Dialogue on the Public Good of Higher Education at the Conference on Globalisation and Higher Education: Views from the South. Cape Town, South Africa.

Soros, G. (1998). *The Crisis of Global Capitalism: Open Society Endangered*. New York: Public Affairs.

Vidovich, L., J. Currie, and H. Pears. (1996). *Trends Report: Accountability and Autonomy: Case Study of Murdoch University*. Unpublished paper. Report from The Changing Nature of Academic Work Project. Perth, Western Australia: School of Education, Murdoch University.

PART II

A Closer Look

INTRODUCTION

OUR ATTENTION so far has been focused on the macro level of analysis, the nature of globalization and its consequences for higher education. In this section, our authors look more closely at the microprocesses and at some details.

All too typically, people think of globalization in terms of marketization—extending market "logic" across the globe, including, therefore, the increasing marketization of many institutions, including higher education. Charles Smith's essay is a frontal assault on the generally uncritical views of markets. He argues that both friends and foes of markets misconceive them, with disastrous consequences for our understanding. Instead, then, of assuming that both parties to an exchange know the value of what is to be traded and that the "price" is the intersection of the two curves representing this evaluation, he argues that we need to see that "markets are rather first and foremost definitional systems. They do not just reveal the preferences of the participants; they constitute the social process whereby participants determine such preferences/values. Put slightly differently, they are mechanisms for establishing a consensual definition of goods and services under conditions of ambiguity." Thus, we "don't have to agree on why we value a given object for a hundred dollars in order to exchange it for that sum."

Moreover, instead of thinking of markets as disembedded and morally neutral, there is no good reason to believe that the rules identified in mainstream neo-classical theory either do fit or should fit all markets. Indeed, once this is acknowledged, we can see that the problem is not markets as such, but the failure to notice that little attention has been paid to how markets currently function in allocation decisions in higher education and how they might function to resolve current and growing ambiguities. These include, importantly, ambiguities regarding the "products" of higher education—what is being produced and for whom?—ambiguities regarding the roles of relevant participants—who are the producers and what competences do they have?—and the rules that should govern allocation processes, including, critically, being clear about priorities and increasing transparency over questions of cost. Smith concludes his essay by arguing against some misguided "solutions" to the current ambiguities.

Most academicians, we may guess, have a low opinion of the for-profit institutions of higher education: they are diploma mills, with low-paid, overworked faculties, and tyrannical administrations. Their students, often paying more tuition than students in public institutions, are not getting the value that they believe they are getting. Richard Ruch's essay will not convince the inconvincible, but it ought at least to shake up our thinking—especially if we suffer from a distorted view of practices of the nonprofits.

Ruch is the first to acknowledge that "as a guardian of institutional integrity and quality, the marketplace is limited in terms of what it reveals about an institution and how it functions to improve quality." He continues: "The market alone cannot determine educational quality." Indeed, the success of (say) the Phoenix University may be a fluke, or a case of duping the unsuspecting public. But even if this is the case—and this is doubtful—there can be no doubt that Phoenix is filling an articulated need. As others in the present volume would seem to agree, Ruch offers that, at a minimum, "the for-profit providers represent another form of institutional and missional diversity, one that serves a useful purpose and contributes to the overall vitality and breadth of the higher education industry." Similarly, as he notes, it is not clear whether useful purposes are being served when institutions take for granted the "luxury of inefficiency," a sentiment shared by Charles Smith. As suggested by his thoughtful consideration of the goals of higher education —the theme of Part III of this volume—Ruch is not an uncritical advocate of "efficiency," especially as defined by neo-classical theory, but he does argue that there are things that might be learned from the practices of the for-profits.

Scott Thomas offers us some detail of the structure of higher education in the United States. He examines the idea of "a knowledge-based economy" and the growth in postsecondary opportunities. Both, he argues, are consequences of the globalizing of the economy. He looks at the dramatic shift in motivation of students toward vocational success, suggests an explanation for this, and assesses what would seem to be, in fact, the "economic value" of college, directly addressing a problem raised by Ruch and Smith. But his conclusions are not heartwarming. Indeed, the increase in opportunity, considerable though it was, may not have resulted in either an individual or social benefit. Not only has this increase attended an increasing stratification of opportunity, defined in terms of the relative "prestige" schools, but also it is now more accurate to view "life with a high school diploma or less as a much, much greater disadvantage than before." Those lacking credentials are in deep difficulty while, in contrast to the recent past, postsecondary education is no longer "the ladder of ascent" it once was. While the rich get richer (having a superabundance of "cultural capital"), most people need to run faster just to stay in place! One might like to believe that if increased participation in postsecondary education has not been an engine of mobility and decreased stratification, it has promoted among a larger group of students increased individual capacities "to develop a meaningful philosophy of life." Obstacles to this development under present arrangements are discussed in Part III.

CHAPTER 4

GLOBALIZATION, HIGHER EDUCATION, AND MARKETS

Charles W. Smith

GLOBALIZATION IS UNDERSTOOD by most people to entail an ever-increasing dominance of markets and market ideology worldwide. In the case of higher education, this dominance is formulated in numerous ways, including the commodification of education, greater reliance upon corporate management styles, greater sensitivity to "customer" interests, and "bottom-line" decision making. Those favoring this process see it as leading to not only more rational resource allocation and cost savings, but also greater responsiveness to the educational needs of both students and the society at large. They further see it as a welcome attack upon entrenched educational hierarchies, including faculty governance prerogatives. Critics, in contrast, see the increased emphasis on direct financial benefits as impinging negatively on the integrity of the educational process, causing a loss of faculty input, and undermining long-term developmental, civic, and cultural goals.

In the give and take of these debates, it has become clear that not all participants share the same vision of what higher education is, let alone what it ought to be. This is not surprising given the many and varied functions that higher education has assumed over the years. Today, depending upon whom you ask, higher education is expected to provide students with a wide range of technical skills, access to numerous types of accepted knowledge sources, critical thinking capacity, cultural and civic values and beliefs, as well as certification in scores of different disciplines. It is also expected to provide students with access to numerous other students both similar to and different from themselves, a diverse and highly skilled faculty, job training, and instruction in lifestyle skills that will assist in upward social mobility. Nearly all institutions of higher education, at the same time, are also supposed to serve the community at large by providing, among other things, future workers, informed citizens, and new knowledge.

Numerous other questions emerge in these discussions and debates. Whom is higher education meant to serve—individual students, potential employers, the state, humanity, or some other entity? Is education meant primarily to preserve existing cultures and societies, or to serve as an agent of change? Is higher education meant to be primarily a personal experience, an economic apprenticeship, civic training, or moral enlightenment? To what extent is higher education meant to preserve and sustain the received wisdom and knowledge of the past, and to what extent is it responsible for generating new knowledge? Is it primarily a public good or a private good? As the sayings go, are professors meant to be "guides on the side" or "sages on the stage"? Is the education provided, to use another set of pithy sayings, meant to be "just in case" or "just in time"?

Given such varied and often conflicting visions of higher education, it is not surprising that people react differently to the effects that they perceive increased marketization within higher education is generating. Most might favor the promised efficiencies and increased choices that such marketization is thought to bring, but most are also concerned about what the associated long-term economic, social, and moral costs might be. Not surprisingly, those who tend to perceive higher education primarily in instrumental terms are usually more favorably disposed toward what they see as the results of marketization, while those who place greater emphasis on higher education's civic, political, and cultural facets tend to be more negative.

Various factors, as revealed in the chapters contained in this volume, can have a significant influence on how these issues and questions are framed, understood, and decided. In this chapter, I focus upon one factor that I believe tends to be misconstrued by nearly all participants in these discussions and that results in a good deal of confusion and faulty conclusions. I refer to the marketization process itself, or more simply to the way markets actually function in contrast to how they are often assumed to function by both proponents and opponents. I argue that both proponents and opponents of marketization tend to hold a profoundly inaccurate conception of how real markets function. I should note that this faulty understanding of how real markets actually function is not limited to discussions regarding higher education; it is also pervasive throughout most discussions about markets.

Markets are generally assumed to be the basic means whereby goods and services are allocated. Markets govern who gets what, and in the case of price-setting markets associated with neo-liberal capitalism, for how much. While markets clearly play a central role in the allocation of goods and services, it is important to recognize that they are only one type of allocative system. As Polanyi (1957) noted some time ago, and as is quite obvious to anyone who thinks about it, many goods and services, gifts, for example, are allocated through a system of reciprocity. Goods and services are also allocated by nonmarket reallocation systems. In socialist or other central planning economies, in fact, most goods and services are allocated in this manner. In most so-called market societies, tax funds continue to be reallocated in a similar manner.

It is important to recognize that there are alternatives to markets, if for no other reason than the recognition sensitizes us to the fact that markets tend to thrive in some environments more than in others. This, in turn, should alert us to the fact that markets may not always be the best means for allocating goods. If, as seems to be the case, markets appear to thrive with the advent of globalization, the question we need to ask is why. Taken together, these factors would seem to suggest that price-setting markets are significantly more complex than the comparatively simple allocative systems, described by many economists, which merely allocate goods and services to those willing to pay the most for them.

I would argue that markets are rather first and foremost definitional systems. They do not just reveal the preferences of the participants; they constitute the social process whereby participants determine such preferences/values. Put slightly differently, they are mechanisms for establishing a consensual definition of goods and services under conditions of ambiguity (Smith, 1989).

The pricing and search practices associated with markets, in fact, are unnecessary when values and possession rights are established. This explains why in more traditional societies, where values tend to be more fixed, markets play a more secondary role than they do in modern society. People often incorrectly assume that price-setting markets and auctions were common thousands of years ago. In actuality, they tended to exist only when conditions put accepted values in question such as was the case with war booty. The so-called *sub hasta*—under the spear—auction where Roman soldiers sold their war booty was an example of this. These objects fell somewhere between stolen goods and home-produced goods and were consequently of ambiguous value.

The link between markets and ambiguity also explains why markets flourish on cultural/social boundaries, where agreements regarding values and definition of ownership are not likely to be the same on both sides of the boundaries. Marco Polo and Lewis and Clarke brought items to trade with them to support their interactions with the "natives." Teenagers often go shopping together as a means of exploring and solidifying their values regarding not only specific goods, but also styles. People traveling in foreign lands often go shopping for similar reasons. Markets, in short, allow participants holding different values to engage in exploratory interaction. Markets similarly allow people to work through shared differences and ambiguities. As one respondent put it some forty years ago when I asked him to sum up what the stock market—perhaps the purest example of a price-setting market—was all about: "The stock market is about defining value." He could have been describing almost any auction/price-setting market.

While markets may be definitional processes, they never operate, as suggested above, in a vacuum. Differences and ambiguities do not result from a lack of beliefs and opinions, but normally from a multitude of such beliefs and opinions. As such, markets are not meant to generate prices out of nothing, but rather to bridge differences in values that the participants already hold. If one listens to the bargaining that normally goes on in a flea market, for example, prices per se are not what buyers and sellers primarily discuss. Rather, they discuss such things as the age of the item, what it is made from, the quality of the workmanship, its rarity, and so on in an effort to discover the parameters that will either increase or decrease the value of the item being bargained over. In short, markets function as practices that allow participants to explore each other's views and to seek a consensus sufficient to allow for an exchange. We do not have to agree on why we value a given object for a hundred dollars in order to exchange it for that sum.

This brings us to a third major facet of markets that is also generally overlooked. Markets not only resolve issues of value and ownership, they also set, or more correctly continue to reproduce, the rules for doing so. Neo-classical economists might argue that their paradigm sets what such rules should be in all cases, but in actuality each market continually reproduces the rules governing its own functioning. Moreover, the dominant principle guiding the reproduction of these rules is that the resulting market decisions be seen as legitimate (Smith, 1989). This explains why the rules governing different types of auctions and markets vary so dramatically. It is not illegal, for example, if competing buyers at a thoroughbred horse auction agree to jointly buy a given horse in the middle of the bidding, because buyers are seen to operate at a disadvantage to the sellers in such auctions. If two antique dealers decided to do the same thing at a New York antique auction, they would end up in jail if caught because in these auctions the buyers are seen already to have an advantage. Markets do not function in a moral vacuum. In fact, tendering to the governing normative structure is often privileged over the allocation process per se. The process tends to be one of minor adjustments over time generated by trial and error.

So how does all of this impact on higher education? Perhaps, first and foremost, it suggests that, even assuming that a greater reliance on market processes might be appropriate, before anyone begins to rethink, or even worse, retool a particular educational system, they need to determine what, if any, factors are in dispute. What are the various goods and services that are vying for resources? Besides the various academic departments that are always vying for additional resources, in most educational institutions there are also numerous special academic programs, various athletic programs, adult education, alumni affairs, faculty unions, community outreach programs, buildings and grounds, a wide range of artistic performances, and multiple student activities, to name just the most prominent, striving for both more resources and greater recognition.

Before these conflicting demands can be addressed, it is necessary to establish one's governing priorities. What is the primary purpose of the particular institution of higher education whose structure and charge is in question? Is the primary function of the institution meant to be vocational training? Is it meant to service the larger society or the individual student? How should economic, political, personal, and cultural objectives be weighted? Does this particular institution of higher education serve as some sort of gatekeeper? Does it have a responsibility to promote upward mobility? Does it have a responsibility to preserve the dominant culture? Is its role primarily to disseminate knowledge or generate new knowledge? Who, if anyone, in this particular case is responsible for what students learn? I could go on, but these questions indicate just how complicated and problematic the mission for any institution of higher education can be.

Who should be considered as legitimate participants in this decision-making process? In most institutions, students, faculty, and alumni tend to be privileged, but there are often major differences of opinion regarding their respective importance. Administrations, trustees, students' families, and the larger society also need to be considered. Should all voices be given equal weight? The answers will clearly differ from one institution to another, with the responsibilities and rights of participants varying in significant ways. In this context, it is worth noting, however, that markets seldom function on a level playing field. Some participants are always at an advantage. What sets one market apart from another is the extent to which such advantages are permitted or constrained. There exist no markets that I know of where anything goes.

In the case of higher education, additional questions arise regarding who should pay what. How much of the cost of higher education should be carried by the student, how much by the family, how much by the state, the charitable public, the faculty and employees? To complicate things further, all of these various questions and issues are clearly interrelated. Moreover, what might be a satisfactory solution in one situation is quite likely to be unacceptable in another. The normative context of a business education is unlikely to be the same as that for a member of the clergy.

Given the multiple factors at play in higher education, it is highly probable that the market processes described above will generate a number of quite distinct higher education markets. In fact, such multiple markets have been emerging for some time. The problem has been that we keep trying to impose the same set of rules on inherently very different markets. Critical thinking skills, library access, online introductory technology courses, and face-to-face interaction with faculty members are not the same products. Teenage students, employers, retired students, and parents of students are not the same customers. Research faculty, adjunct faculty, technical staff, and administrators are not the same workers. Students, parents, the state, and educational institutions themselves not only have different resources to invest in the educational process, but also have different objectives. Despite all of these differences, nearly everyone associated with higher education continues to look for one model that will fit all. A good part of the present problem facing most institutions of higher education is that over the past few decades many of these institutions have taken on new projects under the heading of education that really have nothing to do with their primary mission.

In light of the numerous complicating factors noted above, one might legitimately question the wisdom of even attempting to derive market-based solutions to any of these questions. It is here that we confront the catch-22 nature of markets. Markets may be unruly, but in situations of limited resources that lack a strong governing consensus—the situation in higher education today—the traditional hierarchical structures of most institutions of higher education are likely to prove wanting. The situation is further complicated by the fact that most institutions confront reallocation pressures at the same time that there is increased demand for general resources, which often must be covered by revenues. In short, whereas most institutions of higher education were once confronted primarily with questions of setting allocation priorities, they must now reassess these priorities in terms not only of costs, but also income-generating capabilities. Most of the tried and true allocation formulas of the past will no longer work.

Simply allowing market demands to determine who gets what, however, will not work either. There clearly needs to be a greater reliance upon market-related factors, but these factors need to be filtered and structured through a governing set of educational principles and goals, which in turn need to be subject to constant review. Such principles and goals, or more accurately a historical reflection of such principles and goals, I would suggest, already exist. They are built into the allocation system presently in place. Unfortunately, since most people are unaware of how present allocations are made, no one seems to be aware of the principles presently being followed. Though there is no need to generate the principles and goals that should guide this market process, knowing what things presently cost is essential.

There really is nothing unusual about this. In fact, the same situation characterizes practically every ongoing market that exists. Put slightly differently, no concrete market actually functions as depicted by the neo-classical paradigm. Each market tends to be governed by its own peculiar set of nonmarket rules that have evolved over time and are subject to continual revision. Real markets, as noted above, recognize that the playing field is not level and participants are not all equal. The objective of the governing rules is to offset these inequalities in a manner that will allow the market to fulfill its social, that is, collective, purposes. At the same time, nearly all markets start from where they are. An emerging consensus might dictate that one item should be valued higher while another should be valued lower, but in both cases the consensus will begin with the present price. So in education, it might be decided that more resources need to be invested in technology and less in athletics, but any transformation needs to begin with where the institution presently is. Much the same can be said for funding new programs and cutting back on existing programs. And to reiterate a point made earlier, different institutions will evolve in different ways.

Given the complexity entailed in maintaining a healthy market, would it be more efficient to impose a modified hierarchical, rational decision-making apparatus? This, of course, is the classical hierarchy versus market question that confronts most economic organizations. It also underscores the contradictory nature of many suggestions coming from some major critics of higher education. When they argue that higher education should be run more like a business, contrary to conventional wisdom, they are usually not proposing greater reliance upon market mechanisms. They are rather arguing for greater reliance upon some form of hierarchical central governance structure similar to the more traditional academic hierarchies that they simultaneously criticize.

They want a stronger administration, but one that is more sensitive to financial rather than academic issues. In some cases, they even want financial officers to have control over academic programs. The irony here is that historically higher education, even when it relied heavily upon its own form of hierarchical leadership, has tended to be financially more efficient than many, if not most, businesses. Academic hierarchies have tended to be fairly flat and faculty and students have participated in various forms of shared governance, especially regarding nonfinancial matters. The reason for this is that academic hierarchies have tended to share, or at least have been seen as sharing, the values of the community at large more so than has been the case in most business institutions. That such governing hierarchies shared or were seen as sharing the basic values of the community was due to the fact that within these institutions was a vibrant market for ideas. In short, the market of ideas legitimated the hierarchy of control.

If higher education hopes to be successful in adapting to the multitudinous changes associated with globalization, moving toward greater top-down leadership structures is folly because the present market of ideas is not sufficient in and of itself to maintain the legitimacy of any hierarchical leadership. The market of ideas needs to be augmented with information regarding the financial implications of different programs. More specifically, institutions of higher education will need to apply the same market principles it has employed for centuries in resolving curricular and personnel issues to financial issues. Historically, most academic debates have dealt with largely everything except financial issues. Debates focused upon curricula matters, hiring and tenuring, and parking. Most engaged in these debates assumed that if they could resolve the questions regarding what should be taught and how it should be taught, someone, somewhere, be it the state, rich alumni, or someone, would find the money to fund the institution.

The large numbers of students presently receiving higher education and the increased costs of providing such an education no longer make this assumption feasible. Expenditures and revenues have become linked in a way that was not obvious in the past. As such, curricular and personnel decisions are inexorably linked to their financial, both cost and income, implications. While this may lead to situations where some historically favored, but expensive programs will be cut back, it should also underscore the need to institute new programs, whatever their cost might be. Costs by themselves should not determine the issue. Higher education is expensive. In many cases the only solution will be to find ways of increasing funding.

Linking financial factors to traditional academic discussions will require, among other things, ensuring the highest level of organizational, including financial, transparency as possible. Economic information needs to be available to all involved in academic decision making because decisions regarding the allocation of financial resources have taken on a whole new level of importance. As in any market situation, guidelines also need to be established regarding who should and who should not participate in specific decisions. All markets have participation rules. Sometimes these rules are very restrictive and at other times they are very inclusive. The deciding factor in each case is what is required to ensure the legitimacy of the process to the participants. Finally, higher education, like any market process functioning in an ever-changing environment, must be open to internal transformational change.

While such guiding principles need to be in place if market processes are to be of any use in higher education, it clearly does not settle any of the current debates within and about higher education. It does, however, enable us to identify a number of clearly wrongheaded suggestions being pursued. I begin by simply noting some of these suggestions coming from those who see themselves as promoting market principles, but who, in fact, are doing just the opposite. I then say a few things about those who feel that they are defending the academy from market incursions, but are actually merely abandoning the field.

Among those claiming to be market defenders, one of the most active and loudest groups is actually trying to convert institutions of higher education into corporate hierarchies, with disastrous results. Nearly all of their proposed initiatives, whether they focus on eliminating tenure, cutting back on research, relying more on central management or on external funding, have actually increased costs and lowered productivity (Smith, 2000). Many of these critics aptly embody the "cost of everything, value of nothing" depiction attributed to them. Whereas markets have traditionally served as a means for allowing new products to be introduced, many of these critics promote economic efficiency as a means for maintaining the status quo or for promoting pet projects. Despite praising the merits of the market, few seem willing to let a self-regulating market actually function. Under the guise of economic efficiency, what one normally discovers is that these critics actually have a very narrow conception of what higher education should be. They have little or no interest in the best "products" emerging in the marketplace. Generally, they are already in possession of a product and it is that product they want everyone to buy.

At the same time, these naïve assaults have stimulated a categorical rejection of market-sensitive systems of accountability and allocation of resources from those who wrongly fear any adjustments to the traditional way of allocating resources. Such responses have, in turn, limited the ability of many institutions to adapt to changing conditions in a creative manner. Many of these market critics fear that marketization means that every course and every program will have to compete on an equal footing for funding. Similarly, they fear that salaries and tuitions will be determined by external supply and demand factors. Students will become customers and faculty will become workers. Physical resources will be allocated to departments or programs willing to pay the most for them. We have all heard the litany. The reality is, however, that while such outcomes might be inherent in certain simplistic market models, real markets have both the ability and the proclivity to establish their own standards. The give and take of any market always occurs within normative parameters acceptable, if also negotiable, to all participants. The real danger that exists for those refusing to become involved in allocation decisions is that these decisions will be made without their input.

Ironically, what both proponents and critics fail to recognize is that American higher education institutions have traditionally functioned in an extremely market-sensitive manner when it has come to resolving differences of opinion and allocating resources. To assert that higher education institutions have traditionally been sensitive to market principles admittedly goes against general opinion. Rather than being sensitive to market and financial matters, institutions of higher education have for the most part appeared quite indifferent to financial/market factors. They seem to spend what they want and simply increase tuition costs to cover their expenses. In reality, this is far from the case. When adjustments are made for general inflation, especially long-term inflation and increased costs due to new, quite expensive frills such as enhanced athletic facilities and computer access, true costs prove to have remained fairly constant.

The dramatic increases that have caught most people's attention have not been in costs per se. They have been in tuition costs that have doubled, tripled, and even quadrupled in some cases even when corrections are made for inflation. The reason for this has been a significant reallocation of costs from endowments and state support to tuition. The irony in all of this, of course, is that these reallocation decisions were not market-driven, but rather politically orchestrated. It seems as if the decision was made that in turn for making higher education more available to poorer students, the percentage of the cost that students would pay would be dramatically increased.

We find another market-related anomaly associated with recent changes in the structure of higher education. Traditionally most institutions of higher education functioned with relative small and flat hierarchical administrative structures. Such structures helped enable most higher educational institutions to produce an inherently very expensive product at a quite reasonable price. As noted earlier, they were able to survive in this form because they relied upon a high degree of institutional consensus maintained through the institutions' marketplace of ideas. This consensus also allowed most institutions to function in large part as voluntary organizations. By this I mean that a great deal of the day-to-day management was done by faculty members on a voluntary basis, be it serving as chairpersons of various committees and programs or simply doing various administrative chores. In return for their labors, these volunteers expected to have a say in what got done. Given the numerous different opinions on what and how things should be done, the system required a good deal of give and take as well as all sorts of trade-offs. In short, both opinions and resources were subject to *market* principles. As in any market, this process often seemed disordered and chaotic because markets flourish when there are differences of opinion and conflicting demands. Markets prove quite efficient in these situations, because they are ideally suited for resolving, or minimally dealing with, conflicting demands for resources in nonconsensual contexts.

So what do we find as one of the major changes brought about in recent years by attempts to make higher education function more like a business? We find a quite profound growth in the size of academic administrations, produced under the principle of attempting to make the institution more efficient. Not only has this growth in administration entailed significant direct costs, it has also served to undermine both the historical voluntary ethic of many of these institutions and the governing consensus that legitimated whatever governing hierarchy existed. The truly sad part of this story is that those in the academic community who continue to refuse to become involved in the broader debates governing economic resources because of their hostility to markets are only serving to speed this process of administrative growth.

None of the above is meant to imply that higher education is perfect or cannot profit from innovative fiscal management changes. The types of changes being proposed by most critics, however, have and will only make things worse. What we need to do is properly price the various components of higher education, determine what our priorities are, and resolve how we will cover the resulting costs. In short, we need to decide what types of education should be provided to whom and how the costs of these various packages are to be allocated between students and their families, the state and taxpayers, and the institutions themselves through their own private fund-raising initiatives.

We need to do all of this in an open and informed forum. While most markets have their own boundaries, within these boundaries, healthy markets favor more open systems. Similarly, while subject to rules, healthy markets also tend to be open to experimentation. A sense of play is operative in such markets, which explains in part their power to attract participants, be it the stock market or simply shoppers. Perhaps most important, we must convince faculties that it is in their interest to accept fiscal responsibility for their own actions and institutions and to participate in such forums. If the public and boards of trustees actually want to get a handle on the economics of higher education, they will need the cooperation and involvement of the faculty.

I must admit that after thirty-five years in academic life dealing with fellow faculty, administrators, parents, and legislators, I am not as optimistic as I once was that the types of changes needed will occur. The financial and managerial challenges confronting higher education are many and serious. Faculty bashing, half-baked organizational and fiscal innovations, and denial will not resolve them. On the other hand, there is evidence that some recent innovations not only can save money but also may enhance the educational experience. As in any marketplace, the best is not always the most expensive. On the other hand, it is also true that you normally get what you pay for. This is only one of the paradoxes of real markets. It is time that we come to grips with this reality as it applies to higher education.

REFERENCES

Polanyi , Karl. (1957). "The Economy as Instituted Process." In *Trade and Market in the Early Empires*, ed. K. Polyani and C. Arensberg. Glencoe, Ill.: The Free Press.

Smith, Charles W. (2000). *Market Values in American Higher Education: The Pitfalls and Promises*. Lanham, Md.: Rowman and Littlefield.

———. (1989). *Auctions: The Social Construction of Value*. New York: The Free Press.

CHAPTER 5

LESSONS FROM THE FOR-PROFIT SIDE*

Richard S. Ruch

THE BEAT POET Allen Ginsberg visited my campus in the fall of 1969, when I was an undergraduate English major at a large state university in the Midwest. He spoke in a kind of prose-poem about the purpose of American universities, characterizing them as giant warehouses designed to occupy the time of young people that society did not know what else to do with. A proper college education, he suggested, was simply a way of efficiently housing people who were too young to be adults and too old to be children. Most of the assembled students, myself included, identified strongly with Ginsberg's straightforward explanation of our own experience.

The giant warehouse metaphor may still work in some of the large, state university systems, but in general it no longer describes reality. For one thing, the demographics have radically changed. Half of the college students in America are adults, and only about 7 percent are eighteen-to twenty-two-year-olds living on campus and pursuing liberal arts degrees. Perhaps even more dramatic, it has become increasingly common to tie the outcome of a college education to the economic earning power of graduates, and that is how the payoff is measured in many studies. The earning power of graduates is in turn tied to regional and national economic health. The National Center for Education Statistics (NCES) now tracks the relationship between national productivity, the educational attainment of individuals, and individual earning power, which it uses to demonstrate the tangible benefits of investing in

---

* An edited version of Chapter 6, of Richard S. Ruch, *Higher Education, Inc.* (Baltimore: Johns Hopkins University Press, 2001), reprinted by permission of the author and publisher.

education to the economic well-being of the nation. One recent NCES report (1997) asserts that improvements in worker productivity in the United States are the result of increases in educational attainment and that the "best available measure of a worker's productivity is that of worker's wages."

The focused educational missions and values the for-profit provides fit harmoniously into this conversation about the relationship between educational attainment, the earning power of graduates, and national productivity. These institutions thrive on providing an efficient and cost-effective route to a degree and job placement in a high-demand field at a good salary. This, in essence, is what they do as educational providers. Allen Ginsberg might have described it as mass assembly-line job training tied to the needs of the market. A small but growing proportion of students (ca. 400,000 in 2000) and, to a lesser extent, faculty (ca. 3,000 full-time faculty in 2000) are choosing to study and teach in these pragmatic, applications-oriented colleges and universities.

The rise of the for-profit model in higher education, and in particular the growth of the large, publicly traded corporations that offer accredited degree programs at the associate's, baccalaureate, master's, and even doctoral levels, will continue to have a profound influence on the higher education industry in America. I seek to accomplish two primary goals in this chapter. The first is to frame the for-profit model within the larger context of the continuing development of higher education in general and to identify how for-profit institutions are influencing our evolving understanding of what constitutes a college education. My second goal is to identify some of the lessons that traditional higher education institutions may learn from the reemergence and growth of the for-profit providers. By understanding what seems to be working well in the for-profit model, in particular, by observing how the for-profits are addressing needs that are not being met by some traditional colleges and universities, traditional institutions may be able to more clearly understand and articulate their own values and purposes.

Blurring of the Lines

To begin, it is useful to identify some of the ways in which the lines are blurring between for-profit and nonprofit institutions.

At the level of the classroom, the for-profit and nonprofit sectors are indistinguishable. The better for-profits, such as Strayer University, in the Washington–Baltimore corridor, Education Management Corporation, which owns and operates the art institutes, and Argosy Education Group, which offers doctoral programs through the ten campuses of the American Schools of Psychology and the University of Sarasota, are legitimate and viable academic institutions. Meanwhile, growing numbers of well-known nonprofit universities are adapting their organizational structure to create for-profit arms, focused on adult continuing education and venture-capital formation. Clearly, the growing number of new for-profit ventures within nonprofit universities are indicators that the terms *for-profit* and *nonprofit* are becoming less meaningful in making distinctions among institutions of all types and at all levels of quality. This blurring of the lines began to escalate during the economic boom of the 1990s, when major improvements in educational quality and significant new growth occurred in the for-profit sector, while at the same time the traditional model of higher education was being questioned from within and criticized from without for its inefficiency, unresponsiveness, and resistance to change.

As a result of this blurring of the lines, the higher education institutional landscape is changing significantly. College students of all ages and at all degree levels now have a broader menu of options to choose from in pursuing their educational goals. Faculty members too have a new set of career options to consider, which replaces the tenure track with stock options, sidesteps the scholarly productivity game altogether, and provides them with clearly defined institutional roles. Further, the stigma associated with being "proprietary" is slowly disappearing.

Still, one of the concerns within the traditional academy about the for-profit providers is whether they provide a legitimate college education or merely job training. Here again, however, the distinctions have blurred. The difference between what we call teaching and what we call training is not particularly clear except, perhaps, in the extreme. Cosmetology schools provide training, not education. Medical schools provide a combination of training and education, as do schools of law, engineering, art, and architecture, among others. Without question, good trainers engage in teaching and good teachers use training techniques. Training implies mastering skills through learning. As educators, we expect and we hope that teaching accomplishes something greater, something more like "opening minds." If someone's mind is opened while being taught, we might naturally want to attribute that to effective teaching (and perhaps to effective learning). If someone's mind is opened while getting trained, however, we might be reluctant to attribute that to effective training.

The question of what constitutes a legitimate college education—what should be studied and learned and how it should be taught—is part of an evolving conversation that continues to be shaped by both traditional ideals and the pragmatic appetites of the market economy. Perhaps this has always been the case, especially in American higher education, which emulated but did not exactly copy the European university model and which could not ultimately survive in total isolation from the influences of the economic marketplace. Alongside the first classical colleges in the United States were also thriving alternative, often subversive, and sometimes underground proprietary schools whose existence was sustained by needs unmet by the traditional model. Higher education in America, from the classical colleges to the mechanical arts schools, and from the land-grant universities to the correspondence schools, is the product of both tradition and the imperative of contemporary market demands. Many traditional colleges have continued to emphasize the protection of tradition over the response to market demands. The for-profit providers pay homage to academic tradition, and indeed they must do so to gain regional association accreditation, but they place a higher value on meeting market demands. There is room for both of these purveyors of higher education, and although the distinction between them is blurring, both approaches can be carried out with integrity.

MEASURING VALUE BY THE EARNING POWER OF GRADUATES

What the for-profits do exceptionally well is respond to the marketplace. In the case of freshmen students, national survey data indicate that the for-profits provide what many of these customers say they want. The annual survey of freshmen conducted by the Higher Education Research Institute at UCLA, now in its thirty-fifth year, has tracked the increasing level of disengagement with traditional academics and the emerging dominance of the goal of financial well-being on the part of college freshmen. The most recent survey, released in January 2000, asked a sample of 261,217 students to rank order a list of 13 reasons they considered very important in deciding to go to college. At the top of the list were two reasons: "to be able to get a better job" (72 percent of respondents), and "to get training for a specific career" (also 72 percent). Out of 20 goals they hoped to achieve by going to college, "being very well off financially" topped the list (73.4 percent), well in front of the old standard, "developing a meaningful philosophy of life" (39.7 percent).

Such attitudes and expectations have perhaps become so common among college students today that they are taken for granted by the higher education community. In fact, the primary yardstick for assessing the value of an institution's undergraduate degrees has evolved to become a matter of the earning power of graduates. For example, several studies have confirmed that the high price of a degree from an Ivy League university does indeed result in a successful career launch and high-paying employment. One such study, released in late 1999 by the National Bureau of Economic Research, compared the value of a degree from a highly selective institution, such as Yale or Bryn Mawr, with the value of a degree from a less prestigious institution, such as Denison or Tulane. The only variable used in this study to assess the value of the degrees was the average earned income of the graduates. Whether these graduates developed a meaningful philosophy of life was not even considered.

That the value of a college degree is assessed on the basis of how much money graduates earn and that such assessments are regularly conducted by researchers both inside and outside academia would seem to offer strong support for the conclusion that higher education in the United States is essentially becoming a process of providing credentials, whose value is measured in terms of economic return. On that particular score the for-profits rank highly, as do the elite, highly selective institutions.

TWO GUARDIANS OF QUALITY AND INTEGRITY

Two distinct guardians of institutional quality and integrity are at work in the higher education industry. One is the accreditation process. In simple terms, accreditation verifies that a "proper college education," consistent with the institution's mission and meeting or exceeding thresholds of approved standards of education quality, is attainable at an institution. The accreditation process is not perfect, but the vast majority of institutions appear to find it helpful in addressing problems and improving overall quality.

The for-profit providers treat accreditation as a business objective. They have demonstrated that meeting accreditation standards is essentially the direct result of properly allocating resources. The standards themselves, whether pertaining to faculty credentials or to the adequacy of the library, are surrogate measures of a quality education, but they do not guarantee quality. Within the universe of accredited colleges and universities there is obviously a wide variability in institutional quality, in both the nonprofit and for-profit sectors.

Surely it makes sense that all educational institutions, whether organized on a for-profit or a nonprofit basis, should meet the same standards for accreditation. Historically, however, this has not been the case, and several states and regions still have on their books a different, often more stringent set of standards for the for-profit schools. State licensing standards, too, often hold proprietary institutions to different standards, as in the case of New Jersey, which has separate rules for licensing proprietary institutions and limits the duration of the license to five years (as opposed to a one-time license for nonprofit colleges and universities).

Judith Eaton (2000), president of the Council for Higher Education Accreditation, notes that regional accreditation is "one of the oldest and most frequently used forms of institutional quality assurance in the United States." As the regional associations rise to the challenge of the changing face of higher education, especially the advancements in distance learning and the rapid growth of for-profit institutions and for-profit arms of nonprofit institutions, they are revisiting the core academic values that have long guided the regional association accreditation standards. Eaton summarizes these core academic values as follows:

- institutional autonomy
- collegiality and shared governance
- the intellectual and academic authority of the faculty
- the degree (whether associate's, baccalaureate, professional, master's, or doctorate)
- general education
- site-based education and a community of learning

Regional association accreditation, says Eaton, exists to protect these core values. What must be acknowledged is that for-profit providers operate under a different hierarchy of values, especially as they pertain to the second and third values listed above. Shared governance does not accurately describe how the for-profit universities profiled in this book handle the decision-making process. Faculty participate in some decisions, and not in others. For example, the faculty at DeVry, Strayer, Education Management, and others do not decide which degree programs are offered by their campuses, and often they do not even participate in discussions on this topic. In addition, the intellectual and academic authority of the faculty, by which Eaton means responsibility for the curriculum, course content, and academic standards for evaluating student performance, differs significantly in the for-profit environment. In my experience, although the faculty in the for-profits have some influence over these areas, they do not have final authority over the curriculum, course content, or academic standards.

The other guardian of institutional quality and integrity is the free market economy itself. At its best, the marketplace functions as a system of checks and balances in which good products and services are sustained by the buying public, while poor products and services eventually lose their markets to better competitors. Products and services that are responsive to the needs and demands of the market are consumed, and those that are not responsive are not consumed.

In the simplest of terms, *marketplace* in this context refers to the relationship between the demands that exist for certain kinds of higher education and the response of institutions to address these demands as measured by enrollments. In other words, the marketplace is a point of exchange between providers and consumers of higher education. For example, the fact that 100,000 adult students have enrolled at the University of Phoenix, when they obviously had many other choices of educational providers, indicates that the marketplace is confirming that what Phoenix is offering addresses the needs and demands of certain consumers. Whether Phoenix's success is a fluke, a matter of watered-down standards, or a case of duping the unsuspecting public is not readily revealed by this information alone.

Indeed, as a guardian of institutional integrity and quality, the marketplace is limited in terms of what it reveals about an institution and how it functions to improve quality. The market alone cannot determine educational quality, particularly if educational quality is defined in terms of fulfilling the needs of society, for the market is entirely attuned to current demands and does not necessarily account for the larger needs of society. Perhaps tensions between individual perceptions of need, such as one's economic earning power, and the needs of human community and society are inevitable. Consequently, it may be reasonable to assume that some institutions must swim upstream against the current tide of the marketplace in order to preserve values that extend beyond such goals as improving individual economic earning power. The consumer marketplace itself is somewhat valueless; it reflects whatever values consumers themselves bring to the exchange.

THE LUXURY OF INEFFICIENCY

One of the questions traditional educators sometimes ask me about the for-profit universities is, where is their intellectual center? I am not always certain what they mean by this question, but the concern behind the question has to do with the apparent departure of the for-profits from the traditions of tenure, academic freedom, and shared governance.

In the traditional model, the intellectual center of the institution lies with the full-time faculty, who are entrusted with authority over the curriculum, instruction, and course content and who are granted considerable voice in all major decisions that affect institutional life. In this model, a large amount of release time from classroom teaching—as much as one-third or one-half of the standard teaching load—is often defended on the basis of its direct and indirect contributions to the institution's mission and, more to the point, to the health of the institution's intellectual center. Certain forms of instructional inefficiency in the deployment of full-time faculty, such as team teaching and very small classes, are tolerated and even celebrated because it is believed that the "luxury of inefficiency," as Patricia McGuire (2000), president of Trinity College, calls it, is an important investment in the intellectual foundation of the institution.

As attractive as the concept may be, it is difficult to make a sensible case for the luxury of inefficiency for all of higher education. The benefits of being inefficient in the use of financial, human, and physical resources are not clear. The supposed outcomes have tended to be accepted on faith and not on the basis of outcomes measured. Despite the adoption of the language of "assessment of outcomes," there remains a considerable lack of measurement of and accountability for results within many universities. What is sometimes celebrated in the name of the luxury of inefficiency may simply be a form of organizational ineffectiveness. Concerning the emphasis on faculty research in many colleges and universities, for example, Zachary Karabell (1998), among others, has argued that the emphasis on faculty research all across academia has resulted in the duplication and triplication of the research already being carried out by faculty at the major research universities. And while it is presumed that faculty research contributes to better classroom teaching, this has not been proven and may be true primarily for certain fields only at the graduate level of instruction.

In the classroom, it is presumed that smaller classes, of, say, fewer than twenty students, result in improved learning and better student performance, especially in such subjects as freshman composition. Having taught freshman composition for many years, I admit to clearly preferring a class of twenty to a class of thirty, but I could not offer proof that improved learning and better student performance resulted from my smaller classes. Too many other variables, such as the skill level of the collection of students in a particular class, the classroom dynamics among particular groups of students, and the variability of my own performance as a teacher on certain days and at certain times, were at play. The nondebatable and measurable difference between a freshman composition class of thirty and one of twenty was the amount of work I had to do, for reading thirty student papers unquestionably involves more work than does reading twenty.

Not that the for-profit providers have very large classes; they do not. Even the standard-bearer of efficiency, the University of Phoenix, has an average class size in the teens and a student-to-faculty ratio of 18 to 1. Of course, these are primarily part-time faculty, and this brings us back to the question of the location of the institution's intellectual center.

DEFINING THE INTELLECTUAL CENTER

In the for-profit model generally, the full-time faculty occupy the intellectual center of the institution just as they do in traditional universities. The students, who are generally older, working adults with families, also significantly contribute to this intellectual center, just as they do in traditional institutions. Unlike in traditional nonprofit institutions, however, the authority of the faculty in for-profits over decisions that affect institutional life is more controlled. Without tenure and lacking many of the standard trappings of shared governance, such as faculty senates and promotion-and-tenure committees, the faculty in these institutions are deployed to teach, not to govern the institution.

At Educational Management, Argosy, Strayer, and DeVry, the full-time faculty generally teach 50 to 70 percent of the credit hours taught during an academic year. Release time from teaching for curriculum development, professional development, and continuing education, as well as time off from teaching responsibilities during sabbatical leaves, is available to the full-time faculty who work in these for-profit providers.

At DeVry, for example, in addition to a paid sabbatical every five years, faculty have the option of banking extra teaching hours (usually by teaching an additional course in the evenings or on weekends) and then cashing them in for release time. In a typical academic year, release time from teaching responsibilities on my DeVry campus constitutes about 10 percent of the total full-time workload, or about 350 hours of release time out of a total workload of about 3,500 hours, which translates into the equivalent of eight full-time faculty positions released from teaching. About half of this release time is for sabbaticals, and the other half is for curriculum development and administrative responsibilities for department chairs. Faculty at DeVry are seldom released from teaching for research projects, except when those projects are related to the completion of a Ph.D. dissertation, in which case they may be released from 50 to 100 percent of their teaching load.

Based on my work in and study of the for-profit universities, I believe a strong argument could be made that the intellectual center at some of these for-profit campuses is at least as viable as that at many traditional institutions, even though the for-profits do not place as high a value on faculty research. This is certainly the case at Argosy's American Schools of Professional Psychology, where the faculty are required by contract to be on campus four days each week and are held accountable for the delivery of instruction and for the learning outcomes of the courses they teach, which they themselves develop. Instead of research and publication, Argosy's psychology faculty are actively involved in clinical practice, which clearly informs their teaching and shapes the curriculum. At the art institutes of Education Management, the faculty are on campus five days a week and work closely together and with their students to build and maintain a strong sense of a community of artists. At the DeVry Institutes of Technology many faculty are deeply involved in ongoing discussions of pedagogy and student learning styles, especially in the areas of general education, which on my New Jersey campus comprises 50 percent of the coursework in each technical degree program. What is noteworthy about the full-time faculty in these institutions in terms of their contributions to the intellectual center is that they are present, on campus, four or five days each week.

But what about the intellectual center of an institution like the University of Phoenix, which employs part-time faculty almost exclusively? Can there be an intellectual center at an institution where nearly all the faculty are "adjuncts"? Jorge de Alva, Phoenix's president, recently addressed this question at a meeting of the Council for Higher Education Accreditation. He drew an interesting distinction: "To me," he said, "the fundamental difference is not between full-time and part-time faculty, but rather between practitioner faculty and self-employed faculty." Phoenix does not refer to its faculty as "adjuncts" because they are not "adjunctive" but are rather the instructional centerpiece of the institution. A condition of employment as a faculty member at Phoenix is full-time engagement as a practitioner in the field being taught. Phoenix's founder and CEO, John Sperling (1998), puts it this way: "If you don't do it by day, you can't teach it at night."

De Alva (2000), reflecting on his years as a tenured professor at Princeton and as the holder of an endowed chair at Berkeley, says, "The full-time faculty of many traditional institutions are essentially self-employed, independent agents, who are expected to advance their careers and bring acclaim to their institutions through scholarly publications, grants, fellowships, and prizes." Operating under such expectations, argues de Alva, these faculty are often absent from their campuses, absent from the classroom, and absent from direct involvement in governance, and they are therefore contributing not so much to the institution's intellectual center as to their own careers and to the advancement of knowledge in the disciplines. He suggests that Phoenix's faculty are actually more present and engaged than the full-time faculty at many traditional universities and therefore more able to contribute to the institution's intellectual center.

Whatever our conclusions about the intellectual center of the University of Phoenix (and the other for-profit providers), we must ask whether it matters at all to most undergraduate students. One suspects that it does not.

LEARNING FROM THE FOR-PROFITS

"Now, and even more in the future, what goes on in the university is inseparable from who we are as a nation," writes Zachary Karabell (1998) in *What's College For?* Karabell suggests convincingly that U.S. higher education is undergoing a revolution, "becoming mass education and in the process being radically democratized." Access to higher education by students of all backgrounds and ability levels is one of the strengths of the U.S. system.

Surely another strength is the diversity of colleges and universities within the system itself, providing students with choices and options for pursuing their education. The diversity of institutional missions allows many institutions to excel in particular areas, whether basic scholarship in certain fields or serving the local community with associate's degree programs. The for-profit providers represent another form of institutional and missional diversity, one that serves a useful purpose and contributes to the overall vitality and breadth of the higher education industry.

In my involvement with for-profit institutions I have often thought about what the nonprofits could learn from the for-profits. From the other side, it seems clear that the for-profits have taken cues from traditional institutions, for they have essentially taken the traditional model of higher education—students seated in the classroom and a professor up front—and subjected it to modern principles of operations management, cost accounting, financial management, and marketing. The result has been an efficient, cost-effective, alternative route to a college degree, albeit with a somewhat limited focus on pragmatic, applications-oriented instruction. In considering what traditional nonprofit colleges and universities may learn from these successful for-profit institutions, four areas for change suggest themselves:

- responding to market forces
- adapting the organizational structure
- redefining shared governance
- developing a strong customer orientation

RESPONDING TO MARKET FORCES

Reflecting on the remarkable growth of higher education in the United States and the apparent preeminence of the U.S. university system worldwide, some observers have suggested that while the traditional university has been slow to change, it has also demonstrated a remarkable ability to adapt and respond. Others have faulted the academy for its inherent resistance to change. Of course, change is inevitable, whether in the demography of students, the economy, or the uses of technology, and the impact of change is variable in terms of its pace and scope. But in the area of market responsiveness many traditional colleges and universities have been resistant to change, responding slowly and adapting reluctantly. This becomes especially apparent when one looks at how quickly and effectively some of the for-profit education companies have responded to change, particularly regarding curriculum development, new program offerings, alternative instructional delivery, and academic decision making. Having lived and worked in both environments, I have found the contrast striking.

Perhaps some traditional nonprofit institutions have resisted change out of a sense of mission to protect values that are assumed to be essential to human society. Some may have been less concerned about the need for change in areas other than those stemming from scholarly advancements in the academic disciplines themselves. Others have simply paid little attention to the need for change, suffering from what William Tierney (1999) calls "organization attention deficit disorder." Many simply lack a mechanism for addressing change. At one liberal arts college where I helped to develop a strategic plan, enrollments in the humanities had declined steadily for ten years and then remained low, while the scope of the humanities curriculum and the size of the humanities faculty had remained unchanged. Throughout most of its history, this college had geared itself to deal with growth and expansion, but there was no blueprint for how to cut back or significantly reallocate resources other than a cumbersome and unworkable layoff provision in the collective bargaining agreement. The prevailing thinking expressed in faculty meetings was that enrollments were always cyclical and that the pendulum would swing back to the humanities in due time. Now, eighteen years into the slump, enrollments in the humanities have still not rebounded.

"The university's tremendous inertia is the result of a long-standing, well-established system," write Patricia Gumport and Marc Chun (1995), of Stanford University, in their analysis of higher education's resistance to technological change. "The scientific revolution took place for the most part outside of academe, and many academics shunned the industrial revolution." As long as social, economic, and technological change was incremental and evolutionary, the traditional university's complex decision-making structure was not a fatal flaw in responding to market forces. However, as Scott Cowen (2000), president of Tulane University, has suggested, social, economic, and technological change today is discontinuous and revolutionary, and in the face of this new reality the traditional decision-making process of the university "defies the logic of what you would expect of an effective organization."

Aside from the 110 to 120 major research universities and an equal number of premier liberal arts colleges, by far the majority of American colleges and universities today are in the business of educating the workforce. In order to educate the workforce, institutions must be in touch with the needs of the workplace, and the workplace is undergoing profound and constant transformation. One way to document this transformation is to consider how long it now takes new products and services to reach a 25 percent market share. For example, it took an estimated 46 years for household electricity to achieve a 25 percent market share penetration. The telephone took 35 years to penetrate 25 percent of its potential market, and the VCR, 34 years. The personal computer, however, took only 15 years, the cellular telephone, 13 years, and the Internet, 7 years. These increasingly rapid rates of market penetration have not occurred in isolation but have been accompanied by changes in the education and training needs of many large industries and of the workforce generally.

For these reasons, the majority of higher education institutions must become more responsive to the market forces that impact the education and training needs of the students they serve. The question and the challenge is not whether to become more responsive but how to do so in the face of a tradition of resistance, a history of inertia, and a system of decision making that inhibits quick decisions and rapid response to change.

ADAPTING THE ORGANIZATIONAL STRUCTURE

One of the more fascinating developments in higher education at the turn of the twenty-first century is the creation of for-profit arms in several universities, including Columbia, Cornell, Stanford, New York University, and the University of Maryland, with others soon to follow. Why, one might ask, would a nonprofit university want to establish a for-profit venture—which would not qualify for tax-exempt status—as part of its operations? The answer is twofold and further attests to the blurring of the lines between nonprofit and for-profit institutions. First, these for-profit arms provide access to private investment capital, which functions as a kind of endowment in for-profit institutions. Universities with international brand identity, as well as institutions with strong regional or even local presence, are beginning to realize that their names and reputations can be used to attract potentially large sums of investment capital. If they are successful—it is a bit too soon to tell— they will have found a way to attract another form of "donated" income, through the investment of money from both individuals and corporations.

Second, relatively little financial risk is involved in setting up these ventures. Even if they fail, the university itself will not go bankrupt or suffer financial exigency; it will simply continue to rely on its main business. These for-profit ventures are carefully structured to be located at arm's length from the university itself, so that the institution's core academic identity and culture are protected. In a sense, they offer an opportunity to participate in the for-profit game without the full measure of the for-profit risks.

From my own experience on the for-profit side, I would suggest that many colleges and universities should consider the benefits of establishing a for-profit venture as part of their total institutional structure. Establishing a for-profit venture makes it possible for nonprofit institutions to realize the best of both worlds: the tax advantages and fund-raising opportunities of a nonprofit organization along with the capital investment options and operating efficiencies of a for-profit corporation. They can do so without causing harm to their mission or their academic culture. The risks are minimal, and the potential financial rewards are substantial.

REDEFINING SHARED GOVERNANCE

Despite its appeal to traditional academic sensibilities (including my own), the concept of shared governance has evolved into a system of decision making that is unworkable on many campuses. For presidents, provosts, and deans, shared governance reduces leadership to making compromises and finding the "middle ground" in order to appease the loudest and offend the fewest. In practice, shared governance actually makes decision making a delusion altogether, says Daniel Julius, director of the Center for Strategic Leadership at the University of San Francisco.

A new model is needed. The lesson of the for-profits is that a reasonable level of participation and inclusiveness can coexist within a more traditional management structure, in which authority for making decisions is granted to those in leadership positions. In working with faculty at DeVry, I see that less reliance on shared governance does not necessarily result in the destruction of academic culture; many faculty actually feel relieved to be freed from excessive participation in governance so that they can focus on their work as professors. There have also been times when I have felt that DeVry and perhaps other for-profits may have swung too far in the other direction, where the bosses wield power and sometimes fail to include the faculty sufficiently in decisions to which they could make important contributions, such as those involving curricula. I do not believe the for-profit providers have found the perfect solution to the problem of shared governance, but they have demonstrated that a more traditional management culture can work in an academic institution.

Perhaps every institution needs to find its own center of gravity in these matters. I am convinced that shared governance needs to be redefined to allow those in positions of authority to make decisions that are timely and responsive and to break free from what Daniel Julius (1999) describes as the political power struggle in which "decisions go round and round in circles, and the best one can hope for in the political battle is a temporary win."

Developing a Strong Customer Orientation

The strong customer-service orientation of the for-profit colleges and universities is one of the reasons a growing population of students is choosing them in pursuit of higher education. Treating students like customers does not mean that they cease to be students, or that the institution must give in to all their preferences, or that faculty must give away good grades for the sake of happy customers. It simply means that the institution becomes more responsive to its students and makes serving them effectively the highest priority. Failing to do so, I believe, will result in students' taking their business elsewhere.

What Is a Proper College Education?

Any serious inquiry into the changing face of American higher education ultimately leads to the question of what constitutes a proper college education. This question is a decidedly complex one. Its answer inevitably depends on how one answers larger questions concerning epistemology, ontology, and the relationship between education and the greater social good. What can be known? How can it be known? What is the nature of the human knower? What is the purpose of knowledge? What is the meaning of human existence? What is the relationship between individual persons and democratic society? Answers to these fundamental questions implicitly or explicitly inform every attempt to define what constitutes a proper college education. Is it any surprise, then, that this educational question continues to be hotly debated, and consensus remains an impossible dream, both within and between educational institutions?

In his masterful study of the idea of liberal education, Bruce Kimball (1995) analyzes the U.S. debate concerning postsecondary education in terms of the centuries-old debate between philosophers and orators. The origins of the U.S. debate about what constitutes a proper education are situated in ancient Greece and Rome. Both orators and philosophers were committed to the formation of virtuous persons through the pursuit of knowledge, but they disagreed about the shape of the curriculum and the educational processes through which knowledge and virtue could be attained.

The philosophers, Plato and Socrates, argued that truth exists and can be known in itself and, further, that such knowledge will produce virtuous persons. Clearly, not every person in Plato's aristocratic society enjoyed the leisure for such an educational pursuit. But the elite class of persons who did were responsible in this pursuit to the greater good of the whole society.

In contrast to the philosophers, the orators, including the Sophists and such individuals as Isocrates, Quintilian, and Cicero, argued that truth, beauty, and goodness cannot be pursued as abstract ideals, nor can the formation of virtuous persons depend on the contemplative activities of a few. Rather, they concluded that these virtues are discovered and taught through active engagement in the real life of society, which leads to the articulation of practical wisdom. Here again, such learning is primarily available to persons with adequate wealth and leisure to participate, but its fruits are more immediately available to the larger society in which the orators practice their art.

Even this brief sketch begins to make sense of the debates that continue to shape U.S. college and university education. The liberal arts tradition in the United States has been expressed in terms of education both as free inquiry (philosophers) and as the study of received textual traditions (orators). But in the U.S. context the classical debate undergoes some critical permutations, which Kimball (1995) defines in terms of what he calls the "liberal free ideal."

On the one side, the philosopher's commitment to free inquiry is eventually linked to scientific research methodologies dedicated to the objective pursuit of truth as empirical fact. Free inquiry is no longer grounded in philosophy and contemplation as the means to discover truth. Further, it ceases to be interested in the formation of persons who are virtuous in the classical sense—persons who understand and commit themselves to the virtues of truth, beauty, and goodness. The capacity for rational, critical, empirical inquiry becomes the key virtue to be formed in persons. On the other side, texts are analyzed and criticized rather than imitated and appropriated. Virtuous persons do not submit to the authority and wisdom of received traditions—they question them.

I offer no judgment concerning these epistemological and ontological shifts, but rather intend to frame the complexity of the questions that surround U.S. college and university education. Assertions that the best postsecondary education is achieved through the liberal arts tradition must take into account that in the U.S. context precisely what this means for both the content of the curriculum and the processes of teaching and learning is immersed in muddy waters. It doesn't mean just one thing now, and in fact it never did.

Voices are calling for a return to the classical values of a liberal arts education. Howard Gardner (1999) has argued passionately for a return to education grounded in the formation of persons in the virtues of truth, beauty, and goodness. Mortimer Adler (1977) is another outspoken advocate for a liberal arts education. He asserts that liberal learning is that which is not vocational, going so far as to claim that "it is an absolute misuse of school to include any vocational training at all."

What Adler overlooks in making this assertion is that, from the outset, an education in the liberal arts was a vocational education: it prepared philosophers and orators in service to the greater social good. One might argue that these vocations are among the most noble and essential in society, but they are, nevertheless, vocations. Of course, Adler's concern is to speak against utilitarian and pragmatic traditions in U.S. higher education in favor of learning for its own sake. But in the U.S. context, education for agrarian and industrial vocations existed alongside and outside colleges and universities focused on the preparation of persons for the learned and genteel vocations of ministry, law, and medicine. This separation began to shift with the Morrill Land Grant Acts of 1862 and 1890. Driven by the demands of an agrarian economy and growing industrialization, this legislation "supported postsecondary institutions for teaching agriculture and the mechanic arts" and ultimately "introduced more practical, technical, and vocational subjects" (Kimball, 1995) into the mainstream of American higher education. The distinct aims of liberal learning and preparation for a broad spectrum of practical vocations have been uneasy bedfellows for decades in America.

The utilitarian voices in American higher education might appeal to the philosophical tradition of pragmatism in support of their claims. John Dewey was responsible for most fully articulating the implications of pragmatism for education in a democracy. Arguing that social efficiency is among the chief aims of education, Dewey believed that no person could live without means of subsistence and that an individual who was not able to earn a living was "a drag or parasite upon the activities of others." According to Dewey, among other things, education must prepare persons for a vocation and equip them with the ability to make their way economically in the world.

But Dewey's program of education for social efficiency goes beyond individual economic empowerment and vocational training. Dewey understood the human vocation in broad terms, as a vocation to participate fully in society in multiple roles with varying responsibilities. Education must prepare persons to be good citizens, to exercise sound judgment about economic and social principles, to be adaptable in the face of rapid changes, to be flexible thinkers, and to participate in the transformation of social rules and norms. In keeping with the oratorical strand of the liberal arts tradition, Dewey was convinced that education must prepare all persons to engage in persuasive rhetoric, not primarily for the purpose of persuading another to change perspective, but with the goal of creating understanding between a diversity of persons making choices and expressing values on the basis of their own best rationality.

Indeed, the purpose of higher education is a complex question. We are the inheritors of diverse philosophies, multiple educational traditions, and varying practices, a handful of which I have sketched above.

I have attempted to describe the assumptions, content, and practices of for-profit institutions of higher education. I have argued that there may be opportunities for nonprofit educational institutions to examine their own assumptions and practices in light of these new ventures in higher education. But I am also clear that the for-profits are not getting it right at every point. These ventures involve both losses and gains. Nonprofit colleges and universities continue to hold in trust certain age-old educational values and remind us that some of the key benefits of education are simply not immediately measurable as outcomes, economic or otherwise. It is my intention to contribute to the ongoing conversation about higher education in America and to submit my own understanding and experience to the larger community of persons who also dedicate themselves to the human vocation of knowing and sharing knowledge, for the good of individuals and the larger society.

REFERENCES

Adler, Mortimer J. (1977). *Reforming Education: The Opening of the American Mind.* Boulder: Westview.

Altbach, P. G., et al. (eds.). (1998). *American Higher Education in the 21st Century.* Baltimore: Johns Hopkins University Press.

Alva , Jorge de. (2000). "For-Profit and Non-Profit Higher Education." Presentation at the annual conference of the Council for Higher Education Accreditation, Washington, D.C., January 26.

————. (1999–2000, winter). "Remaking the Academy in the Age of Information." *Issues in Science and Technology, 16.*

Blumenstyk, G. (2000, January 7). "Turning a Profit by Turning Out Professionals." *Chronicle of Higher Education*, A46.

Cowen, Scott. (2000). "Leadership, Shared Governance, and the Change Imperative." Presentation at the Eighth AAHE Conference on Faculty Roles and Rewards, New Orleans, La.

Dewey, J. (1920). *Democracy and Education: An Introduction to the Philosophy of Education.* New York: Macmillan.

Eaton, Judith. (2000). *Core Academic Values, Quality, and Regional Accreditation: The Challenge of Distance Learning.* CHEA Monograph Series, 1.

Gardner, Howard. (1999). *The Disciplined Mind: What All Students Should Understand.* New York: Simon & Schuster.

Geiger, R. (1995). "The Ten Generations of American Higher Education." In Altbach et al., *American Higher Education in the 21st Century.*

Goldstein, Michael B. (2000). Dow, Lohnes & Albertson. Washington, D.C., interview by author, January 25.

Gose, B. (2000, January 14). "Measuring the Value of an Ivy Degree." *Chronicle of Higher Education*, A52–A53.

Gumport, Patricia, and Marc Chun. (1995). "Technology in Higher Education." In Altbach et al., *American Higher Education in the 21st Century.*

Higher Education Research Institute, University of California at Los Angeles, Graduate School of Education and Information Studies. (2000). "The American Freshman: National Norms for the Fall 1999." Retrieved from <www.gseis.ucla.edu/herilheri/html>. See also *Chronicle of Higher Education*, January 28, A49–A52.

Julius, Daniel. (1999, October 7). "Case Studies from the Floor: Getting Down to Brass Tacks." Presentation at the "Market-Driven Higher Education" conference, hosted by *University Business* magazine, New York.

Karabell, Zachary. (1998). *What's College For? The Struggle to Define American Higher Education.* New York: Basic Books.

Keller, G. (1999–2000). "The Emerging Third State in Higher Education Planning." *Planning for Higher Education, 28*, 3.

Kimball, B. (1995). *Orators and Philosophers: A History of the Idea of Liberal Education* (expanded ed.). Princeton, N.J.: College Entrance Examination Board.

Krueger, A., and S. Dale. (1999). "Estimating the Payoff to Attending a More Selective College: An Application of Selection on Observables and Unobservables." Working paper W7289, National Bureau of Economic Research, August.

Lynch, Merrill. (1999). *In-Depth Report: The Book of Knowledge, Investing in the Growing Education and Training Industry.* Report 1268 (April 9), *44.* The figures originally appeared in a study by the Miliken Institute.

McGuinness, A., Jr. (1999). "The States and Higher Education." In Altbach et al., *Higher Education in the 21st Century.*

McGuire, Patricia. (2000). "For-Profit and Non-Profit Higher Education." Presentation at the annual conference of the Council for Higher Education Accreditation, Washington, D.C., January 26.

McPherson, Michael. (1999, spring). "Balancing Competing Values: The Market and the Mission." *The Presidency*, 2.

National Center for Education Statistics. (1997, March). "Education and the Economy: An Indicators Report," NCES 97-939. Retrieved from <www.nces.ed.gov.puhS97>.

Runte, Roseann. (2000, January 8). "How to Succeed in Academe: A Question of Degrees." *Chronicle of Higher Education*, B8.

Sperling, John. (1998, August 25). Quoted in D. Stamps, "The For-Profit Future of Higher Education." *Training.*

Tierney, William. (1999). *Building the Responsive Campus: Creating High Performance Colleges and Universities.* London: Sage.

CHAPTER 6

GLOBALIZATION, COLLEGE PARTICIPATION, AND SOCIOECONOMIC MOBILITY

Scott L. Thomas

THE EMERGENCE of a truly globalized economy has had far-reaching consequences for labor and training in the United States. Among the more visible impacts of this new economy are expanding participation in postsecondary education and a corresponding growth in the number of colleges and universities offering baccalaureate degrees. While this expansion of opportunity and participation is generally viewed as a positive and desirable development, a closer look at the qualitative nature of today's postsecondary opportunities reveals a highly stratified landscape that serves to filter the rewards typically associated with college attendance. This chapter explores this recent growth in participation and the general beliefs driving it.

The chapter comprises four sections. In the first, I examine the economics of the changed economy and its need of more highly skilled labor. Trends in the growth and contraction of institutions of higher education in the United States are considered in the second section, while the changing economic value of the college degree is the focus of the third. The fourth section of the chapter considers the role the university plays as a social institution and the ways in which that role changed over the latter part of the twentieth century. The chapter concludes with thoughts about the potential impact of college participation on socioeconomic mobility in the United States.

A KNOWLEDGE-BASED ECONOMY

National education systems have been dramatically affected by globalization, particularly in those nations, such as the United States, most closely tied to the globalization process. Education in the United States has long been understood as a principal vehicle for socioeconomic advancement, and recent changes in the economy seem to make higher education more important than ever.

It is no longer news that in the United States postsecondary education and credentials are viewed as necessary to better ensure attainment of a middle-class standard of living. The baccalaureate degree, once seen as an advantage for many, is now understood as a necessity for access to quality jobs and economic opportunities. Underlying this realization is a radically transformed U.S. economy. Consider that:

- The proportion of nonagricultural employment in goods-producing industries declined from a peak of 47.4 percent in 1943 to a low of 18.3 percent in 2002.
- The proportion of jobs in the private service industries grew from a low of 38.3 percent in 1943 to a peak of 65.6 percent in 2002.
- The proportion of jobs in government/public service increased from 12.8 percent in 1941 to a peak of 19.1 percent in 1975, and declined to 16.2 percent in 2002 (Bureau of Labor Statistics, 2002).

These shifts have profound implications for the educational attainment requirement of Americans. Projections by the U.S. Bureau of Labor Statistics show that employment in areas that generally require a college degree or other postsecondary award is expected to grow faster than average across all occupations. Jobs generally requiring a college degree constituted 29 percent of all jobs in 2000 and are expected to account for 42 percent of projected new job growth across the coming decade.

So while new "educational technologies" such as computers and advanced telephony are frequently used to symbolize the impact of the globalized economy on education, sole focus on such physical manifestations distracts attention from the much larger impact globalization has had on education vis-à-vis the perceived press for a more highly educated workforce.

GROWTH IN COLLEGE PARTICIPATION AND POSTSECONDARY OPPORTUNITY

INCREASING ENROLLMENT

These economic realities are not lost on the American public. While attending college was always a cornerstone of the twentieth-century "American dream," never before has such a large proportion of the population had such relatively easy access to the college campus. Today, almost 65 percent of high school graduates enroll in college within 12 months of receipt of their high school diploma or GED certificate—up from 49 percent in 1980. During the 2000–2001 academic year, roughly 9 million students were enrolled full-time at degree-granting institutions in the United States and another 6.3 million were enrolled at these institutions on a part-time basis. The most recent projections from the National Center for Education Statistics show that enrollment will grow by roughly 14 percent through the coming decade.

A GROWTH IN COLLEGES

While there exists some question about the degree to which institutions of higher education have themselves driven the demand defining recent increases in enrollment, there is no question that there are many more degree-granting institutions than was the case roughly twenty years ago. By 1980, at the end of an unprecedented expansion of higher education in the United States, there were close to 3,200 degree-granting colleges operating across the country. Today there are nearly 4,200. While traditional colleges (i.e., public and private not-for-profit) granting baccalaureate degrees grew around 11 percent over the 1990s, a newer class of for-profit baccalaureate-granting institutions also emerged, growing from 53 institutions in 1990 to 263 in 2001—or 461 percent (National Center for Education Statistics, 2002). While these new for-profit institutions still constitute a small fraction of colleges, their rapid growth and unique appeal speak to what many see as their potential to transform the traditional higher education model.

What is especially noteworthy about this more recent expansion is that it occurred across a period in which demographers and those monitoring college enrollments were projecting radical declines in the college-age population—declines that were expected to translate into a full-blown enrollment crisis by the late 1980s. The inevitable crisis was obviated, however, by college officials turning their attention and energies to the recruitment of so-called nontraditional populations (e.g., people from ethnic minority backgrounds, those older than twenty-five, and many with less rigorous academic preparation—in short, those who were traditionally underrepresented from college campuses) that now constitute a substantial proportion of today's student body. The net result was a significant enrollment growth across a period that would have otherwise been marked by a major oversupply of classroom space. This growth in the nontraditional student population also created a demand for a host of new student services, many of them academic in nature, which colleges and universities had theretofore had little experience with.

THE ECONOMIC VALUE OF COLLEGE

While the actual dynamics of educational attainment and its interaction with future labor market experiences is clearly understood by few, the basic extrinsic economic returns to college credentials are much more widely accessible and appreciated. Charts 1 and 2 illustrate two of the most visible labor market benefits of postsecondary credentials: higher incomes and a lesser likelihood of unemployment.

Although the benefits of college attendance have been shown to be far-reaching, ranging from enhanced self-esteem to improved health, the very frequently (if not most often) cited reason for attending college is simply to get better jobs that yield greater incomes. And of course this financial interest is manifest not only in students' decision to attend college but also by their subsequent choice of academic major. Student awareness of the marketability of particular majors is evidenced by a notable increase since the late 1960s in the number of degrees awarded in professional areas. Colleges' heightened attention to this demand has been shown to have fundamentally impacted undergraduate curricula at many traditionally liberal arts colleges, leading some scholars to conclude that many such schools today are liberal arts in name only.

By keying on the extrinsic value of the baccalaureate degree, col-

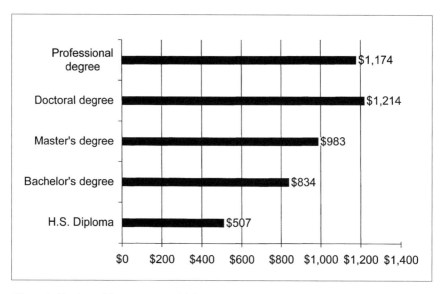

Chart 1. Real weekly earnings of full-time wage and salary workers aged twenty-five to sixty-four by educational attainment, 2000.

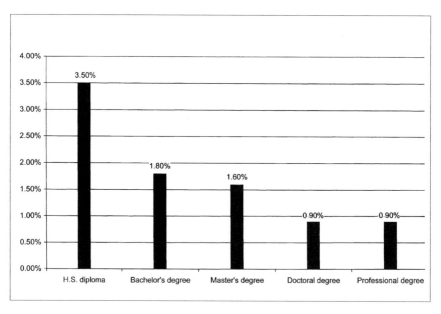

Chart 2. Unemployment of workers aged twenty-five and over by highest level of educational attainment.

leges and universities were able to open new markets, buoying enrollments and revenues during a period in which both were precarious.
Colleges' highlighting the monetary value of their degrees played right
into broader trends of student orientations to college. Students themselves are today more likely to identify extrinsic motivations for attending college than were their counterparts of thirty-five years ago. Data
collected annually by the Higher Education Research Institute at the
University of California at Los Angeles show that roughly 84 percent
of incoming freshmen they surveyed in 1966 (the first year of their survey) indicated that a primary life goal was "to develop a meaningful philosophy of life." During that same year 44 percent of students surveyed
identified "to be very well-off financially" as a primary life goal. By
1990 those proportions were almost exactly reversed and have remained
relatively constant since. The period in which these trend lines reached
their plateaus was eerily coincident with the fall of business tycoons Ivan
Boesky and Michael Milken and the emergence of the unscrupulous
movie character, Gordon Gecko—all perhaps symbolic of our country's
preoccupation with material acquisition.

Further fueling this extrinsic orientation has been the tuition hyper-
inflation over the past fifteen years. As state budgets have been unable to
keep pace with growth in college and university expenditures, more of
the total cost of education has been shifted to students and their families
during this period. In an effort to ameliorate critics of these increases—
critics that included not only students and their families but the Congress of the United States and many higher education groups—college
officials are quick to point out that these increases are necessary to
ensure educational quality and argue that the long-range "value" of the
investment in a baccalaureate degree pales in comparison to its still relatively inexpensive price. Such logic in turn fueled the much lamented
"consumer mentality" among today's students—a mentality much at
odds with intrinsic notions of the undergraduate years being devoted to
the "life of the mind," a devotion presumed to confer rewards beyond
monetary remuneration and to yield a more civil and productive society.

But a closer examination of the material return-on-investment argument is much more complicated (and interesting) than realities such as
those shown in Charts 1 and 2 might suggest. Yes, college attendance
influences one's experiences in the labor market. But a host of other
factors beyond simply deciding to go to college qualify the economic

value of this investment. Three of the more important of these factors shown to impact one's career choices and income are (1) choice of college, (2) choice of major, and (3) academic performance during the undergraduate years. Students face real constraints when dealing with each of these important factors—constraints that are tightly bound to socioeconomic background, race, and gender.

COLLEGE CHOICE

Outside of the most elite institutions exists a buyer's market as better qualified prospective students weigh their alternatives in the higher education marketplace. Research has examined two distinct phases of this choice process. The first phase centers on the decision whether or not to attend college after high school. Ability and achievement, family socioeconomic status, academic orientation of the high school program, and student aspiration are among the factors that have a demonstrable impact on students' decisions to attend college in general. Once having decided to attend college, prospective students are then faced with a second phase of decisions that focus on the choice of institution. Sociologists and economists have identified many factors affecting students' college choice, which include the net cost of attendance (tuition and cost of living adjusted for financial aid), perceived academic quality of the target institution, individual academic ability, and family social class background.

At both of these decision points, prospective students are likely to also be weighing the economics of college attendance. While immediate considerations such as how one is going to meet personal costs associated with tuition, books, and living expenses are likely to occupy the attention of those contemplating college attendance, broader assessments of the payoff to college are also likely to be taking place. However, relatively few young people contemplating college are capable of employing a reasonably accurate return-on-investment (ROI in today's parlance) analysis that would include not only those direct costs noted above but also items such as the forgone earnings resulting from time devoted to attending college or the costs associated with financing college attendance through any number of student loan programs that will likely be used.

Equally complex is the other side of the ROI equation. One's potential postgraduation earnings are impacted by a variety of factors, many of which are likely unknown to the prospective college entrant. Student choices of academic majors and institutions are two of the more obvious decisions that can have dramatic impacts on career development. Perhaps a person has decided upon a major field of study from which likely postgraduate earnings could be reasonably extrapolated. But college does indeed impact students—and in ways that often radically alter initial intentions and goals. These changes might occur during the window in which many students are allowed to choose their academic majors or quite some time after an initial major has been declared. It is also important to acknowledge that majors that students choose among have distinctive patterns in terms of race and gender that serve to encourage or discourage particular students. Of course, a student must choose an institution (and negotiate acceptance and matriculation) before he or she can choose a major. Institutions will be more or less closely aligned with various labor markets that can have a direct impact on both the employability and the quality of jobs for their graduates. The reality of unknowns such as these fundamentally compromises any accurate assessment of just how good an economic investment in college might be for any particular person. The claim by college officials that despite the rapidly rising prices a baccalaureate degree is still a great investment is likely true for many. But given the much wider participation in higher education and the rapid expansion of institutions it becomes increasingly necessary to ask how these benefits vary across groups and to what degree these benefits actually enable meaningful upward socioeconomic mobility.

Unlike systems of higher education in many countries, in the United States it is comprised of institutions that vary dramatically in terms of size, geography, sector, selectivity, and mission. These institutions take the form of campuses ranging from flagship state universities to private liberal arts colleges and two-year community colleges. Through these institutions students take a variety of paths to the baccalaureate—paths often marked by periods of stop-out and/or attendance at multiple institutions. The diversity of institutional type and relative freedom of mobility among these institutions ensure most Americans access to some facet of higher education. But as many observers have noted, not all college experiences are equal, and this is manifest in part in the differential labor market experiences of graduates from different academic majors and different types of institutions.

In fact, over four decades of research focusing on economic outcomes of college demonstrate that graduates from high-demand majors (e.g., business, economics, health, and engineering related fields in the late 1990s) at more prestigious colleges enjoy distinct advantages in terms of access to good jobs and income. Academic performance as expressed through one's cumulative grade point average has also been shown to be associated with earnings but to a much lesser degree than major and institutional prestige. So assuming that our adolescent econometricians wished to maximize the ROI on the baccalaureate degree, they would be best advised to enroll at a prestigious college, subscribe to a high-demand major, and earn grades better than that of their peers.

It is important to acknowledge the reality that, while the economic value of college is a consideration for most, for at least some students the choice of college may be based on other, less extrinsic factors. For example, the plethora of relatively anonymous religiously affiliated colleges across the country suggests the existence of a market that is making decisions based less on financial considerations and more on the intrinsic value of a faith-based environment while at college. Research shows that these colleges, while considerably more expensive to attend than public institutions of similar prestige, confer no notable economic advantages to their graduates relative to those they would have received by attending a comparably distinctive public institution. One might conclude that, after factoring in the reality that most students attending these institutions are financing some significant proportion of these costs through student loans, attending such institutions is actually somewhat of an economic disinvestment.

Another reality deserving acknowledgment is that some students make their institutional choices based less on their evaluation of the career prospects associated with a baccalaureate degree from that institution and more on what economists like to call the "option value" of those degrees. It has been widely noted that the baccalaureate degree is sometimes perceived as the new high school diploma and that in order to have a competitive edge one must have an advanced degree to better ensure career success. Some schools are better known than others for their ability to place their baccalaureate recipients in the most competitive advanced and professional degree programs around the country—programs known for providing their graduates entrée to extremely powerful and well-paid positions. Baccalaureate degrees from such feeder institutions are therefore said to better provide the option to attend graduate school. Thus, the option value of degrees from those institutions is higher than that of degrees from institutions producing graduates less prone toward graduate school attendance. For some, then, the baccalaureate is merely a stepping stone to advanced degrees with which career success can be much better assured.

A final group worthy of attention here is comprised of more technically oriented students with clear extrinsic aims. Students in this group are less likely to be concerned about the traditional college experience and instead are more likely to be seeking a distinct set of technical skills that can be immediately applied in the workforce. For these students in particular, interests in general education take a back seat to the development of demonstrable technical mastery of particular areas. While such training has typically been provided by employers, the acceleration of technical complexity associated with many positions and the willingness of firms to shed the costs of such in-house training have encouraged new institutions to address this emerging need. Community colleges have long provided a base for such training and have now begun to offer advanced technical certification and in some instances four-year degrees to those in this market. In addition to the expansion of the role of community colleges, a new class of for-profit institutions has emerged largely to capitalize on this market. Finally, many of those firms retaining their training programs have expanded these to offer special technical certifications. So large has this segment of higher education grown that Clifford Adelman of the U.S. Department of Education has labeled it a "parallel universe" and noted that despite its awarding of upwards of 1.7 million certifications in 1999 it remains very difficult to track its growth.

Howard Bowen's 1977 book entitled *Investment in Learning* reminds us that "returns" on college investment need to be considered at two levels, individual and social. To this point in the essay I have focused on the private returns to college, in an effort to suggest that a variety of influences have come together to encourage the preoccupation with this dimension. Despite the matter-of-fact fashion with which we tend to treat higher education opportunity in the United States, access to particular segments of the higher education system is highly unequal. Given the impact of higher education on life chances and its potential to enable socioeconomic mobility, this inequality should be of great concern. In the remainder of this chapter I shift attention to the structural dimension of college attendance and the importance of the college as a social institution.

COLLEGES AND UNIVERSITIES AS SOCIAL INSTITUTIONS

STRATIFICATION OF OPPORTUNITY

Many researchers have focused on the structural factors that define how students are sorted into specific institutions and majors. One might assume that the diversity of institutions and freedom of major choice would create myriad opportunities that could be realized purely on the basis of merit—where the most talented and qualified could freely avail themselves of the most resourced colleges and universities. And, to be sure, the nation's most prestigious institutions—as is true of most institutions—do have a vested interest in attracting the best and the brightest regardless of their social station or ability to pay. But this assumption belies the reality that children from less affluent families are still considerably less likely to attend college, even after controlling for aptitude and preparation.

This is also related to the question of how we define "merit" in our society. Sociologist Jerome Karabel states that "meritocracy's dirty little secret is that 'merit' in any society is defined by the powerful." Invoking elements of Michael Young's *The Rise of Meritocracy*, Karabel reminds us that meritocracy is by design a means by which the existing class structure, replete with its inequalities, is preserved while at the same time providing a rationale that everyone, regardless of where they may sit in that class structure, deserves their lot. Merit, at least as it relates to college opportunity in the United States, is a unique hodgepodge of standardized test scores, grades, and extracurricular activities that are highly correlated with particular schools, which in turn are highly correlated with the socioeconomic status of the families of the children that populate them.

While the stratification of opportunity is evident in general college-going patterns it becomes much more pronounced when one examines the relative prestige of colleges attended by students of different socioeconomic backgrounds. Much of this is the direct result of students' experiences at primary and secondary schools. K–12 schools in the United States vary widely in their orientation to college and this variance is often problematically correlated with the socioeconomic and racial composition of their student bodies. Students bring to school certain values and predispositions to education in general and to college in particular and these values and predispositions are importantly magnified by the primary and secondary school systems.

We can draw on French sociologist Pierre Bourdieu's concept of cultural capital to help explain how students and families interpret the value of education. Leveraging much of Max Weber's work on status groups, Bourdieu argues that society's elites have a highly developed sense of proper educational pedigrees that are symbolic of one's station and advantage. Cultural capital provides the means by which those symbols are recognized and the ways in which students and families act in order to maximize their value. Those capable of decoding the symbolic power of education are more likely to find themselves with others who share this same power, thus magnifying its already substantial effect. This common insight then translates into learning environments that nurture collegiate aspirations and provide the intellectual and counseling resources necessary to prepare and predispose children for the rigors of relatively elite educational opportunities—opportunities that help ensure the intergenerational transmission of knowledge, power, and status.

This is a process that unfolds over the course of one's childhood and early adult life and is therefore resistant to interventions that might occur at the late high school or college admissions junctures. Given the long-term nature of this process, primary focus on financial barriers that restrict students' collegiate choices somewhat misses the mark. As important as it is to make college affordable enough to be seen as a realistic option, this does little to address the larger structural bias discouraging students from families of lesser economic means from attending the best resourced and most prestigious institutions—those that are presumed to convey the largest economic advantages.

But let us not lose sight of the reality that a greater proportion of people in all age groups are attending college than ever before and a record number of degree-granting institutions are serving these students. While this might be cause for celebration, it masks two important realities. First, while a college degree can confer distinct economic advantages, it comes at a real price—even at the nation's most affordable colleges. More often than not students seeking financial assistance to help pay for college costs find themselves mired in significant amounts of education-related debt upon graduation (excluded from this consideration are those students failing to graduate after semesters of loan-financed attendance). Simply put, the cost borne by students—especially when financed over many years—can significantly undercut, and in extreme cases eliminate, any economic advantage realized. The degree to which this is a concern is determined in part by one's choice of major and in part by how closely one's alma mater is aligned with good jobs.

A second reality that might qualify our enthusiasm over increasing participation in postsecondary education is that many of these educational opportunities might be better understood as little more than what Stephen Brint and Jerome Karabel (1989), writing about the community college, referred to as "diverted dreams." Some have noted that these new educational opportunities have served to take pressure off the nation's most prestigious institutions, those that have traditionally served as credentialing bastions for the country's—indeed, much of the world's—elite. So by some accounts the growth in institutions, most of which can be accounted for by demand from students from nontraditional backgrounds, can be viewed as a bulwark protecting the institutions traditionally serving the nation's most economically privileged families. These two realities, when taken together, help explain why many economists note that rather than understanding college as providing greater advantage today than was the case in the past, it is often more accurate to view life with a high school diploma or less as a much greater disadvantage than ever before. Expanding opportunities in this fashion does little to address the growing problems associated with economic inequality in the United States.

The major point in all of this is that the real value being accorded to increased opportunity and participation in postsecondary education may be somewhat misplaced. While a college degree helped assure previous generations that they would move forward socioeconomically relative to the previous generation, the reality for the current generation is somewhat different. For most, the new economy has helped make the college degree a necessity for maintaining one's rung on the socioeconomic ladder. Career options for those without college credentials are increasingly bleak. Those unable to attend or complete college are often limited to relatively menial jobs in the service sector that are marked by low pay, few if any benefits, and unstable employment terms. Those who do go on to college will experience wide differences in both the costs and benefits of their degree programs.

Consider as an example of the uneven distribution of costs and benefits of college attendance results from my own work examining the earnings and student loan indebtedness in 1997 of a nationally representative sample of baccalaureate recipients from 1993. Chart 3 summarizes the earnings advantages (or lack thereof) experienced by students graduating from colleges at three distinct levels of selectivity (which is often used as a proxy for prestige) in the public and private sectors. The dollar values are the earnings of graduates in each group relative to

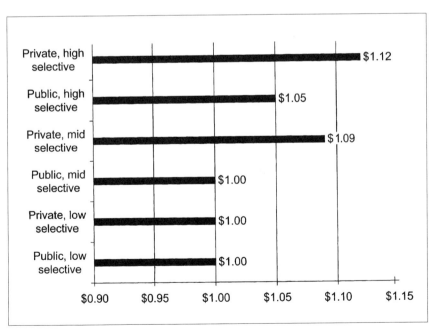

Chart 3. Relative average earnings of baccalaureate graduates from different types of colleges.

those graduating from public colleges in the lowest prestige tier. So, for example, graduates from the most selective private colleges (see the top bar) earned $1.12 for each dollar earned by their counterparts graduating from the least selective public institutions (see the bottom bar), four years after graduation.

A couple of important qualifications must accompany these figures. First, these values have been adjusted to account for the reality that institutions vary in terms of the makeup of their academic majors, gender and racial compositions, and a number of other factors that are known to influence earnings. I have in a real way statistically equalized the graduating classes of these institutions to enable more accurate measurement of earning differences attributable just to the institution. Second, these numbers represent the earnings of what we call "terminal baccalaureates"—that is, they exclude any graduate who has gone on to full-time graduate study between receipt of a diploma in 1993 and when these data were collected in 1997. As many of the most prestigious colleges in the country are used as conduits to the most competitive advanced and professional degree programs, this snapshot of the earnings of terminal baccalaureates in all likelihood significantly understates the economic advantages associated with graduation from these high-prestige institutions. Terminal baccalaureates from these schools do not convert the option value of degrees from these colleges and therefore forgo a substantial component of the real benefit.

While the relative earnings advantage enjoyed by graduates from higher-prestige institutions is interesting, perhaps more interesting is the lack of advantage associated with graduation from private institutions of low selectivity. The lack of a relative earnings reward from low selectivity private colleges is of particular importance because these institutions are considerably more expensive to attend than most public colleges.

Over one-half of these graduates from 1993 relied on student loans to meet their college expenses. Graduates from private institutions were more likely to have borrowed and on average borrowed about half again as much as graduates from public colleges. Consider that in 1997, those 1993 graduates who borrowed to finance their degrees from private colleges owed roughly $11,000 while indebted graduates from public colleges had balances of just below $7,400 on average. Breaking this out across levels of prestige reveals a striking pattern of indebtedness and raises questions about the net economic advantages associated with attending prestigious schools if one must borrow substantial amounts of money to do so. Managing this debt after graduation has been shown to negatively impact opportunities relating to home purchases and early career investment decisions that compound over one's lifetime to provide significant long-term financial advantages.

Another interesting finding about the earnings and labor market experiences of graduates from different types of colleges is that there are effectively no earnings differences among graduates one year after they have received their degrees. The earnings advantages seem not to accrue in any meaningful way until several years after graduation. This further complicates the financial challenges of a student who has borrowed significant amounts of money to obtain a degree from a prestigious (and expensive) college.

Chart 4 shows that compared to graduates from all schools in the public sector, four years after graduation private college graduates had debt burdens between 34 and 47 percent higher. In terms of extrinsic incentives, taking Charts 3 and 4 into consideration, the best investment

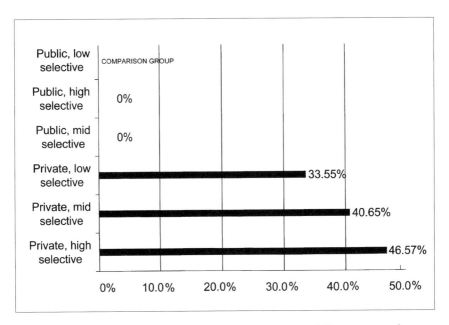

Chart 4. Relative average debt burdens of graduates from different types of colleges.

(when also considering financing costs) would be at a high-prestige public institution. This of course assumes one is academically qualified to gain admission into a college in this sector—an assumption importantly qualified by one's socioeconomic background. Conversely, these numbers suggest that the worst investment is in a degree from a relatively high-cost, less selective private college. And this is one of the fastest growing postsecondary sectors.

This is not to say that college does not still offer a "leg-up" for many. I wish only to suggest (again) that (1) some colleges provide a greater advantage than others, and (2) access to the colleges that provide the greatest benefits is unequal and this inequality is problematically tied with family socioeconomic status. Consider that the stratification in higher education is marked in part by a small set of elite institutions that have changed little in their student composition and another rapidly expanding set of less prestigious institutions attracting populations of students that have been traditionally underrepresented on college campuses.

EXPANDING PARTICIPATION AND SOCIOECONOMIC MOBILITY

While difficult to quantify, colleges, being institutions of the dominant class structure, tend to offer benefits in proportion to the cultural capital students bring to their campuses. This speaks to advantage far beyond that gained through technical skill acquisition. Prestigious institutions more greatly magnify the effects of one's cultural capital than do institutions of lesser prestige (prestige, after all, is a subjective assessment based on the values of the dominant culture). To the degree that this is true, relative to graduates from less prestigious colleges, all students will benefit more greatly from experiences at more prestigious institutions. Those bringing more cultural capital to the institution will benefit the most, however. And this benefit is more likely to be exponential than linear. High-prestige institutions therefore might be understood as superchargers of one's cultural capital. Whether this happens through greater development of human capital or through the signals that a credential from a prestigious college (or any college for that matter) sends to others, research shows that students from more affluent families tend to receive a greater boost from higher-prestige colleges than do students from families of more modest means.

Higher education in the United States has always been greatly stratified. But throughout the twentieth century it facilitated the fundamental belief that it serves as the primary vehicle for socioeconomic advancement. This, especially in the face of the widening abyss between the rich and the poor in this country, provides a symbol of hope that no matter how great the inequities of wealth and power clear "ladders of ascent" remain for those who are ambitious and hardworking. But the expansion of educational opportunity through a dramatically increased number of institutions has for many new entrants to the higher education system attenuated the linkage between educational attainment and socioeconomic mobility. To the degree that this becomes evident to the population as a whole, faith in higher education as a primary ladder of ascent will be eroded and class conflict will heighten.

Finally, the form being taken by this expansion is marked by another less recognizable threat. As more colleges come on line and new post-secondary sectors emerge, the desire to more clearly separate, or decouple, knowledge production from knowledge dissemination becomes much greater. Distance education and for-profit institutions will thrive if they can only perfect the delivery of knowledge content developed at our more cost-intensive traditional universities. Such endeavors will ultimately require only experts in the delivery of standardized content and have the potential of generating tremendous revenues—revenues that in traditional settings would be used to underwrite research and teaching efforts in areas that are considerably more expensive or less popular in terms of student participation. At some point the historically symbiotic relationship between knowledge production and knowledge dissemination will break down further, discouraging investment in fields deemed less popular or too expensive. This of course will have little impact on our most prestigious campuses, but poses a significant threat to those campuses competing in markets for less qualified students, further eroding the quality of opportunities available in the more quickly expanding nonelite segment of higher education.

Combating these realities will require systematic and sustained attention to the great variance in the quality of K–12 schools, the widespread expansion of effective college outreach programs, and a philosophical shift in state and federal financial aid policies that can make college truly affordable for students from less affluent families. As importantly, policies need to be developed that better ensure the quality of postsecondary educational experiences being made available— especially those that the public is subsidizing through direct appropriations, student financial aid, or publicly funded research grants and contracts. Our current system of institutional accreditation and government oversight as regulatory mechanisms is being overwhelmed by the rate of institutional growth, the new forms of higher education becoming available, and rapid technological change affecting the ways in which education is being delivered. Now faced with a much less supportive fiscal environment and heightened competition for funds, state and federal leaders will find it even more difficult to marshal the ideological and capital resources necessary to address these issues. The magnitude of economic inequality in the United States has become sufficiently great, however, to necessitate just such an effort.

REFERENCES

Adelman, C. (2000). "A Parallel Universe: Certification in the Information Technology Guild." *Change, 32*(3), 20–29.

Astin, A., et al. (1997). *The American Freshman: Thirty Year Trends, 1966–1996.* Los Angeles, Higher Education Research Institute, Graduate School of Education and Information Studies, University of California, Los Angeles.

Bourdieu, P., and C. Passeron. (1977). *Reproduction in Education, Society, and Culture.* London: Sage.

Bowen, H. R., and Carnegie Council on Policy Studies in Higher Education. (1977). *Investment in Learning: The Individual and Social Value of American Higher Education.* San Francisco: Jossey-Bass.

Bowles, S., and H. Gintis. (1976). *Schooling in Capitalist America: Educational Reform and the Contradictions of Economic Life.* New York: Basic Books.

Brint, S., and J. Karabel. (1989). *The Diverted Dream: Community Colleges and the Promise of Educational Opportunity in America, 1900–1985.* New York: Oxford University Press.

Bureau of Labor Statistics. (2002). *Occupational Outlook Handbook,* 2002–2003 edition. Washington, D.C.: U.S. Department of Labor.

Delucchi, M. (1997). "'Liberal Arts' Colleges and the Myth of Uniqueness." *Journal of Higher Education, 68*(4), 414–426.

Karabel, J. (1999, October 23). "What the Deserving Deserve and Whether They Get It." *New York Times.*

National Center for Education Statistics. (2002). *Projections of Education Statistics to 2012*. Washington, D.C.: U.S. Department of Education.

National Commission on the Cost of Higher Education. (1998). "Straight Talk about College Costs and Prices." Washington, D.C.: American Council on Education.

Pusser, B., and D. Doane. (2001). "Public Purpose and Private Enterprise: The Contemporary Organization of Postsecondary Education." *Change, 33*(5), 18–22.

Thomas, S. (2000). "Deferred Costs and Economic Returns to College Major, Quality, and Performance." *Research in Higher Education, 41*(3), 281–313.

———. (2003). "Longer-term Economic Effects of College Selectivity and Control." *Research in Higher Education, 44*(3).

Young, M. (1958). *The Rise of the Meritocracy*. London: Thames and Hudson.

PART III

Implications for Pedagogy

Introduction

ALL OF THE WRITERS in this volume raise questions of pedagogy and curriculum: what is teaching and learning, and what is to be taught. But in this part, these questions are addressed directly. John McDermott does not deny that globalization is a force, or that the new technologies will demand a serious rethinking of both pedagogic and curricular matters. But ultimately, for him, the question of pedagogy comes down to the relation between the teacher and the student. He acknowledges uses for the new technologies, but does not see them as being capable of replacing the face-to-face encounter of student and teacher. This is not because such technologies are less efficient or powerful modes of providing knowledge. Rather, for McDermott, as for Socrates, pedagogy can be transformative only if it involves a direct engagement of minds —student's to teacher's. For him, teaching is a process of helping people construct a whole way of life, a goal which, he insists, is always under attack. He does not object to vocational training, enhancing skills, including "the basics," or promoting "civics." But these ought not dominate the academy. Nor does he object to "research." But, he asks, why do all professors have to make breakthroughs? Indeed, the "research university is a euphemism for trashing undergrads."

Charles Karelis, sharing many of the values urged by McDermott, focuses on the curriculum. He does not see that the tension between the university as a "used car dealership" with its eye on the market and the university as "a church" with its eye on the highest of human aspirations is necessarily fatal. He takes aim at faculties and the curriculum. His striking observation that most undergraduates lack even the vaguest idea why they must satisfy a "general education core" suggests that faculties have failed to communicate "the educational purposes of the university," not only to students, but to their parents and to the larger communities of which they are a part. Thus, "within the educational agenda, seen broadly, only the values of research and broadening access to education itself seem clear and compelling today. Notions such as 'the larger significance of things,' 'meaningful lives,' and 'social criticism' seem too vague or dogmatic to rally strong support among students, trustees, or the general public. Indeed a kind of silence about larger educational purposes seems to have created a partial vacuum in the agenda of universities, which has allowed consumer agendas to loom unduly large." But, curiously perhaps, that this has happened should not, he says, be seen as "the fault of the academy." Rather, he offers that the problem relates very much to what Delanty (below) sees as a crisis of modernity. Karelis concludes with some very positive suggestions: "Let us stop all this nostalgic dogmatizing about the coherence of reality and just ensure that the undergraduate experience itself is coherent enough to allow students to come to their own conclusions about the world." "Interdisciplinary programs, learning communities, capstone courses, student portfolios—even today's subsidized campus snack bars" are straightforward reforms within the compass of current faculties and their administrations.

Jaishree K. Odin has had considerable experience with online teaching and is on top of the current research literature regarding its uses and potential. Odin sees the necessity for a paradigm shift in the educational process in response to the new technologies and the concomitant "creation of networks, multidirectional flow of information, diversity, and instant access." She compares these changes to the transformations ultimately produced by the printing revolution. But online education, for better or for worse, has become entangled in difficulties that predate its use, difficulties well documented by other authors in this volume. These include not merely corporatization of the university, declining academic standards, decreasing faculty governance and commodification, but also a shift in the meaning and function of knowledge.

Odin agrees with McDermott, both following John Dewey, that good pedagogy is student- and not teacher-oriented, and that learning, as Odin puts it, involves "a continual reorganization, reconstruction, and transformation of experience." But for her, the new technologies can play a critical role responding to these challenges. This requires, most critically, a much deeper understanding of how learning goes on. Only then can we see how the new technologies can be exploited for effective learner-centered pedagogies. She argues that "current research on learning effectiveness in the online classroom shows that the new technologies allow us to create an interactive learning environment where course participants communicate genuinely, listening as well as responding to others in a mutually collaborative fashion." "Contrary, then, to the already conventional view, new technologies in higher education are not of significance just for their power to create virtual spaces, but for the fact that their incorporation in the university makes possible a totally different conception of teaching and learning. The heightened communication without restrictions of time and space enables the creation of local, national, or global communities of learning and research." But this is not to say that what is possible will be actual. That will depend on a host of contingencies, including the readiness of faculties and administrations to face up to the challenges.

CHAPTER 7

THE EROSION OF FACE-TO-FACE PEDAGOGY: A JEREMIAD

John J. McDermott

Their foot shall slide in due time.
—Deuteronomy 32:35

THE JEREMIAD is rooted in wisdom literature and has many variations. Nominally, in this chapter I use that which has come to us courtesy of the prophet Jeremiah—neither a full lamentation nor a Cassandra-like prophecy of doom, but rather a "dew-line," an early warning system, or the ever-present and ever-dangerous "tipping phenomenon."

In modern times, the jeremiad is an American cultural staple, first appearing in the election sermon of Samuel Danforth in 1670. Two recent major jeremiads have to do with the subject at hand, high technology, electronic technology, or more directly, with the potential loss of our sense of person as primarily felt, as embodied. The first is the 1995 Unabomber Manifesto of T. J. Kaczynski, which linked technological prowess with the systemic destruction of the environment necessary to sustain and foster human life. Surprisingly, a guarded sympathetic response to the concerns of this manifesto was presented by Bill Joy, a major technology wizard and founder and chief scientist of Sun Microsystems. Although clearly opposed to the person and violent activities of the Unabomber, Joy nonetheless sees merit in that section of the manifesto, "The New Luddite Challenge," where Kaczynski writes: "If the machines are permitted to make all their own decisions, we can't make any conjectures as to the results, because it is impossible to guess how such machines might behave." Bill Joy adumbrates this worry by stating,

> Perhaps it is always hard to see the bigger impact while you are in the vortex of a change. Failing to understand the consequences of our inventions while we are in the rapture of discovery and innovation seems to be a common fault of scientists and technologists; we have long been driven by the overarching desire to know—that is the nature of science's quest, not stopping to notice that the progress to newer and more powerful technologies can take on a life of its own.

The language in both documents is simple and straightforward. The message is identical. The issue is consequences and the worrisome context is that consequences can yield both amelioration and disaster. How do we know which of these upshots is forthcoming? Can we know which will emerge? Most often we think we do know. Yet, frequently we do not. Think here of the baleful consequences of so-called side effects in the use of pharmacological regimens to treat assorted afflictions and diseases.

CONSEQUENCES

In the *Meno* of Plato, Socrates is pressed to answer the following questions: How do you know what you are looking for? And if you find that, how do you know that it is what you sought? At this point, Socrates backpedals and appeals to a priestess, who has a claim staked on knowledge beyond our experience. That will not do. One is reminded here of that telling and poignant piece of dialogue in Eugene O'Neill's *Long Day's Journey into Night*. After chastising her son, Jamie, Mary Tyrone opines: "But I suppose life has made him like that, and he can't help it. None of us can help the things life has done to us. They're done before you realize it, and once they're done they make you do other things until at last everything comes between you and what you'd like to be, and you've lost your true self forever."

This is how I view contemporary technology: dazzlingly creative, exponentially explosive in its speed, spatial shortcuts, and shrinking of equipment necessary to the endeavor. Nonetheless, the working strategy is single-minded and often oblivious to consequences beyond the ken of immediacy. For an increasing number of us, the dominance of this approach to technological "breakthrough" is foreboding. The difficulty here is a paramount problem for all pedagogy, namely, how to build an awareness of consequences into the fabric of *all* decisions.

Infrequently considered in discussions of these matters are the underlying philosophical assumptions. For many, the point of departure is that we, human beings, "belong," inherit a purpose, and have a fixed end that is both explanatory and exculpatory. In this view progress, however one-dimensional, is good and the nefarious instances of fallout are the price we pay. Or, contrariwise, we could work off a different philosophical bedding, one that holds that we do not so belong and therefore have to create, to build, to protect, and to endow as sacred a human place, a human abode. If this is so, as I hold it to be, then we as the human community are responsible for all that has taken place and for all that we choose to take place from here forward. Given that, the consequences of all thoughts and actions are inseparable from the quality, the merit, the worth of what we think and do. Scoping and scaping, evaluatively, is a major task of pedagogy. Echoing Dewey here, "it is the quality of the experience which counts."

In order to understand how one assesses consequences we must have an awareness of processes as they press into future experience. Put simply and directly, we have to grasp the ongoing web of relations that adhere, inhere, cohere, surround, penetrate, obviate, float, shrink, squash, deceive, render inert, cause perversion, erupt idiopathically, iatrogenically, and just lurk as a buried landmine. These are some of the sensibilities and concerns that should be at the forefront of the present attempt to impose electronic technology as the prime medium for pedagogy. Lamentably, for the most part none of these beacons for spotting consequences are under consideration.

Who among us has the temerity to sound an alarm with regard to the overwhelming explosion of computer technology as addressed to matters educational? The term *distance learning*, in a remarkably short time span, has become a talisman for the resolution of educational problems, globally. The claims of accessibility to online education are astounding. We have been told that in one area of India more than 700,000 persons are online. In that conversation, we have not been told that in the very same geographical area, several hundred thousand women rise very early to squat on the railroad tracks before the arrival of the commuter trains, for they have no toilet facilities. This conjunction of glaring opposites can be played out over and again when technological prowess is set against the dolorous circumstances that plague the lives of most people on the planet.

Such is the larger setting. Here, I address a more immediate question, namely, should we be distressed by the escalating influence of computer technology in the affairs of pedagogy? How seriously are we to take the erosion of face-to-face encounters in the pedagogical environment? And how seriously are we to take the obsoleting of our language, our embodiment, and our intentional communities, the latter understood here as the teaching classroom, the seminar room, and the counseling session?

Surely, even a neo-Luddite, of whom I am not one, cannot gainsay the extraordinary achievements of computer technology. In many areas of concern, accessibility has been increased dramatically, or in some cases made available for the first time. One thinks here of families separated throughout the nation and from other nations, for whom the opportunity to exchange information, relay messages of affection and announcements of disaster, act as a binding hitherto never seen. Analogously, we recall the difference between the sending and arrival of letters before the advent of the telephone. We cite as well the contributions of medical informatics such that health care professionals in areas egregiously distant from the most advanced diagnostic equipment can have virtually immediate access to information protocols and advice that would otherwise be hidden from them. True, also, is it that the arrival of the computer-generated database has enabled us to store vast sources of information easily retrievable and yet without needing the existence of comparatively vast physical space. (I mention here a small example of the space question. By domestic standards I have a large personal library. Recently a student acknowledged the size of the library and waggishly stated that in a short time I would be able to put all of it in a shoebox.)

So, I repeat, who among us would display the audacity to stand up, chafing in the face of this scientific and technological power? Yet, apace, there emerge demurrers. We isolate here the dilution of embodiment and the worship of speed.

EMBODIMENT

Thinkers as different as Aristotle, Freud, and Dewey warned against patterns of disembodiment as a vestibule for conducting and understanding human life. Even the mystics, in spite of their constant and intense concentration on the ever-present sensuality of the spiritual, were persons in bodies. Unless one is an orthodox Cartesian or embraces some other type of psycho-physical dualism, all knowing is irreducibly and patently embodied. A colleague once remarked to John Dewey, "The trouble with you, Dewey, is that you think philosophy is done with the hands rather than with the eyes." Dewey responded, "Thank you for the compliment." Following Alfred North Whitehead, we are prehensile animals. And as such to touch is to be touched. To obviate the tactile whether it be of the face or of the hand is to run the risk of severe disconnection from the way in which we experience ourselves as organisms. To fly in an airplane from Honolulu to New Zealand is not to be a Polynesian voyager, nor is it even to be outrigging. To fly from St. Louis to San Francisco is not to be a mountaineer. In fact, in both instances one has traveled through space but has neither traversed nor overcome space. In these travels neither the ocean nor the mountain has been experienced as embodied, only seen from afar. Put simply, no feet, no hands are at work.

Certainly it is impressive and, upon reflection, startling to "travel" distance online. And, as we have noted, much is salutary about this revving up of accessibility. Yet, citing the insight of Whitehead, we must be wary here of committing the fallacy of "misplaced concreteness." An e-mail message to Bangkok has its "place," but we are not in Bangkok, not in Thailand, nor for that matter anywhere but where we are. The fallacy of misplaced concreteness tells us that contemporary physics holds there to be no solids, so this table on which I write is a rush of electrons. Coming up from this table hurriedly and awkwardly, I hit my knee. The resultant hematoma tells me that though some things may be true, they are not so. Consequently, I hold that the "traveling" of distance by online technology is true but there is a crucial way in which it is not so. By analogy, and with regard to the anecdote above, my "library" may very well be reprised in a shoebox. In what sense is it still my library if I say goodbye colors, goodbye scents, goodbye shape and size, goodbye touch, and goodbye the personal history of *this* book?

Since the time when the first human beings evolved or emerged, speaking generically, all humans have experienced the same bodily functions, physiologically and emotively. Defecating and urinating, laughing and crying, sweating and breathing are constants, among other responses appropriate for a "natural" in the world. In this consistent mix are the presence and the activity of the human face, which is not the sole way but the most revealing way by which we communicate with each other. To wit: I can see it in her face; his face is tight, grim, lined, furrowed, distressed; her face is laced with mirth; he uses his face to hide his depression, or to reveal his depression; she has the look of confidence; I see rage in his face; ad infinitum. The human face is not flat. The human face is not one-dimensional. It is textured, contoured, and expressive beyond words. The human face has reach and finds its way into the voice, the smile, the hands, and even the gait. Our face sends messages by a myriad of gestures, some continuous, some discontinuous, some mysterious, answering and resonating to affects deep within our person. The human face is rarely bland and if so, that, too, is a messaging. Human facing connotes joy, sorrow, guilt, shame, fright, repression, anxiety, alienation, anomie, perplexity, curiosity, and intellectual hunger, an attitude incomparably more profound than the seeking of information.

I am aware that faces are beginning to show up online. Such a development, no matter how sophisticated it becomes, cannot gainsay the implacable power of face-to-face, physiognomically undergone. The wider the physical gap, the more indirect the experience. Following William James, we have knowledge only "about" rather than "by acquaintance." As an example of the diluting character of distance, I point to the distance between voice-to-voice and "voice" mail, another technological marvel that has a negative hook. Quite aside from the mounting complexity of the "convenience," of the "step-(fast)-forward," and the ensuing corporate strategy for its use to deter messages rather than accept them, I find that the protected person on the other end of the voice mail carousel frequently welcomes a live, personal voice with whom to speak. By now, all of us know how it goes with voice mail. After pushing anywhere from five to twenty buttons in response to Byzantine directions, the caller is chastised for hitting the wrong button, providing information that does not compute or simply for falling off the carousel. Obviously irritated with our incompetence, voice mail tells us, tough luck, call back. Still, once in a while the system will give up on us and track us into the voice of a live person. Usually, they are friendly, sympathetic with our voice-mail travails, unabashedly confessing that they also are unable to navigate the system. Sometimes it is my lead, sometimes theirs, whatever, the conversation slowly transcends the business at hand, yielding conversations about geographical location, the weather, medical ailments, and sports, embodied concerns, all. Although these conversations are not face-to-face, they are not voice-to-machine nor communication by password. We do not hold that voice mail, especially for personal reasons, does not have a salutary place in our lives. The problem is that having such a place, it has quickly ratcheted itself up to an overarching place, thereby replacing my place and replacing your place with a place that is no place. In the interest of efficiency and on behalf of speed, we have further enervated embodiment herein found as the human voice.

The just noted marriage of efficiency and speed is a reigning characteristic of the revolution in electronic technology. On closer look, this marriage sits on very rocky soil. In the history of American attitudes, efficiency has been a frequent target of critics who hold that when used single-mindedly, "the cult of efficiency" blocks imagination, innovation, and, ironically, when locked up in its stubbornness, fails to see the inefficiency of efficiency. I cite but one illustration. Now rarely heard, less than ten years ago, we were told that e-mail would lighten our workload and introduce us to efficiency undreamt of. That rhetorical nostrum has vanished, taking its place as one of the truly authentic canards.

What, then, of the second partner in this efficiency-speed conjugation? One of the more misleading, actually treacherous, American mantras is "safe at any speed." Not so. Speed is deceptive on two accounts. First, it is not simply an arithmetic progression. Speed picks up force, exponentially, as we know from our attempts to stop an automobile when adding five mile-per-hour increments. We quickly proceed from difficult to perilous to impossible. In a different vein, writing longhand, typing, and computer word processing is not only a question of speed. These three viaducts for sentences, paragraphs, and pages are working under a very different timing gear, sufficient to result in a very different outcome. Yes, speed is energizing. Yet, we must beware of its impatience, its reluctance to stop, to reconnoiter, and to maintain those boundaries that cannot be violated with impunity. For instance, I note the execrable prose of e-mail communication. This is now a genre overrun with abbreviations, many intelligible only to self-styled initiators, and well on the way to a private language ostensibly on behalf of widening and extending connections.

A second deception is that increased speed has an endless future, and, in time, ironically, all speed barriers will evaporate. Think of poor Mr. Bernard Lagat, who won the fabled Millrose mile run in the year 2003. He was criticized for running that mile in a "slow" 4:00.36. Now, it is just several decades since the centuries' long-standing barrier to the 4-minute mile was broken. Today, that speed is slow. So determined are we to go faster, we have added hundredths of seconds to our measurements and then thousandths of seconds. Soon we will measure our human speed in millionths of seconds, billionths? trillionths?—in a word, using a measurement that has no connection to how fast we are going, as experienced by us. We then have a measurement that relates only to itself, namely, the heightened speed, the heightened capacity that is the hallmark of computer worth.

COMMUNITY

To cut to the quick, here is my response to the aggressive takeover of pedagogy by variant, ever-more powerful, and intrusive versions of electronic technology. The fundamental claim is that contemporary technological innovation forges, widens, and intensifies connections between human beings, especially in a pedagogical setting. That this can happen and, at times, does happen has some evidential support. That it always happens is false. That it most often happens is also false. To the contrary, paradoxical though it be, this vaunted claim on behalf of generating connections has fostered, in reverse, an abiding pattern of disconnections. In my understanding of pedagogy, a systemic move away from interpersonal embodiment is a move away from who we are and how we experience ourselves as human beings, ineluctably.

In his work, *The Hope of the Great Community*, Josiah Royce (1967), a philosopher committed to globalization long before that term was coined, writes of the danger of becoming a "detached individual." He has in mind a person who, despite access to communication and information, remains isolated from the burdens and nectar of social union, in short, the community. I do not see us obviating this warning if we shed embodiment and face-to-face intentional community life. To bypass, to transcend, or to move beyond the pace, the gait, the deliberate, the considered, the slow, is to ignore the taproots of genuine communal growth. Fructification has no future without roots. Globalization is hollow if it does not embrace the centrality of an affective, liturgical, and aesthetic binding, none of which seems to be the province of the mavens of speed, heightened capacity, and communication absent reflection. A plethora of information and electronic contact will not suffice for comprehending the issues in globalization that demand simmering rather than boiling, watching and waiting rather than seizing and managing by intrusion. Is that why, traditionally at least, we always shake hands, even in times of tension? I repeat, to be touched is to touch.

Pedagogy is at its best when one person touches another by virtue of imaginative and intelligent reconstruction of experiences had and experiences novel. For me, teaching is a response to the most fundamental of all human questions, "Can you help me?" I believe that you can see the existential urgency of this question in the faces before us, given, of course, that we remain face-to-face.

References

Dewey, John. (1925). *Experience and Nature, Later Works, 1925–1953.* Vol. 2. Ed. Jo Ann Boydson. Carbondale: Southern Illinois University Press.

Joy, Bill. (2002). "Why the Future Doesn't Need Us." In *Ethics and Values in the Information Age*, eds. Joel Rudinow and Anthony Graybosch. London: Thomson Learning.

McDermott, John J. (1985). "The Stethoscope as Talisman: Medical Technology and Loneliness." In *Technology and Freedom*, The Proceedings of a New Liberal Arts Symposium, *4*.

Royce, Josiah. (1967). *The Hope of the Great Community.* Freeport, N.Y.: Books for Libraries Press.

CHAPTER 8

THE USED CAR DEALERSHIP AND THE CHURCH: ON RESOLVING THE IDENTITY OF THE UNIVERSITY

Charles Karelis

THE ECONOMIST GORDON WINSTON memorably and mischievously called the modern university a cross between a used car dealership and a church. This caricatures on both sides, but it suggests an important question: can the value of consumer sovereignty coexist with more purely "educational" values in the modern university? More ambitiously, can the two be resolved into a consistent identity or agenda? Or is it the fate of the modern university to be pulled in opposite directions, with progress toward one pole undoing progress toward the other?

GIVING CUSTOMERS WHAT THEY WANT

In practice, the goal of giving the customer what the customer wants at a good price means giving students engaging courses, accessible professors, sports teams to cheer for, lavish dorms and student centers, and a hedonistic social life outside of class—or at any rate, a relaxed level of law enforcement. It means giving out a prestigious diploma, and maybe most important, enabling new graduates to find a high-paying first job. It evidently does not mean making sure students develop a meaningful philosophy of life, as surveys have repeatedly shown that students care little for that. To provide all this at a good price, the university tries to maximize efficiency. This has sped the search for capital/labor substitutions. (Though it can be argued that the universities' favorite capital investment, technology, has done little to increase bang for the buck, given a price tag that looks disproportionate to even the rosiest estimates of its educational impact.) It has led to more and more outsourcing, not just of food services and janitorial services but now, with the coming of distance education, the outsourcing of teaching itself. Notably too, the efficiency agenda has seemed to justify the shifting of faculty slots away from tenure track to adjunct status. (With doubters contending that axing the basically costless fringe benefit of job security compels the university to spend many more salary dollars to attract and keep a faculty of any given level of quality.) Whatever the strategic mistakes of its supporters, consumer-friendliness is indisputably central to the contemporary university.

Giving Students What They Need

At the same time, as Winston's image suggests, the modern university finds itself driven by aims and values other than consumer satisfaction —in short, "educational" values. There is no clear common denominator for the values that go by this name, but prominent among them are research and scholarship, learning that is not career-specific, teaching students the larger significance of things, independent social criticism, preparing students for meaningful personal and professional lives, and extending all these benefits to nontraditional students. To the degree that these agendas are not the first priority of its paying customers, the university tries to get support for them from outside sources such as foundations, government research grants, donors, and taxpayers. If efficiency means satisfying the customer at the best possible price, the pursuit of these agendas also means departing from the aim of maximum efficiency. For instance, when universities are thinking in this mode they do not necessarily evaluate their investments in technology according to whether they help students learn what they wish to learn.

The Arguments in a Nutshell

In the international conversation on higher education we find an endorsement of one or the other of these aspects of the university. The supporters of the market model make at least three plausible points. First, they argue that the supporters of "educational values" have no right to impose their ethical/political agendas on generations of vulnerable, because grade-dependent, students—or for that matter their middle-aged conceptions of a good time. Second, they say that the grubby-sounding goal of efficiency makes it possible to expand access to higher education by stretching dollars. Third, they note that the whole dilemma is moot anyway because the market just is; it is a reality that sooner or later will punish any providers that fail to serve the customer efficiently.

On the other side, the supporters of "educational values" remind us with equal plausibility that the independent academy has historically provided critical perspective in times of change; that even in our materialistic times, recent graduates do not live by bread alone; that altruism aside, offering educational opportunities to nontraditional populations is prudent for any society; and that basic research, however impractical it may seem, has often turned out to bestow unforeseen benefits.

As for the supposed inexorability of market forces, the advocates of educational values are fond of responding that universities have flourished without rational prices, rational salaries, balanced budgets, or conspicuous attention to consumer preferences since before capitalism was invented. It is a safe bet they can do so a while longer. One indication of how forgiving the market has been to universities is that while something like half of all new businesses fail, universities almost never go out of business. They may be better-managed enterprises than their critics realize (Smith, 2000), but their amazing invincibility must stem from something deeper. Ernest Boyer (1987) was surely correct that society sees universities as virtually priceless.

Overcoming the Dilemma

All this having been said, my thesis is that the tension between the used car dealership university and the university-as-church can be overcome. The two facets can be reconciled. Like a great orchestra that stays true to itself while it keeps the people dancing, the academy can have it both ways. But to see how, we have to probe deeper into both sides of the dilemma than we have been used to doing.

Consider the university's desire to serve the market—real enough, whether essential to its survival or not. Does it have to mean taking customers' current tastes as a given and trying to accommodate those tastes, like a candy manufacturer or a pop music label? Surely there are other models. A serious art dealer, for instance, normally devotes a great deal of time to elevating and refining customers' tastes, in short, to education. Only *then* does the art dealer present wares that purport to satisfy the customers' tastes. As this suggests, universities do not have to choose between pandering to seventeen-year-olds and dictating to them. A third option for universities is to start educating students by explaining why they propose to educate as they do, maybe mixing this "meta-education" with first-order education throughout the four years. When I was the director of the Fund for the Improvement of Postsecondary Education, I traveled around the country talking to groups of first- and second-year undergraduates about the general education requirements at their schools, and I rarely found a student who could even parrot back an official rationale for general education, much less talk intelligently about it. Their schools had not taken the students' "meta-education" very seriously, and so predictably these schools found themselves faced with a distasteful choice between trying to satisfy intellectual tastes that were quite immature and requiring unwilling students to choke down general education courses like spinach—"for their own good."

For that matter, we might probe deeper by asking, just who is this customer that needs to be served? While the immediate benefits of education go to the students, one could argue that parents and taxpayers are customers too. But if so, the academy is probably in a much stronger market position to push some of its own educational values than it realizes. How many parents or taxpayers would withhold support from universities that reinstituted 8:00 A.M. classes or foreign language requirements?

But if the idea of consumer sovereignty can be refined to become more compatible with educational agendas, the same thing holds in reverse. There is a great opportunity to reconcile market values and educational ones by developing our understanding of the educational purposes of the university. Within the educational agenda, seen broadly, only the values of research and broadening access to education itself seem clear and compelling today. Notions such as "the larger significance of things," "meaningful lives," and "social criticism," seem too vague or dogmatic to rally strong support among students, trustees, or the general public. Indeed, a kind of silence about larger educational purposes seems to have created a partial vacuum in the agenda of universities, which has allowed consumer agendas to loom unduly large. Why, for example, have not the leaders of America's liberal arts programs come together to propose an alternative to consumer-oriented ranking systems like that of *U.S. News and World Report*? It may not be too much of an overstatement to say that the "educational" elements of the university agenda will not get their due weight in the practical operation of the institution until the university succeeds in modernizing its own "educational value proposition."

That this has not happened must not be seen as the fault of the academy. It is mainly due to historical and cultural developments beyond the control of the academy. As a brief historical note, the problem started around 1900. The old, postcolonial value proposition of the colleges was that they would teach students the larger significance of things, and what comes first in life and what comes second—and hence enable students to do well and good in their adult lives. What this originally referred to, of course, was the coherence of things according to a divine plan: our duties form a neat system, history moves forward sensibly and compatibly with moral values, nature is a solvable jigsaw puzzle likewise compatible with human aims, and the quasi-divine invisible hand reconciles even selfish economic behavior with common social purposes. But around the turn of the twentieth century, if not before in German-influenced research universities like Johns Hopkins, this consensus was coming apart. By the time Woodrow Wilson was president of Princeton, in the first decade of the century, this preacher's son had to grant that religion had become a private matter and was no longer available to shape the curriculum and general program of the university. A generation earlier, college presidents had talked confidently about the learning of spirit. But in his Phi Beta Kappa address of 1909, Wilson was reduced to waffling about the spirit of learning. A few years later, by the end of the war Wilson helped get us into, popular skepticism about the coherence of the world had degenerated still further into something like confidence in the incoherence of the world.

This put those who wished to talk about aims of undergraduate education other than research and preparing students for graduate school in a difficult position. If college was about the way things fit together, and things did not fit together, then college was not about anything at all. There seemed only two possible ways out. One was just to hold onto meaning-giving dogmas despite the skepticism that pervaded the broader culture. Colleges and universities that took this reactionary route had the option of taking a right fork in the road or a left fork—which is to say, church-based education or what would now be called political correctness. The second way out, and surely the only route that is truly compatible with liberal values, was throwing the whole issue of meaning back into the laps of the students by forcing them to shop in a free and well-stocked marketplace of competing ideas, and justify their eventual purchases. Students in this model are called upon to determine for themselves the larger meaning of things, or reject the very existence of such a meaning. At mid-century, the usual pedagogy for enabling students to make this judgment was survey courses covering the diverse books and ideas that survived in the referendum of history. Paradoxically, these courses were later attacked as "conservative."

But this second, fundamentally liberal approach has had to contend with obstacles besides misguided criticism. The organization of undergraduate experience into distinct, compartmentalized knowledge-modules called courses has made it hard or impossible. Gerald Graff (2003) tells the story of the young woman enrolled in an existentialism course and a course in behaviorism who is asked where she comes down in the free-will/determinism debate. "No problem," she says. "The existentialism course meets on Monday and Wednesday, and the behaviorism course meets on Tuesday and Thursday, and I am pulling A's in both." The prophet of the decompartmentalized undergraduate experience was a president of Amherst College named Alexander Meikeljohn, a Scotsman like his friend Woodrow Wilson. Meikeljohn's message was simple: let us stop all this nostalgic dogmatizing about the coherence of reality and just ensure that the undergraduate experience itself is coherent enough to allow students to come to their own conclusions about the world. Today's interdisciplinary programs, learning communities, capstone courses, student portfolios—even today's subsidized campus snack bars—are echoes of Meikeljohn's idea.

As for those high-paying jobs, Meikeljohn might have added that such an education is the best preparation for the kinds of broad and responsible roles that most students ultimately seek. For the undergraduate who has been trained to compare and weigh competing paradigms and competing conceptions of the good is the readiest to lead and organize specialists at mid-career, and the readiest to find a personal truth that will see him or her through the vicissitudes of life.

References

Boyer, Ernest L. (1987). *College: The Undergraduate Experience in America* (The Carnegie Foundation for the Advancement of Teaching). New York: HarperCollins.

Graff, Gerald. (2003). *Clueless in Academe: How Schooling Obscures the Life of the Mind.* New Haven: Yale University Press.

Smith, Charles W. (2000). *Market Values in American Higher Education.* Lanham, Md.: Rowman and Littlefield.

CHAPTER 9

New Technologies and the Reconstitution of the University

Jaishree K. Odin

IT CAN HARDLY be doubted that higher education is being reconstituted at many different levels. The way this reconstitution unfolds is intricately linked to the extent universities are cognizant of the potential of new technologies to radically transform the production and transmission of knowledge, along with teaching-learning practices. Trying to adapt to the new reality without changing the university's outdated structures is not going to take universities very far as far as their survival and effectiveness as teaching institutions are concerned. In order to change the culture of higher education, which is characterized today by student apathy and faculty frustration, nothing short of a paradigm change in the educational process is required. Any reform in the curriculum needs to be integrally related to pedagogical objectives as well as teaching-learning practices. The role of information and communication technologies needs to be central to this thinking, both in terms of how these are changing the disciplines and their relations to one another, as well as how the new technologies are transforming the cultural matrix within which they are embedded.

New Technologies and Higher Learning

The impact of information and communication technologies can be compared to the changes brought about by the printing revolution, which transformed how knowledge was produced, preserved, and disseminated. Elizabeth Eisenstein argues that even before the close of the sixteenth century, the procedures for charting the planets, mapping the earth, synchronizing chronologies, and codifying laws or compiling bibliographies underwent a major change. The old knowledge was retrieved and given typographical fixity, which made it available for broader study and perusal. Printing made possible simultaneous viewing of identical data by people geographically separated, which was analogous to a communication revolution. It was the accumulation of knowledge through the preservative powers of print that distinguished the print era from the preprint era.

The introduction of new computer-based technologies marks another transition, which is characterized by creation of networks, multidirectional flow of information, diversity, and instant access. New modes of delivery as well as interaction become possible that were unheard of in the print era. Furthermore, new technologies have dramatically impacted how knowledge is created, stored, and accessed and this, in turn, is transforming writing, reading, and research practices. The creation of distance-independent communities of learning allows people in geographically distant places to come together and interact online at any time, both synchronously and asynchronously. The Internet has led to the democratization of knowledge in all areas by increasing access globally. Two decades ago we saw computers as word processors, but now they are integrally involved in the field of knowledge making, enabling the user to switch back and forth between the roles of creator, transformer, communicator, and receiver of knowledge.

As part of this change, a burgeoning online education industry has emerged, along with new educational organizational models. Corporations are unbundling the educational process and repackaging it to suit the educational needs of their prospective students. Educational integrators or meta-universities are emerging that bring together courses and programs from traditional colleges and universities along with student support services (including academic advising and technical support). This educational experience is made available to students through their online portals. No need for bricks and mortar campuses, as educational experience itself has become a service to be marketed and sold as efficiently as possible. Promoting their products as providing integrated learning experiences and support services in a single cohesive environment, such enterprises present themselves as efficient and flexible alternatives to traditional academic institutions of higher learning. A common characteristic of these new organizations is extensive use of information and communication technologies to overcome the space and time barrier to create distance-independent communities of learning and to provide efficient support services that can be accessed from anywhere at any time.

The traditional colleges and universities have also joined in the fray to stay competitive and to increase access without recourse to building more campuses. Many innovative arrangements have emerged as colleges and universities have entered into intrauniversity as well as interuniversity partnerships to offer online courses and programs to greater numbers of students. The online partnerships are making the hallowed walls of place-bound colleges and universities permeable, as students can easily click their way from one institutional portal to another to enroll in a program or take courses without leaving their homes. As increasing numbers of students access courses, library resources, and support services online, the traditional meaning of the university, the classroom, the curriculum, and even the commonly held beliefs about the teaching-learning process are going through a change.

Online courses are quite popular even among on-campus students because of their convenience. The boundaries separating regular and distance students are thus slowly dissolving, too, as both types of students might be enrolled in the same online courses. Hybrid courses and programs are also making their appearance, where on-campus students are enrolled in courses or programs with some components or courses face to face and others completely online so students spend only some of the time in the classroom and the rest online. As hybrid courses and programs spread, the practice in higher education of equating teaching time with students' seat time is bound to be eroded as new types of flexible class management arrangements emerge for on-campus courses.

Even as new technologies are transforming the fabric of academic institutions, the underlying crisis in higher education, attributed to the increasing corporatization of the university, declining academic standards, and decreasing faculty governance, continue to raise concerns. (See Currie and Margolis.) Online educational institutions and practices have especially caused alarm because they have become a mirror for traditional institutions, but without the accompanying accoutrements of campuses, buildings, extensive libraries, and classrooms. As alternative education providers, both online and campus-based, attract increasing numbers of students, traditional colleges and universities need to ask themselves seriously what it is that sets them apart from the institutions that cater to the market. (See Karelis.)

American colleges and universities have regarded their primary mission as preparing students for civic and democratic citizenship while at the same time serving the utilitarian purpose of preparing the students for the workforce. However, market forces operating indirectly or directly on the university and its response to these forces have created an academic culture where the value of university education is perceived only in terms of its instrumental function; students increasingly associate university education with getting credentials. This is intimately linked to the general trend in contemporary consumer society, where the production as well as transmission of knowledge has shifted toward its instrumental value. In what follows, I concentrate on two interrelated aspects of this challenge: the best use of appropriate technologies and the question of the curriculum.

RETHINKING THE CURRICULUM

The meaning and function of knowledge has been dramatically transformed in the past few decades. The major Western master narratives of humanism and social emancipation have been increasingly undermined by various social movements beginning in the 1960s. In the era of delegitimation of metanarratives, Jean-François Lyotard notes, legitimation in both production as well as transmission of knowledge has shifted toward performativity criteria. The truth value of knowledge has been displaced by the exchange value either in terms of its function as a saleable commodity or in terms of its use for acquiring power or growth. As the same knowledge is accessible to everyone, any increase in performativity is dependent on new configurations of data and new uses that can be devised for it. Thus, imagination becomes important in discovering new configurations of the data, which are equally accessible. So it is not information in itself that is meaningful in this age, but how it is connected to other pieces of information. The zealously guarded disciplinary lines thus continue to become blurred as imaginary reconfigurations transcend boundaries. Interdisciplinarity, Lyotard argues, will be the characteristic of the information age.

Though Lyotard uses *competency* and *performativity* interchangeably, a distinction can be made between the two terms. Whereas competency results in reproduction of skills, performativity leads to higher-order skills of imaginative reconfigurations that include competency as well as critical thinking skills to organize and evaluate information to create new knowledge. Thus, performativity in education could lead to power/growth when its economic implications are considered (again Lyotard uses it only in this sense) or in knowledge acquisition in the social context, where it manifests as empowerment/growth. Higher education has a meaningful role to teach students the connections and relationships among ideas in a discipline and between disciplines, or going beyond that, to the broader social context of the role disciplinary discourses play in shaping individual lives.

John Dewey pointed out years ago the necessity of taking the broader social context into consideration if any successful reform is to take place. Thus, both "the method and curriculum of education is as much a product of the changed social situation, and as much an effort to meet the needs of the new society that is forming, as are changes in modes of industry and commerce" (Dewey, 1976). This is obvious when we look at the history of reforms conducted in North American colleges and universities. Christopher Lucas's study *Academy in Crisis* shows that the fixed curriculum based on classical learning of the first half of the nineteenth century was changed in the second half as the knowledge areas multiplied with advances in science and technology that created the need for new courses in the curriculum. A new elective system was introduced so students could choose what they wanted to take. However, after three decades, educators realized that moving away from the prescribed fixed curriculum to an elective system where students could choose what they wanted to take had its pitfalls. This especially affected the liberal arts component of the curriculum.

Consequently in the first half of the twentieth century, the reformers abandoned the two extreme positions of prescribed fixed curriculum and elective anarchy, and instead sought a compromise: the undergraduate curriculum was divided into two areas, the concentration or the major, and a distribution requirement or general education requirement. Whereas the concentration area allowed students to get an in-depth knowledge of the area of their specialization, the distribution requirement afforded them breadth of knowledge as they took courses from various departments. This is the system that has come down to us in different variations. Colleges and universities are still juggling with the balance between the liberal arts component and the major concentration. Since the liberal arts requirement is presented to students in a cafeteria-style menu offering, it ultimately results in a very fragmented curriculum, all too often a meaningless hodgepodge to students. As Karelis argues, students have very little understanding of why they need to take these courses, and how they are related to one another or to their area of concentration.

The evolving curriculum, of course, was motivated by a rethinking of its goals. Historically speaking, the modern university, founded in continental Europe, saw its mission as transmitting the unity of culture. Humboldt envisioned the role of the university as a place for self-cultivation, or *Bildung*. In recent years the notion of the unity of culture has been subject to intense debate. Henry A. Giroux (1993) says:

> This debate raises new and important questions regarding the social and political implications of viewing curriculum as a historically specific narrative and pedagogy as a form of cultural politics. What must be asked about these specific narratives is whether they enable or silence the differentiated human capacities that allow students to speak from their own experiences, locate themselves in history, and act so as to create liberatory social forms that expand the possibility of democratic public life.

The university's mission to reproduce the unity of culture has been contested on many fronts. Can the university create and maintain an autonomous public space? Can it serve as a locus of critical dialogue and cultural exchange, so that students are trained in cultural, democratic, and technocratic citizenship? Bill Readings (1999) in *The University in Ruins* notes that the university is a place of dissensus as it brings together a community of scholars who identify with a plurality of cultures. To keep itself from becoming a transnational bureaucratic organization, the university must assume the role of fostering communication so students can explore interconnections between cultures and between disciplines, especially the relationship between knowledge as science and knowledge as culture. The university needs to become an effective site where students learn about the interconnections among all forms of knowledge and the connections between knowledge and the cognitive structures of society. The university thus has a critical role to play in imparting both technocratic and cultural citizenship to students in a global society.

RETHINKING TEACHING-LEARNING PRACTICES

The new technologies can play a vital role in this effort. Jonassen, Peck, and Wilson (1999) note that technology is a tool that can be effectively used to shape and transform the cognitive engagement of learners. Cole points out that cognition does not take place in a vacuum, but cognition and culture are intricately connected; technology can shape the processes of cognition and impact the cultural dimension of communication, task analysis, and problem solving.

In the studies that have come out on the crisis in higher education, very few have dealt with the crisis from the perspective of a fundamental change in the mental makeup of the new generation of students. The university has been quite oblivious to the changing demographics of the student population, as it has been with the experiences that working adults bring with them to the university when they enroll in a program. Both the demographics of students as well as students' attitudes toward life, work, and education have undergone a dramatic change in the past few decades. In addition, in a knowledge-intensive society, lifelong learning is not a matter of choice, but a necessity, which brings a large percentage of older adults to the university.

In order to make higher education meaningful to more students, educators need to determine in what ways the twenty-first-century student is cognitively and emotionally different from a nineteenth- or twentieth-century student. The current generation of students is always plugged in to one technical gadget or another. Studies have shown that extensive exposure to television and videogames changes how the brain receives and processes information. Marc Prensky (2001) calls today's generation of students "digital natives" in that their formative years are permeated with technical artifacts, such as videogames, cell phones, and computers, which have an impact on their thinking patterns and how they process information. The digital natives, Prensky notes, are taught by faculty who are "digital immigrants," as they have learned to adapt to the digital world, some better than others. The problem in the classroom arises when digital immigrants, using their predigital language as well as teaching methods, teach the digital natives who work best in a visually stimulating environment that allows multitasking. Sitting in a classroom, listening to the professor on the podium is not very appealing to the new generation of students.

James Duderstadt (2000), ex-president of the University of Michigan, points out, if a nineteenth-century physician were to time travel to a twenty-first-century surgery suite with all its modern technological equipment, he would not recognize it and would not be able to function in it. On the other hand, if a nineteenth-century college professor walked into a twenty-first-century university classroom, he would find everything basically the same—the podium, the professor, and the students taking notes. The fundamental question that educators need to ask is whether a new paradigm of teaching-learning is needed that is more appropriate for today's generation of students. With the changing modes of knowledge and the changing role of students, the role of the professor must change, too. However, in most classrooms, the older instructional model prevails, where the role of the teacher is to transmit knowledge.

The traditional classroom is teacher-centered in that it is planned with teacher's teaching rather than student's learning in mind. This pedagogy is linked to the original mission of the university to transmit a fixed body of knowledge. The assessment activities that accompany traditional instruction accordingly test students on their ability to reproduce what they learn in class. The course materials are seen in isolation from the context, and knowledge is regarded as extrinsic to the learning process. The traditional instructional model is not effective in creating a learning environment where students are expected to go beyond passively absorbing information to evaluating it critically and making it meaningful to themselves.

John Dewey pointed out that the learning process involves a continual reorganization, reconstruction, and transformation of experience. More recently, Lev Vygotsky (1978) has commented on the social negotiation of meaning and the role of the teacher as a coach and a facilitator in the learning process. Modern research in cognitive science has shown that the mind is not an information processor. Both memory and cognition involve construction and reconstruction out of the building blocks of experience. The meaning-making process is an individual endeavor, which must be taken into account when designing an effective learning environment. Constructivist theorists note that learning involves the construction of internal representations of knowledge, which can be best accomplished in a collaborative situation where learners are given opportunities to encounter other knowledge representations or perspectives that allow them to review their own perspective, evaluate and assess it, and revise it if doing so is more meaningful to their situation.

Current research on learning effectiveness in the online classroom shows that new technologies allow us to create an interactive learning environment where course participants communicate genuinely, listening as well as responding to others in a mutually collaborative fashion. Students thus acquire knowledge in a social context where they are given opportunities to articulate what they have learned on a regular basis. Roxanne Hiltz (1990) notes: "Collaborative learning means that both teachers and learners are active participants in the learning process; knowledge is not something that is 'delivered' to students in this process, but something that emerges from active dialogue among those who seek to understand and apply concepts and techniques." The validation of the new knowledge by the peers and the instructor leads to the transformation of learners' mental maps. Whereas traditional teaching methods generally promote reproduction of fixed maps of knowledge, the learner-centered classroom gets students actively engaged in the learning process. There is a multidirectional flow of information as students formulate their own thoughts, share them with others, and in the process create new knowledge.

Dillenbourg and Schneider (1995) further analyze the mechanism of collaborative learning as they explore various types of transactions that are accomplished in a collaborative environment. Following Piagetian and Vygotskian socio-constructivist theories, they explore the dynamics of collaborative learning from different perspectives. In a collaborative situation, as students make sense of the assigned tasks, a series of negotiations occur at several levels, some of which are conflict or disagreement, self-explanation, and internalization. As group members work together, they are exposed to perspectives that are in conflict or disagreement with their own. Even though the group members might not be in agreement all the time, in order to have the group function smoothly, each member will tend to reassess his or her own perspective in order to see if, in the light of new information or new perspectives, it needs to be revised. Similarly, the power of explanation can be an effective collaborative working tool as more capable students explain the problems or problematic issues to their less able peers. It benefits both —the one who is doing the explaining and those for whom it is being done. The process of internalization, yet another aspect of collaborative learning, involves internalization of new perspectives as one articulates one's views and compares them with those of others for agreement and disagreement, eventually internalizing the new perspective if it is more meaningful.

McLoughlin and Oliver (2000) propose a multiple cultural model of technology-mediated instructional design "that caters for diversity, flexibility and cultural inclusivity in the design process and affirms the social and cultural dimensions of constructed meaning." Their model identifies ten design principles for culturally inclusive web-based instructional design:

- constructivist pedagogy based on active learning
- authentic learning activities
- flexible tasks and tools for knowledge sharing
- different forms of learner support
- responsive student roles and responsibilities
- communication tools and social interaction
- tasks for self-direction, ownership, and collaboration
- flexible tutoring and mentoring roles that are responsive to learner needs
- access to varied resources to ensure multiple perspectives
- flexibility in learning goals, outcomes, and modes of assessment

Multiple modes of peer interaction as well as knowledge sharing among course participants are possible by using web-based communication and knowledge-sharing tools. The asynchronous and synchronous technology tools available allow the instructor to create an active learning environment that promotes perspective sharing among students. As all interaction in the online environment is text-based, students can read each other's work and thus learn from one another. The instructor can also provide models from previous classes in the form of best student papers or insightful archived student discussion. Online debates can be easily organized as students take opposite sides to understand the complexity of issues under discussion. Students can collaborate in searching and sharing resources on the web. They can build electronic portfolios or study guides, or engage in studying real-world cases. Role-playing can easily be organized in the online environment, where students take on the role of the theorists they are studying and present their point of view to get a better grasp of the material. The assessment of learning can also be done in a variety of ways to find out if students have mastered the basic knowledge, concepts, or ideas and whether they have engaged in higher-order thinking and problem solving on a regular basis. Student performance can be assessed based on the online portfolio of student work, discussion forum participation, online mentoring, and weekly reflections on the readings or completion of problem-solving assignments. Other quantitative forms of assessment are possible through quizzes, tests, or exams. Students' active use of the web resources for research and exploration as well as group work can also be evaluated.

Detailed analysis of the course transcripts of online courses has shown that selecting a course management system and creating the course overview documents or other course materials is only one aspect of the project of creating an effective online course. The other aspect is the organization of the weekly multimodal teaching and learning activities. The electronic medium is unique in that it can be transformed easily into a dynamic virtual space that is capable of sustaining the social presence of both the teacher and the students through a variety of carefully crafted teaching activities. These activities, when combined with complementary learning activities, can become instrumental in creating a highly interactive learning environment. Guy Kemshal-Bell's 2001 study *The Online Teacher* involved surveying online instructors and students from primarily Australia and the United States. Online instructors were asked to rate twenty-one generic skills or attributes that were identified as indispensable in effective online teaching. The survey results revealed that online teachers regarded facilitation skills as essential "to harness the power of technology" to achieve learning. On a 0–3 scale, eight of the eleven facilitation skills that the respondents noted as critical were the ability to provide effective online feedback (2.86); the ability to engage the learner in the online learning process (2.84); the ability to provide direction and support to online learners (2.82); the skills in "online listening" (2.76); the ability to use e-mail effectively (2.70); the ability to motivate students (2.66); positive attitude to online teaching (2.66); and skills in effective online questioning (2.65). The respondents rated technical skills as less important than facilitation skills in order to be an effective online teacher. The three skills or attributes that the respondents considered most important for an online teacher were the ability to engage the learner, the ability to motivate the online learner, and the ability to build relationships. The survey thus shows that the teacher's role in actively engaging the student in learning is an important part of online teaching and this can be achieved through a variety of direct or indirect teaching acts. In the student survey, the student comments on the positive side regarding online learning were: intense, challenging, emotional, dynamic, addictive, fun, stimulating, flexible, empowering, and intellectually stimulating. It is obvious that the focus on getting students actively engaged in an online course creates a learning environment that students find challenging as well as intellectually stimulating.

At this point, we might ask what strategies from the online teaching-learning experience can be utilized to make the face-to-face campus-based courses more challenging for students. By adding online components to an on-campus course, can students be encouraged to become active participants in the learning process? Since large introductory classes, big revenue generators, have the highest enrollments and the least faculty-student and even student-student interaction, some have suggested that such classrooms need to be rethought dramatically to increase the quality of student learning. Problems in large classes, as many have pointed out, arise from a high faculty to student ratio as well as the lecture format of the course delivery, which turn these courses into empty rituals without the participants' meaningful involvement. If communication technology and instructional technology were properly incorporated in the courses with high enrollments and the course format changed from a lecture to studio-type of delivery, the faculty time could be more effectively utilized in designing and managing learning situations where students are actively involved in the learning process. Furthermore, instructional technology can be used in the classroom as a tool to explain and illustrate and as an aid to visualization. Even though the investment in instructional technology has gone up tremendously over the years, most of the faculty still have not integrated it into the curriculum. Investing in technology is not going to lead to any substantial changes in desired educational goals if the incorporation of technology continues to be based on the traditional assumptions about teaching and learning.

THE FUTURE UNIVERSITY

The modern university has operated on the same model for about two centuries, with a certain organizational structure, typical administrative and teaching/learning practices, and a given conception of knowledge. Over the decades, the university has responded to various economic, social, and cultural transformations, but the reforms have always been piecemeal, fixing the problems rather than rethinking the traditional model. The creaking system of mass education can neither explain away the growing misdirection resulting from current practices or the effectiveness of teaching and learning in the online classroom. The use of new technologies in higher education has problematized the current outdated practices and the misdirection is leading finally to new directions in higher learning.

The hyperlinked nature of the Internet allows easy contextualizing of course materials to promote interdisciplinary as well as intercultural inquiry. Combined with this contextualized inquiry, the communication tools allow multiple channels as well as forums of communication. The course materials and activities can be organized in such a way that students from differing backgrounds make meaningful contributions as they become actively engaged in the co-construction of knowledge. The teacher's presence through multimodal teaching can serve to promote self-motivation and self-direction among students. In such an integrated teaching-learning environment, the teacher can see to it that the construction of knowledge is not only personally meaningful to students, but that it also meets the collectively understood standards of disciplinary or interdisciplinary inquiry. The students can be encouraged to relate what they learn to their own knowledge base and, through various learning tasks, given opportunities to transfer what they have learned to real-life contexts. The knowledge that students internalize is not thus acquired in the form of isolated ideas or facts, but as part of real-life situations where they appear in their complexity. The multimodal teaching and learning activities in a technology-mediated classroom thus promote a complex mode of interaction among the learners, the instructor, and the content of the course.

Contrary, then, to the already conventional view, new technologies in higher education are not of significance just for their power to create virtual spaces, but their incorporation in the university makes possible a totally different conception of teaching and learning. The heightened communication without restrictions of time and space enables the creation of local, national, or global communities of learning and research. This fact alone is beginning to loosen the hold of the geographical university on people's imagination. In addition, the university is no longer the sole transmitter of professional knowledge, as multiple sites of knowledge production as well as distribution have emerged outside the university. A greater dissemination of knowledge through television, the Internet, and other technologies has immediate implications for the traditional role of the professor as the transmitter of knowledge. As a consequence of the new technologies, linear modes of presentation and learning are beginning to be replaced by nonlinear modes of presentation and hyperlearning. The electronic media, unlike television, is highly interactive in nature; it can allow explorations based on the user's interests and goals—the user can skim through the material quickly, focus on each detailed section, or skip it all to follow a lateral digression, which has pedagogical implications. In short, the current technological shift is characterized by a shift from learning to hyperlearning experiences; from faculty-centered classroom to learner-centered classroom; from individual learning to interactive collaborative learning; from sequential fragmented to interconnected interdisciplinary or multidisciplinary curricula; and from the university for reproducing the unity of culture to the university for communicating the diversity of culture.

This is not to say that universities should give in to technological determinism. The current transformations in the university arise from multiple and complex interlinked causes. It would be more appropriate to say that new technologies are problematizing the traditional practices of the university and providing us with tools to rethink these practices so they are more appropriate for the twenty-first century. The university will continue to be the site of learning, both in bricks and clicks classrooms, where technology-based learning objects as well as online collaborative learning communities will increasingly become an integral part of the learning environment. Even though higher education in the twenty-first century is going to include a spectrum of arrangements made possible through the use of new technologies, as regards teaching in contrast to research, the singular mission of the university will continue to be the creation of an autonomous public space that fosters critical dialogue to impart cultural, democratic, and technocratic citizenship to students.

REFERENCES

Cole, M. (1985). "The Zone of Proximal Development: Where Culture and Cognition Create Each Other." In *Culture, Communication and Cognition: Vygotskian Perspectives*, ed. J. V. Wertsch, 146–161. New York: Cambridge University Press.

Dewey, John. (1976). *School and Society: Middle Works, 1899–1924*, vol. I. Ed. Jo Ann Boydston. Carbondale: Southern Illinois University Press.

Dillenbourg, P., and D. Schneider. (1995). Collaborative Learning and the Internet. Retrieved December 26, 2001, from <http://tecfa.unige.ch/tecfa/research/CMC/colla/iccai95_1.html>.

Duderstadt, James J. (2000). *A University for the 21st Century*. Ann Arbor: University of Michigan Press.

Eisenstein, Elizabeth. (1983). *The Printing Revolution in Early Modern Europe*. New York: Cambridge University Press.

Giroux, Henry A. (1993). *Border Crossing: Cultural Workers and the Politics of Education*. New York: Routledge.

Hiltz, Roxanne Starr. (1990). "Evaluating the Virtual Classroom." In *Online Education: Perspectives on a New Environment*, ed. Linda M. Harasim. New York: Praeger.

Hirsch, E. D., Jr. (1987). *Cultural Literacy: What Every American Needs to Know*. Boston: Houghton Mifflin.

Jonassen, D. H., K. L. Peck, and B. G. Wilson. (1999). *Learning with Technology: A Constructivist Perspective*. Upper Saddle River, N.J.: Merrill.

Kemshal-Bell, Guy (2001). *The Online Teacher*. NSW Department of Education and Training, TAFE NSW. Retrieved January 16, 2003, from <http://cyberteacher.onestop.net/final%20report.pdf>.

Lucas, Christopher J. (1996). *Crisis in the Academy: Rethinking Higher Education in America*. Griffin: St. Martin's.

Lyotard, Jean-François. (1989). *The Postmodern Condition: A Report on Knowledge*. Minneapolis: University of Minnesota Press.

McLoughlin, C., and R. Oliver. (2000). "Designing Learning Environments for Cultural Inclusivity: A Case Study of Indigenous Online Learning at Tertiary Level." *Australian Journal of Education Technology, 16*(1), 58–72.

Odin, Jaishree K. (2002). "Teaching and Learning Activities in the Online Classroom." In *Proceedings of Educational Multimedia, Hypermedia and Telecommunications (Ed-Media 2002)*, ed. Philip Barket and Samuel Rebelsky, 3:1484–1498. Denver, Colo.: Association for Advancement of Computing in Education.

Prensky, Marc. (2001). "Digital Natives, Digital Immigrants." *On the Horizon.* NCB University Press, Vol. 9, No. 5. Retrieved January 16, 2003, from <http://www.marcprensky.com/writing>.

Readings, Bill. (1999). *University in Ruins.* Cambridge, Mass.: Harvard University Press.

Vygotsky, L. S. (1978). *Mind in Society: The Development of Higher Psychological Processes*, ed. Michael Cole, Vera John-Steiner, Sylvia Scribner, and Ellen Souberman. Cambridge, Mass.: Harvard University Press.

PART IV

SOME REGIONAL
RESPONSES TO
GLOBALIZATION

INTRODUCTION

THE FOCUS of the following three essays is the consequences of globalization as regards higher education in some parts of the less developed world. We wish, of course, that we could have included authors from Africa, the states of the former Soviet Union, and the Middle East. We are sure that there would be further important differences that would have been most interesting to pursue.

What is most striking about the three authors in this part of the book is the huge differences among them, both in perspective and in their analyses. This begins with differences in how they understand globalization, what they see to be the key issues raised for higher education by globalization processes, and ultimately how they understand "knowledge."

For Su Hao, looking from Beijing, "globalization has made the world a global village" and thus, for him, "political elites need a global worldview." He sees new missions for the university and is encouraged by the fact that "international organizations, nongovernmental organizations, multinational companies, foundations, and individual entrepreneurs have also become providers of higher education." Finally, he seems enthusiastic regarding the capacities of the new technologies. His account, accordingly, if perhaps ironically, squares neatly with the neoliberal picture.

Looking from Latin America, Garnier is much less sanguine. As he sees it, the relation between globalization and knowledge is a contradictory relation, a paradoxical relation. In its 1999 World Development Report, entitled "Knowledge for Development," the World Bank began by saying that "knowledge is like light. Weightless and intangible, it can easily travel the world, enlightening the lives of people everywhere. Yet billions of people still live in the darkness of poverty—unnecessarily."

"Unnecessarily" since, for Garnier, "the globalization of commercial and financial markets and the increasingly concentrated character of the global economy have produced a quite different and opposite tendency toward the commodification of knowledge." "If knowledge is like light, the commodification of knowledge manages to capture that light, sealing it out of reach of those unwilling, or unable, to pay for its use."

Garnier offers a review of recent developments in Latin America, and argues that investment in higher education is critical for economic development. He develops a critique of neo-classical economic theory and of policies based on the assumptions of this theory, concluding his essay with a penetrating criticism of the idea that knowledge is a commodity.

Drawing on his experience in South Asia and Taiwan, the essay by Sohail Inayatullah provides yet another perspective on globalization and higher education for the less developed world. His essay is also emphatically future-oriented, so he also provides a neat transition to the final part of this volume.

Inayatullah focuses on "corporatization" and "virtualization," paralleling much of the more extended argument of Margolis. But Inayatullah will not be boxed in. "As academics," he writes, "we should never . . . lose sight of our responsibility to create new futures, to inspire students, to ask what-if questions, to think the unthinkable, to go outside current parameters of knowledge." Following his own advice, he allows himself the freedom to think imaginatively.

One possibility spurred by globalization is a multicultural turn: "Deep multiculturalism challenges what is taught, how it is taught, the knowledge categories used to teach, and the way departments enclose the Other. It provides a worldview in which to create new models of learning and new universities that better capture the many ways students know the world." This will not be easy, however. With his eye primarily on the academics of South and Southeast Asia, he identifies four "Big Ms" that define their possible career paths, falling in line with the Ministry of Education, the Mullah, Microsoft, or McDonald's—or some combination of these. But again, he will not be boxed in. He concludes his very provocative essay with an account of three possible choices for universities and three possible scenarios.

INTERACTION OF GLOBAL POLITICS AND HIGHER EDUCATION

Su Hao

THE NEW WAVE OF GLOBALIZATION, having emerged in the latter decades of the last century, impinges upon us now with an even stronger force. Globalization influences directly both international and domestic politics. It is obvious that the 9/11 tragedy in the United States, as a negative effect of globalization, has made world politics more complicated. Politics, both domestic and international, has become real global politics, further complicating the interrelated hierarchical structure of local politics, national politics, and international politics. In this context, it is necessary for politicians and other elites to become "globalized personnel," traveling overseas frequently, and, if they are to participate successfully in world affairs, they need to acquire a wide range of knowledge and a cosmopolitan worldview. As a consequence, globalizing international politics promotes higher education aimed at adapting students to modernization and internationalization. Bringing global standards to higher education will be conducive to making the whole of the globe an interconnected and interactive community. This chapter explores the interaction of the global politics and higher education in this period of dramatic globalization.

WORLD POLITICS AND GLOBALIZATION

Globalization is real and everybody experiences it. It impacts every corner of the earth. As Anthony McGrew (1992) argues: "globalization has two distinct dimensions: scope (or stretching) and intensity (or deepening)." That means that globalization processes spread not only over the entire world but that they penetrate into the daily lives of individuals. Under the effects of globalization, the dimensions of world politics have changed considerably and some new connotations of politics have come into being.

The late fifteenth and the early sixteenth centuries saw the beginning of the first wave of globalization. The exploration of new sea-lanes and the new geography made the scattered world a real unit with its different parts linked closer together. After the industrial revolution in the eighteenth century and electronic innovation in the late nineteenth century, the second wave of globalization devastated the geographic barriers of communication. Transportation stretched out over the global surface; the colonial system expanded to almost all parts of the world; immigrants moved from the Old World to the New World and people with different cultural backgrounds were regularly meeting with each other in one geographical place. Wars waged by countries in Europe extended not only to Africa and Asia but also to the American continent. These genuine World Wars brought unprecedented disasters to people. We are now facing the third wave of globalization, which along with the information revolution, was inaugurated in the 1980s and 1990s. As Marshall McLuhan remarked many years ago, one of the defining characteristics of the modern age is the developing realization that we live in a "global village." In this global village, life is increasingly lived in a kind of "homogenous society." People share a common space, communicate with each other by many sophisticated means, entertain the same cultural products, link their economically productive activities, and both promote and restrict reciprocity among the nations in the global polity.

The global village determines politics. Global politics means not only traditional international politics, dealing with the interstate affairs in the world arena, but also transnational relations among states. As McGrew (1992) notes, global politics has become "a focus for intellectual curiosity because it cuts across the traditional boundaries that separate the study of international politics from the study of domestic politics, comparative politics and political economy."

Global politics has the following dimensions. First, globalization makes international politics critical to all other politics. Whatever the interstate politics or the domestic politics, there are inherent interactions with each other. Following Modelski, we can say that world politics can be understood in terms of four levels, which link reciprocally with each other in the hierarchical framework of local and national affairs and regional and global affairs, to form a political entity. According to the idea of a "butterfly effect," events in one country could have dramatic consequences in other parts of the world. An example might be the Tiananmen Square incident, which occurred in 1989 in Beijing, and dominated television viewing everywhere; it promoted the tremendous changes in Eastern Europe and the collapse of the Soviet Union, which ultimately ended the Cold War.

Globalization interlaces human political life with homogeneity and heterogeneity. On the one hand, the common standards for judging international affairs have become more and more universal. The principles of democracy, the values of human rights, and other fundamental criteria for international relations have become the common norms with which almost all countries conduct their foreign affairs. But on the other hand, the world's diversity has become more obvious. The different cultural backgrounds and various religious beliefs and diversified political doctrines confront one another in this global village, forcing states to learn how to adjust to diverse national interests if they are to coexist and make possible a world that is stable, peaceful, and harmonious. And certainly, we should be united to fight global terrorism, fascism, and militarism.

Second, international economic affairs have absorbed the attention of political science. The large amount of international trade between countries, the great flow of financial currents around the globe, and the huge sums of foreign investments to some extent shape the pattern of international relations. Since the end of the Cold War, even though different political systems still exist among the states, the mutual intercrossing of national economic interests has tended to dissolve political antagonism between nations. The flow of the global bankroll may strengthen the political power of a government or it might impair a government by destabilizing domestic society. Adding to this, and owing to the consequences of globalization, some traditional employments have lost their pragmatic function. As a result, the issue of unemployment has brought uncertainty to society. As Bordo, Eichengreen, and Irwin argue, commercial and financial integration today is even more pervasive than a hundred years ago. Economic security and financial security have emerged as major concerns for many countries, particularly for the developing countries.

Third, international organizations take increasingly important roles in efforts to resolve international political issues. According to Hedley Bull (1977), an identifiable global political system and global political process embrace a worldwide network of interactions and relationships between not only states but also other political actors, both "above" the state and "below" it. The United Nations not only has the right to express its position on all the international issues and its concerns as regards domestic problems, but it also conducts practical operations to keep or make peace in the world. The World Trade Organization has taken a more important role of arbitrator for many trade disputes between the nations. And many regional and subregional organizations have been formed in all parts of the globe. Almost all the countries of the world are engaged in one or more international organizations. Finally, hundreds of nongovernmental organizations (NGOs) have been active actors in international relations. This earth has been entwined with the organic network constructed by global and regional international organizations.

Fourth, global security has become the hot topic for world politics. Globalization involves heightened movements of capital and human population. These phenomena, on the one hand, are conditions that strengthen global economic and political activities and promote the exchanges of persons from different countries. But these heightened movements also have some negative effects. The free flow of capital makes for great uncertainty in financial markets. In the late 1990s, the financial crisis almost destroyed some countries' national economies and its influences spread to Latin America and Eastern Europe. Hence, economic security or financial security has become the highlight of many governments' working agendas. The movement of population also brings big problems that challenge national security in terms of its nontraditional and nonmilitary implications, including terrorism, transnational crime, drug traffic, disease, refugee problems, and illegal immigration.

The terrorist attack on the World Trade Center on September 11, 2001, has made international terrorism the focus of concern of every government. The majority of states have formed a coalition to respond to terrorist activities and to try to destroy the transnational capacities of the terror network. Consequently, nontraditional security issues are highlighted in the global security agenda. As Clark (1999) concludes, we should adjust our policy-making process from the traditional military security into the dimension of the globalization of the security state.

Fifth, under the wave of globalization, to manage the economic and political conflicts, peaceful resolution and cooperation have become the main option for nations, both internationally and domestically. Alan Mayne (1999) argues that the countries and regions on this earth are interdependent, something like a "community enterprise economy." The use of force to solve these problems harms everyone. The peaceful and rational resolution of conflict makes possible a win-win situation for the nations concerned.

Sixth, new technologies have made possible new modes of conducting relations between nations. Owing to the coming of the information age, which itself impels globalization, new capacities for handling delicate political problems and for enhancing the relations between nations have emerged. Such measures are the use of "hot lines," decision-making transparency, information databases, electronic communication, and so on. Political communication becomes much more convenient and quicker, and political elites get information easier, which increases the efficiency of decision making.

Finally, the capacity of governments to act unilaterally is challenged. Traditionally, domestic affairs fell within the sovereign domain and interference would not be tolerated. But some political norms have turned into universal norms. When politicians make decisions regarding domestic affairs, they must acknowledge that these are subject to norms in the context of a global framework.

POLITICAL ELITES AND HIGHER EDUCATION

History shows that it is always the elites in the society who engage in critical politics. At the present time, the persons who handle politics are the statesmen, legislators, political advisers, senior technical officers in the government, policy-oriented scholars in think tanks or universities, and political critics. Facing globalization, these political elites are required to be persons of exceptional quality—globalized persons. The more knowledge of global affairs and macro-world foresight these political elites have, the better national political affairs and global politics will be. But what kinds of competences should these people have?

Globalized political elites have the responsibility to frame their politics in ways that successfully face the challenges of globalization. Higher education is the major conduit for training the new generation of political elites, since the experience of higher education gives people the opportunity to form their worldviews and to obtain wide knowledge about the world. How does higher education educate this new generation in order to create political elites with globalized worldviews?

First of all, it is critical for the new generation of political elites to have a systematic, macro-strategic worldview. As world politics is dependent on the systematic connection of the global village, the heads of this village should be responsible for maintaining the denizens' safety and prosperity. In this way the whole of the village, in which every family interdependently connects with each other, may be kept secure, stable, and prosperous. Thus, world political elites should understand world trends in terms of politics, economics, and culture. Hence, they can cherish the common values of humanity and adjust to the diversity of the world as well. They can understand and perceive the inherent interaction between the different levels in world politics. They think not only of their nation, but have concern for people in the whole world.

The second competence that political elites should possess is a wide range of knowledge. When Lawrence Summers, the president of Harvard University, gave a speech at Beijing University in 2002, he argued that with the impact of globalization, the world has become smaller and, therefore, that the intention of communication should be enhanced. As knowledge becomes more and more specialized and oriented to practical concerns, students must pay greater attention to the humanities, especially to questions of human nature. It is necessary for the people who conduct politics to have fundamental knowledge of social science and to have as much natural scientific knowledge as possible. Because the Internet is the most significant technological and social force, skill in the use of information technologies is essential. Finally, the ability to speak foreign languages has become an important qualification for political elites.

The third major requirement for political elites is the spirit of coordination and cooperation. In this interdependent world, political elites need to coordinate with their colleagues who come from different disciplines, and they need to communicate with those from other cultures who often have different interests. For example, when dealing with global nontraditional security issues, they must identify broad common interests so that they can coordinate their efforts. Even in the war against terrorism, it is essential for the countries concerned to make a global network of coalitions if we are to eradicate this human evil in the world. If they cooperate, political elites may achieve success not only in their personal political careers but also in dealing with domestic and international political matters.

In summary, in the traditional understanding, the task of education is to pass knowledge on to students. In the traditional Chinese perception of education, education has three goals: handing down knowledge to students, resolving puzzles for students, and giving students life and workplace skills. The function of higher education is, on the one hand, to offer students from the middle schools in certain institutions advanced knowledge, and on the other hand, to conduct scientific research that creates and develops knowledge. But under the impact of globalization, higher education has a new, social global function. This has at least two implications for politics: maintenance of social stability and enhancement of the mutual communication among countries.

THE GLOBALIZATION OF HIGHER EDUCATION

With globalization, higher education also faces the challenge of readjustment. As James van Patten (1999) argues, higher education is in transition to a new role in the educational system. The response of higher education to globalization is the globalizing of higher education. This means that universities should internationalize their teaching and the students they serve, and that higher education must not be conducted within the nation but transnationally.

Three points can be made. First, the content of higher education has been globalized. No matter where the students study in universities, they will share knowledge taught in other parts of the world; they should know the latest developments in their disciplines; and they will have similar methods of doing their research. The textbooks will increasingly be the same for the students in different countries. For example, the universities in China expect their students to have global knowledge. One of the obvious courses is "World Politics and Economy," offered as a compulsory course to almost all students. The courses developing skills in computer technologies are common for all students in universities. These young political elites do not just study social science but some of them focus their study on humanities or natural science. But whatever the subjects they study, they are required to have knowledge of global politics.

Second, through the use of the new technologies, the methods of teaching have improved. For some time, radio and television were used for teaching, and many countries established TV-broadcasting universities. But in the 1990s, Internet technology was introduced and a teaching revolution in higher education occurred. Regarding the impact of this technological revolution, important elements are emerging. The teaching staff has eagerly accepted the globalization of educational resources. Professors easily acquire the materials and the academic viewpoints of countless others via Internet databases. E-libraries, e-books, and e-journals are common. This enables users convenient access to almost any kind of information they want. So-called distance education is also a prominent feature of many famous universities in China and elsewhere. Students may take courses in a university at home over the Internet. The professors, wherever they may be in the world, can instruct their students by e-mail.

Because of globalization, students in universities represent a more internationalized ensemble. The flow of people around the globe is one of the most obvious consequences of globalization. Accordingly, it has become a more and more common phenomenon that college students, especially graduate students, go to other countries to pursue their advanced studies. In the United States each year thousands of foreign students are at hundreds of universities finishing a variety of degrees. In almost all countries, politicians and the majority of political elites have had the experience of studying abroad. World-renowned universities, like Harvard, the London School of Economic and Political Studies, and the University of Paris, have a large number of alumni who have become the leaders of political elites. Even as a developing country, China has more and more foreign students enrolled each year.

Further, so-called continuing education has become an indispensable extension of higher education. With globalization, the world political situation has changed so quickly that political elites have to "recharge" themselves with new information if they are to be current.

Many famous universities now offer diversified training programs for mid-career professionals. The Chinese Foreign Ministry each year has to select senior and junior diplomats to study in China and in foreign countries to get mid-career professional training. The State Department of the United States also has some officers each year on leave at universities getting training or doing research work. Even some politicians go abroad to pursue advanced studies. The famous Singaporean politician, Lee Guan-you, went to the Kennedy School of Government, Harvard University, *after* he had taken the position of premier. The object of higher education has changed not only for traditional students but also for mid-career professionals, government officers, military servants, lawyers, businesspersons, social workers, and technicians.

The main institutions of higher education have also changed. Higher education is conducted not only by universities but also by other institutions. International organizations, nongovernmental organizations, multinational companies, foundations, and individual entrepreneurs have also become providers of higher education. Universities try to link actively with these institutions to expand their influence and reputation.

At present, international organizations take on an increasing role in providing higher education. The United Nations is an active partner with higher education institutions. The United Nations Educational, Scientific and Cultural Organization (UNESCO) has a very important role in promoting education in developing countries. Its major educational activities focus on basic education for all its member states, the renewal of educational systems, and educational advancement and policy. For example, in 1998, its Associated Schools Projects network, which promoted thinking and behavior based on common humanistic and cultural values, increased to 5,600 in 161 countries. In order to teach officers and diplomats skills necessary to handle the complicated international situation, the UN educational bureau offers many training programs, such as peacekeeping and conflict resolution. Sometimes these are joint programs with universities. The author just completed a training program that was a joint program between the educational bureau of the United Nations and Columbia University in New York City. Further, regional organizations have also initiated training programs for the mid-career professionals. The ASEAN Regional Forum is the only one of the official security mechanisms in the Asia-Pacific region. It also has initiated a training program in cooperation with universities. Another regional organization, ASEAN Plus Three, held several workshops on financial affairs. These activities are some of the kinds of continuing higher education that give participants the opportunity to broaden their range of knowledge or to deepen their understanding of certain critical issues.

As the biggest developing country, China is committed to expanding higher education. In the past twenty years, the Chinese government put the development of education on the national strategic level and has developed a strategy of "Reviving the Nation by Science and Education." Two decades ago, China's former senior leader Deng Xiaoping told the nation that education needed to face modernization, the world, and the future. The Chinese government has been vigorous in inviting foreign experts and in sending Chinese experts abroad for studies. Each year, more than 200,000 foreign experts go to China for their work and more than 40,000 Chinese experts go to other countries for their work. China has sent out over 340,000 students at public expense, some at their own expense, and received 10,000 foreign experts in Chinese universities since 1978. China has received about 399,000 foreign students since 1979. Under the guidance of the government, Chinese universities have initiated many reforms to adapt, step by step, their higher educational system to international standards.

The Chinese government has made a special effort to train its senior political elites abroad. The John F. Kennedy School of Government of Harvard University conducted a program for several years that trained Chinese senior military officers, and the Kennedy school will offer another training program to the Chinese senior administrative officers in the coming years. Obviously, it is necessary for governments to promote training programs for their political elites by means of international exchange.

The higher education system in the United States takes internationalization seriously. The most eminent program of international educational exchange in the world is the Fulbright program, which is supported by the U.S. government. Each year, the Fulbright foundation enables about 800 scholars to come to the United States. Almost the same number of American scholars go to other countries. Most of them focus their studies on social science and humanities, which are, to some extent, the disciplines most closely related to policy orientation.

Many of the participants in this program have become political elites in their home countries. During my research work in Columbia University on a Fulbright fellowship, I could see that the university authority implements a policy of internationalization. Many foreign students are taking courses around campus, especially in the School of International and Public Affairs. Some teaching and research programs are conducted multinationally. Tufts University conducted its leadership symposium in three places, Beijing, Hong Kong, and Boston, training international students under the instruction of scholars from different countries. Universities, which are internationalized to a high extent, are excellent institutions for training world political elites.

As the primary institutions of higher education, universities in many countries, especially the developed countries and some big developing countries, have initiated joint programs that involve both colleges and training workshops. In China, for instance, many universities are implementing joint programs with foreign educational institutions. The largest number of joint cooperative programs is in political science. As early as the 1980s, Nanjing University established a Center for Chinese and American Studies with Johns Hopkins University of the United States, and so far, hundreds of young scholars have taken their training courses there. Fudan University and People's University, two very well-known institutions in China, have had joint programs with American foundations to hold workshops on international security and arms control and international political economy. The Foreign Affairs College of China has taken part in the "Chautauqua" project, renowned in U.S. higher educational circles for its short courses for training college faculties, offering courses on China's foreign policy and security policy to some American scholars. To face the challenge of the global economy, some universities in China have developed MBA programs for young business professionals with other universities in Europe and the United States. Some Chinese universities use non-Chinese textbooks and teach in English so that their students can catch up with international standards. China, as other countries, is trying its best to accelerate the internationalization of its higher education.

Nongovernmental actors also play important roles in supplementing higher education, especially in training mid-career professionals. Foundations like the Ford Foundation, the Rockefeller Foundation, and the McArthur Foundation, in this respect are much more active in supporting workshops held at universities and other scholar exchange programs between universities. Some think tanks, like the Rand Corporation and the Institute of Peace Studies, have their own training programs. The Center for Proliferation Studies in the Monterey Institute of International Studies had two sessions of training programs for Chinese university professors on international security, arms control, and disarmament in the past two years. The training programs of NGOs and think tanks clearly wish to enhance political elites' ability to grasp the nature of the global political and economic situation so that they are ready to undertake their political careers.

Communication between nations remains central. In the Asia-Pacific region, the political and security situations are quite complicated. A lack of mutual understanding and trust exists among the countries because of their historical hostility in the past. In order to meet the challenges of globalization after the end of the Cold War, the countries started to pursue economic and security cooperation. In order to let the regional countries work cooperatively, the Joint Center for Security Studies between Toronto and York universities compiled a catalogue of terminology, which listed the accepted meaning of the key words useful in regional security dialogues. This pamphlet has been very important in promoting mutual understanding among countries in the region when the participants of dialogues discussed or did their policy studies. The Institute on Global Conflict and Cooperation of the University of California at San Diego initiated the famous regional security dialogue, the "Northeast Asia Cooperation Dialogue" (NEACD). This subregional security mechanism has become an important vehicle for communication. India and Pakistan have been historical enemies for a long time and lacked any channel to communicate with each other. In the mid-1990s, under the support of the Ford Foundation, the Stimson Center in Washington, and the Center for South Asian Studies at the University of Illinois arranged a series of workshops for training graduate students in South Asia, and invited more than thirty graduate students and journalists from both of these countries and some other scholars from China, Britain, and the United States. These series of training workshops were informal forums for Indians and Pakistanis to exchange their views on bilateral security relations in a setting that made it easier for tensions to be diffused.

CONCLUSION

Globalization has made the world a global village. In this context, traditional world politics has turned into a global politics that has a great impact on the development of higher education. To handle political affairs, political elites need a global worldview. Higher education has the task of cultivating a new generation of political elites for every country. For this purpose, higher education must itself internationalize. As an OECD report (1999) concluded, "internationalization of higher education is one of the ways a country responds to the impact of globalization."

On the way to the globalization of higher education, universities will have their teaching contents globalized, students will become internationalized, and the latest technologies for teaching and learning will be used. Governments will need to push higher education beyond national borders. Universities must actively improve their level of teaching, expand their scale, and strive to improve their reputations by seeking joint programs with partners in other countries. International organizations, NGOs, and other nonuniversity units will continue to play important roles. Finally, higher education will need to acknowledge its new social function via direct attention to social reform and by engaging in political communication among countries. The new generation of political elites, the products of global higher education, will construct a new framework of world politics in terms of a new political understanding and better communication between the increasingly interdependent nations of the world.

REFERENCES

Bordo, Michael D., Barry Eichengreen, and Douglas A. Irwin. (1999). "Is Globalization Today Really Different Than Globalization a Hundred Years Ago?" NBER Working Paper No. w7195. Retrieved July 31, 2003, from <http://papers.nber.org/papers/w7195>.

Bull, Hedley. (1977). *The Anarchical Society*. London: Macmillan.

Clark, Ian. (1999). *Globalization and International Relations Theory*. New York: Oxford University Press.

DeOllos, Ione Y., and David C. Morris. (1999–2000). "The Internet as an Information Resource for Older Adults." *Educational Technology System, 28*(2), 107–120.

Hopkins, A. G. (ed.). (2002). *Globalization in World History.* London: Pimlico.

Magyar, Karl P. (ed.). (1996). *Global Security Concerns: Anticipating the Twenty-First Century.* Maxwell Air Force Base, Ala.: Air University Press.

Mayne, Alan J. (1999). *From Politics Past to Politics Future: An Integrated Analysis of Current and Emergent Paradigms.* Westport, Conn.: Praeger.

McGrew, Anthony G. (1992). "Conceptualizing Global Politics." In *Global Politics: Globalization and the Nation-State,* ed. Anthony G. McGrew and Paul G. Lewis et al. Oxford: Polity.

Modelski, George. (1987). *Principles of World Politics.* New York: The Free Press.

OECD. Program on Institutional Management in Higher Education. (1999). *Quality and Internationalization in Higher Education.*

Patten, James van. (1999). *Challenges and Opportunities for Education in the Twenty-First Century.* Edwin Mellen.

PRC. Ministry of Education's web site. <http://www.moe.edu.cn/cgi-bin/guoji/Chinese/home.php>.

PRC. State Administration of Foreign Experts Affairs' web site. <http://www.safea.gov.cn/>.

Program of Heads of National Defense Colleges. <http://www.gov.an/arf/arfhome.htm>. The program of regional security policies workshops held in universities in different countries. See also the Newsletter of Foreign Affairs College of China, 1999, no. 22.

Rodrigues, Nestor P. (1999). "Globalization, Autonomy, and Transnational Migration." *Research in Politics and Society,* 6, 65–84.

Romeu, Jorge Lius. (1999–2000). "Technology and International Education." *Educational Technology System,* 28(4), 305–310.

Summers, Lawrence. (2002). "The Impact of Globalization on Higher Education." <http://www.people.com.cn>.

Yearbook of the United Nations 1993. (1994). New York: United Nations, Department of Public Information.

Yearbook of the United Nations 1999. (2001). New York: United Nations, Department of Public Information.

CHAPTER II

Knowledge and Higher Education in Latin America: Incommodious Commodities?

Leonardo Garnier

IT WAS ONLY RECENTLY that the tide against investing in public higher education in less developed countries started subsiding. As stated in the report of the Task Force on Higher Education and Society convened by the World Bank and UNESCO, aptly subtitled "Peril and Promise," it is increasingly recognized that, in the context of today's global economy, systematic knowledge has gradually replaced experience in furthering technology, with sophisticated and theoretical knowledge now the predominant path for technical progress. Therefore, the quality of knowledge generated within higher education institutions, and its availability to the wider economy, is becoming increasingly critical to national competitiveness.

Public Higher Education in Latin America: Wasteful and Unfair?

This change of mind is particularly interesting since, for many decades, it has been argued that less developed countries should not waste their public resources on higher education insofar as they still confront both coverage and quality problems at basic educational levels, and given that the rates of return on basic primary education are higher than those of high school and much higher than those of higher education, both in private and in social terms. In fact, Latin American countries had a very difficult time in 1990 at the Jomtien World Conference on Education for All, trying—unsuccessfully—to convince delegates from both most and least developed countries that the Jomtien Declaration should not leave out the importance for all countries, not just of basic but also of technical and higher education, including science and technology and the increasing role of computers and information technology. At the time, as is obvious from the Jomtien Declaration, such pretenses were considered too ambitious and many delegates reacted as if these higher goals were inimical to advances in basic education.

It would take twenty years before a mistake started to be acknowledged. But the damage was done, as the experts of the Task Force on Higher Education admit: "Since the 1980s, many national governments and international donors have assigned higher education a relatively low priority. Narrow—and, in our view, misleading—economic analysis has contributed to the view that public investment in universities and colleges brings meager returns compared to investment in primary and secondary schools, and that higher education magnifies income inequality" (2000).

For decades, Latin American countries confronted very strong internal and external pressure against the use of public resources to finance higher education and, in particular, public universities. International financial institutions were particularly critical of these countries spending public money on higher education, which was regarded not only as inefficient and wasteful, but also as socially unjust, since it supposedly subsidized the rich at the expense of the poor. According to an official World Bank Public Sector Expenditure Report regarding the case of Costa Rica, "the government's commitment to provide free educational services to the whole population from preschool to the university is not sustainable in the future if quality standards are to be maintained. Consequently, the authorities have to: (i) concentrate efforts where social returns are highest and where benefits are more equally distributed among the population, i.e., on basic education; and (ii) encourage private contributions through cost recovery at the university level, developing the possibility of sale of services and raising tuition at the level of private universities" (1989).

That was basically the same position the Bank presented in more general terms in the *1990 World Development Report*, which argues that, in their educational policies, governments have favored higher education to the detriment of services that would have benefited the poor, in spite of the well-known fact that tertiary education offers a much lower rate of return. Thus, the report regrets that many countries invest a disproportionately high portion of their budget in higher education. In particular, they mention that in Costa Rica, Chile, the Dominican Republic, and Uruguay, those who belong to the higher quintile of the population in terms of their family income receive more than half of those subsidies going to higher education, while only 10 percent of those subsidies go to those of the poorest quintile. On the contrary, were public resources to be redirected from higher education toward primary education and basic health, these countries would achieve both higher efficiency and equity.

The Bank (1999) contends, furthermore, that, given "that the distance between basic science and technological application is narrowing or, in some cases, disappearing altogether"; that "for all practical purposes, there are no more logistical barriers to information access and communication among people, institutions and countries"; that there is a "growing importance of continuing education needed to update knowledge and skills on a regular basis because of the short 'shelf life' of knowledge"; and that developing countries will continue to confront a very difficult financial constraint; there would be no viable—or better —alternative to fragmentation and privatization. Universities, public and private, should "organize themselves to accommodate the learning and training demands of a very diverse clientele" that, in turn, reflects the demands from the labor market. At the same time, while the need for some academic leadership is recognized, the response is that "some semblance to the Ivy League or Oxbridge is needed to ensure competent leadership" but that this would be so for only a small portion, about 3 percent, of national higher education enrollments, since, it is said, this is so even in rich countries. In this way, the argument goes, the total cost "for a healthy academic leadership enclave would be modest."

But the arguments do not square with the facts. The assumed dichotomy between politically responsible countries that spend their public money on basic education and health, and others that squander theirs in high-end, inefficient, and unfair programs—like higher education—was not a true representation of what was happening in Latin America. On the contrary, it was precisely in those countries where significant amounts of resources were devoted to higher education that basic education and health were also given priority, while those countries that did not invest significantly in higher education did not invest in basic social services either. With few exceptions, the correlation between general educational enrollment, enrollment in basic education, and enrollment in higher education is significantly positive: the higher primary and secondary enrollment, the higher enrollment at the higher levels, and vice versa. In the same way, clearly an inverse correlation exists between the extension of higher education and illiteracy rates. Finally, there is also a significantly positive correlation between higher education enrollment and better income distribution: those countries with Gini coefficients below the regional average—and, therefore, with a less polarized distribution—are also the countries with higher enrollment in higher education, like Uruguay, Costa Rica, and, until recently, Argentina; while some of the worst offenders in terms of income disparities are also countries where public higher education has received less resources.

While clearly contradicting the financial institutions' received wisdom, these conclusions should not have come as a surprise but as a rather obvious confirmation of a historical tradition: those countries where education had long been a significant priority usually understood education and learning as an integral system and, therefore, tended to invest in the whole system, from preschool to university levels. These were also countries with strong universal social policies aimed at promoting social mobility and social integration. On the contrary, those countries where neither social integration nor public education was regarded as a priority did not bother to invest in either basic or higher education.

Thus, higher education not only does not seem to divert resources from more basic levels of education, but seems to act as a synergic element in the consolidation of the educational system: increasing numbers of teachers and professors are produced by the universities, and a growing awareness of the importance of a good education becomes widespread. In fact, as the UN Economic Commission for Latin America and the Caribbean (ECLAC) has shown, there is a solid relationship in most Latin American countries between educational attainment and both income and productivity. It has been observed, for example, that ten or more years of schooling are needed in order to have a chance of securing well-being and steering clear of poverty. The same is true around the world, and most recent studies show, beyond any reasonable doubt, that education plays a fundamental role in increasing both productivity and incomes. The global estimates of the effect of knowledge in terms of productivity made for the OECD countries roughly coincides with those for the United States, so that typically, between one-fifth and one-third of the variations in income are attributable to the combined effect of education, literacy, and experience acquired in the labor market. This has also been confirmed by the new endogenous growth models, according to which sustainable growth is the result, in a significant proportion, of positive externalities generated by education; new ideas and new technologies are critical to high, sustained growth, and in turn rely on high levels of human capital. Furthermore, it is not only the average amount of education provided that is important, but the equity of investment in education, since the dispersion or inequality of education has been shown to have a clear negative impact on per capita income, and the greater the dispersion, the greater the negative effect. Once again, justice and efficiency seem to work in the same, rather than opposite, directions.

The significance of investing in higher education has been also highlighted by the Global Competitiveness Index, developed by the World Economic Forum. One of its components—the innovation capacity subindex—measures a country's ability to produce new knowledge, based on indicators like the resources devoted to research and development, cooperation between research institutions and business, the proportion of people with tertiary education, and the number of patents registered in the United States. According to this indicator, the percentage of population with tertiary education is the main factor explaining the superior performance of the three highest-ranked countries. Most Latin American countries perform poorly in this index precisely because they have invested a lower proportion of their per capita income in education than countries elsewhere with similar per capita income levels. Conversely, those Latin American countries that are better positioned in this ranking are some of the countries that did invest significantly in their public higher education systems: Argentina (30), followed by Costa Rica (32), Chile (34), Panama (37), Uruguay (41), and Venezuela (42). Another element highlighted by the report as one of the major obstacles to competitiveness in most countries is the prevalence of inefficient and ineffective public institutions that, in many cases, fail to deliver the public goods required from them. As we would expect, there is also a significant positive correlation between those countries with better than average institutional performance and those countries with higher proportional investment in public higher education. Thus, according to the Latin American Competitiveness Report, it is not a coincidence that Costa Rica is one of the few countries, along with Argentina, Chile, Uruguay, and Trinidad and Tobago, that has maintained consistently higher levels of investment in human capital in the region and has stronger institutions as well, so they come out better than most of the rest of the region and are comparable to the most competitive countries in the world, but they are more the exception than the rule. One of the conclusions of this study was, therefore, that in the medium and longer terms, a much stronger commitment to improving access to and quality of public education, especially at the secondary and tertiary levels, is essential for success.

PUBLIC UNIVERSITIES: FROM MODERNIZATION TO CRISIS AND ADJUSTMENT

There is no question about the significance of higher education—especially of public universities—in Latin America's modernization during the second half of the twentieth century. In spite of their many weaknesses and shortcomings, public universities played a key role in producing the technicians and professionals required by the modernization of productive activities, especially in relation with import-substituting industrialization, diversification of agricultural production, and processing of mineral resources; in supporting and promoting the technical and professional transformation of the public sector; and in creating and reproducing an intellectual elite as well as an educated middle class that was the backbone for the development of democratic processes in the past few decades. Public universities were also instrumental for the development of other basic services, like health and education, and of the development of urban (and sometimes even rural) infrastructure for transportation activities, energy, and telecommunications.

Similarly, public universities tended to produce more researchers and professionals than were being demanded by the private productive system, and scientific and technologic education and research was mainly financed, produced, and consumed by public institutions: government and the universities themselves. While for some this was but a public confession of waste and inefficiency in the allocation of public resources, it was in fact the only responsible answer to the distorted or peripheral character of these countries' economic structures.

Public universities were instrumental to the social mobility of the 1960s and 1970s, as reflected in the expansion of urban middle classes in most Latin American countries, and they played a central role in further developing and deepening national culture and national identity, including both its artistic and political expressions. It is estimated that, by 1950, there were about 300,000 tertiary students in Latin America. In the following fifty years, this number grew thirty times so that, by 2000, Latin America had ten million students in its higher education institutions, half of whom were women. Impressive as this expansion was, it remained a limited, mainly urban, and middle-class process: even today, only about 13 percent of the region's population has tertiary education. But public universities remained not just a space for teaching and a space for learning in the more traditional sense—that of acquiring skills and knowledge—but also as a space for critical thought, for understanding, for questioning, for doubt. It is worth noting that public universities in Latin America, being "publicly funded public institutions," nevertheless developed a significant degree of academic and political autonomy, even critical or rebellious autonomy, which also, in the context of politically authoritarian regimes, led to political and military repression.

In the late 1970s, hope and social unrest gave way to crisis, stabilization, adjustment, and disillusion. After three or four decades, Latin America's attempts at national development were confronted by the harsh realities of its own limitations and a new international environment. First, in 1971, the U.S. dollar ceased to function as an international standard of value—and was, in fact, significantly devalued; then, oil prices skyrocketed, with both a dramatic impact on costs of production across the world and on global financial liquidity, thus leading to growing inflation amid the ongoing recession: stagflation. In such a context, the emerging and weak Latin American democracies, either characterized or threatened by populism and revolt, would have been finally confronted with the unavoidable need for adjustment, had it not been for the wide availability of international financial resources. The money was there for the asking, and the governments were quickly asking for it, so they could sail through the crisis without having to either postpone investments or expenditures or increase their incomes through tax reform. It worked well for a few years but, by 1982, it was clear that the ongoing crisis was deeper than just the normal business cycle and that the problems of Latin American countries were structural in nature; the chances of their debts being honored was bleak. Interest rates soared so that the burden of servicing their debts became unbearable and Latin American countries were forced to default. The so-called debt crisis had finally arrived.

With the crisis came the need for stabilization and adjustment and, of course, the help and advice of international financial institutions representing what Williamson aptly termed the *Washington Consensus:* the International Monetary Fund (IMF), the World Bank (BIRF), the Inter American Development Bank (IDB), and, in many cases, the United States Agency for International Development (USAID). Internally, there was also a changing balance of power within most Latin American countries, as the alliance between urban middle class and new business sectors that was mostly behind the 1950s through 1970s reforms dissolved, giving way to the predominance of those interests linked to either exporting or financial activities that, needless to say, had a very similar view of their countries' problems as that of the Washington Consensus: a typically neo-liberal view. Thus, with few exceptions, stabilization and adjustment were understood as merely financial and macroeconomic stabilization, and they were carried on at the expense of both economic growth and social conditions. While no one can deny the urgency of confronting the unsustainable financial situation that had evolved in Latin America during the 1970s, it is equally hard to deny the perverse social effects of the neo-liberal approach to stabilization and adjustment: poverty rates had diminished systematically during the 1970s throughout Latin America, going from an average of 40 percent in 1970 to 22 percent in 1982, which meant a reduction in the absolute number of the poor from 107 million to 80 million. Then, the situation was completely reversed: the poverty rate went up to 34 percent and the absolute number of the poor reached almost 150 million by 1992.

For public institutions in general, and for universities in particular, this meant a radical departure from the realities of the previous three decades. Precisely at the time when the demand for higher education was rapidly expanding in Latin America, the availability of public funds for higher education was being severely questioned and restricted. In many instances, public universities throughout Latin America found themselves with much less money to deal with much larger and more complex demands. The expansion of demand was a result of the tremendous increase in the number of students, not just because of demographics, but also because of the previous success of educational policies at primary and secondary levels, which meant that a larger proportion of youngsters wanted to pursue higher education. But it was also a more complex demand, as the challenge of globalization and the growing importance of knowledge implied, something that was increasingly recognized both within the universities and in the context of more open and democratic societies.

These difficulties were confronted through contradictory processes. On the one hand, they were confronted through the liberalization of higher education markets, the promotion of private universities, and the pressure for public universities to move toward those fields and careers with growing market demand—technical careers, engineering, business administration, and so on—while restricting less appealing careers, mainly in the social sciences. But, on the other hand, they were also confronted through strengthening graduate programs and the research abilities of public universities, and their increasing cooperation with both private productive firms and public governmental entities—activities at which private universities, usually pressured to minimize costs (and quality), did not excel.

As a result of these diverging trends, public universities have expanded even further, in some instances becoming mega-universities —increasingly controlled by administration and bureaucratic-minded academics; in other cases, new public and private universities have emerged, to handle part of the growing demand; and also, new types of educational institutions, mostly private, have been created to supply specific aspects of these growing and diversified demands: technical colleges, specialized schools, and so on.

In most cases, the leading push comes from the market, which has been both good and bad. The market has been good insofar as a necessary sense of realism and social responsibility prevails in universities, which sometimes—even in the name of political commitment— becomes *aloof* from reality. (Compare Smith, above.) And the market has been bad insofar as the ideology of the market penetrates universities in the form of ill-understood competition, commodification of knowledge, and instrumentalizing both the curriculum and research programs in terms of their profitability.

The expansion of private higher education, however, has not necessarily meant an expansion in its quality. By 1930, private universities accounted for only 3 percent of enrollment in higher education in Latin America; they grew slowly, reaching 14 percent by the mid-1950s; but then, the private share grew to 34 percent by 1975 and, according to some estimates, they could account for almost half the students in higher education. Since 1980, more than 80 percent of new institutions have been private, generally smaller than their public counterparts. In Latin America, this is particularly troubling in terms of the pathological explosion of private institutions that call themselves universities— *garage* universities—charging very high fees and offering very low quality in their educational programs. Basically, they are selling degrees— and, of course, people are buying degrees because education is not just important as a source of knowledge, but as a "signal" of labor market demand, so people are willing to "pay for the signal."

Finally, the push from the market has also meant the creation of a few elite universities aimed at supplying the highest academic quality at even higher prices, which would also guarantee—and that is part of the idea—that by studying there you would get not just the best education, but also the best environment in terms of meeting the right people. With public universities confronting the problem of increasing numbers of students with stagnant budgets, this trend toward elite private universities could reproduce at the level of higher education what is already a reality in primary and secondary education, thus consolidating and further reproducing existing inequalities. This is not just a problem in terms of those who are left out, but also in terms of the increasing social detachment of this emerging elite. It is, then, a problem for democracy.

It is true that the globalization of higher education can have beneficial as well as damaging consequences. It opens many opportunities in terms of access to knowledge and learning, but it can also lead to unregulated and low-quality higher education, with the worldwide franchising or marketing of poor quality programs or even fraudulent degrees. However, as the Task Force on Higher Education and Society warned in the *Peril and Promise* report:

Developing countries are currently under great pressure to meet increased demand for higher education, and many are finding it hard to keep up. They are becoming increasingly reliant on fee-based education and private, for-profit providers. In this environment, education becomes more narrowly focused on providing a skilled labor pool for the immediate needs of the economy. Market forces predominate and the public benefits of—and responsibilities for—higher education recede from view. (2000)

GLOBALIZATION AND KNOWLEDGE: A PARADOXICAL RELATION

The relation between globalization and knowledge is a contradictory relation, a paradoxical relation. In the 1999 World Development report, entitled "Knowledge for Development," the World Bank began by saying that "knowledge is like light. Weightless and intangible, it can easily travel the world, enlightening the lives of people everywhere. Yet billions of people still live in the darkness of poverty—unnecessarily." Why unnecessarily? Because, the report argues, while knowledge is often costly to create—which is why most of it is created in industrial countries—developing countries could both acquire knowledge overseas and create their own at home. Why don't they? Would this change with globalization?

It is true that the intertwining of globalization with the ongoing scientific and technological revolution would seem to open wide the opportunities for building a "knowledge society" that could overcome much of the malaise that has confronted the world for centuries. This would mean taking advantage of the essentially public character of knowledge. In the language of economics, knowledge is a good whose consumption entails no rivalry: my consumption does not detract from yours, or vice versa. With the new technologies, it could become a truly global public good, capable of "enlightening the lives of people everywhere," and of ending poverty everywhere.

But globalization is a paradoxical process. As new scientific and technological breakthroughs have come to enhance the free or public character of knowledge, the globalization of commercial and financial markets and the increasingly concentrated character of the global economy have produced a quite different and opposite tendency toward the

192 · *Globalization and Higher Education*

commodification of knowledge. Globalization has showed how enormously profitable knowledge could and would be, if science and technology could be used to produce commodified knowledge, that is, knowledge tied up in a package (or under legal constraints) that could actually be privately owned, bought, and sold.

If knowledge is like light, the commodification of knowledge manages to capture that light, sealing it out of reach of those unwilling, or unable, to pay for its use. A market for knowledge emerges, then, on the basis of an artificial scarcity. It is not, therefore, an efficient, competitive market, but a consortium of legally sanctioned monopolies operating in fields where nonrivalry is the norm. This results in an enormous amount of waste, inefficiency, and, obviously, injustice. In such a context, the commodification of knowledge acts directly against arrangements that would be necessary for knowledge to be efficiently, and equitably, used and produced.

Knowledge is not just information. Knowledge is the capacity to use information to guide specific actions. It is for this reason that, as Paul David has argued, knowledge related activities are usually performed by "knowledge communities," which constitute networks of such shared understanding. These networks operate as public or collective spaces for the shared production and dissemination of knowledge. In fact, as David (2002) emphasizes,

> The knowledge economy's growth into the knowledge society hinges on the proliferation of knowledge-intensive communities. These communities are basically linked to scientific, technical and some business professions or projects. They are characterized by their strong knowledge production and reproduction capabilities, a public or semi-public space for learning and exchange and the intensive use of information technologies. Only when increasing numbers of communities displaying those very characteristics are formed across a wide array of cognitive fields, when professional experts, ordinary users of information, and uninitiated students are brought together by their shared interest in a given subject, will "the knowledge society" become a reality rather than a vision of a possible future.

It is precisely for this reason that the trend toward the commodification and privatization of knowledge is particularly problematic for less developed countries. They could easily be left out, or relegated to the periphery of the social networks that produce and disseminate this increasingly private public good.

THE ROLE OF UNIVERSITIES

Such is the challenge of our universities: to acquire, to create, to share knowledge. And it is a particularly difficult challenge in the context of increasingly commodified knowledge and, in particular, in the context of increasingly privatized systems of higher education—either through fully privatized universities or through increasing pressures for public universities to rely on private funding for their survival. While these pressures have brought some good incentives in terms of an increased awareness of Latin American universities toward the "new realities," they have also produced a further fragmentation of university functions, sacrificing some of its essential functions in order to save and expand what we might regard as instrumental or auxiliary functions.

There are many different ways to classify the functions of higher education, of universities. What should these functions be in Latin American countries? A higher education system should meet many different goals, ranging from satisfying students' demands for acquiring specific skills and a rewarding education to providing the people and environments required by the kind of society people, collectively, want to become. Higher education institutions should produce skilled technicians and graduates in different professional fields who are capable of confronting and solving problems through the application of both technical and scientific knowledge in specific particular situations. Performing surgery, judging a crime, designing a building, and proposing a new economic policy are all examples of the kind of knowledge that university professional graduates should acquire. As with technicians, the production of professionals has a direct relation to the labor market, though at times it is difficult to predict how demand and supply would evolve in the medium term.

An essential function of higher education institutions, public universities in particular, is that of creating scientific knowledge. While some research can be produced by private firms, government institutions, or some nongovernmental organizations, the bulk of scientific investigation in Latin America is performed at or through the participation of public universities with high-quality and expensive graduate programs. Scientific research tends to be costly and risky for private institutions.

But higher education does more than produce graduates with technical, professional, and scientific knowledge. Universities must also produce communities of people capable of critically reflecting on the meaning and significance of current and historical events. These communities need to understand what is happening and why, to locate events in their more general contexts in relation to cultural identities, ethical values, scientific paradigms, and political ideologies. Philosophy, then, remains an essential aspect of higher education. Universities should also provide much of the leadership in society, not just in terms of technical, professional, or scientific activities, or in terms of philosophical understanding, but also in terms of the political and cultural life beyond their own walls. Finally, universities—along with other cultural institutions —have a responsibility for promoting a better understanding and practice of democracy, including the building of a shared memory and a pluralistic cultural identity.

But if these are the functions of higher education, and these functions have to be performed in less developed countries in the context of an increasing globalization and commodification of knowledge, then the question that emerges is whether, in Latin America, higher education can adequately perform these functions merely through private incentives in a market economy, or whether public universities should remain an essential backbone of the system.

HIGHER EDUCATION: A TRUE COMMODITY?

Latin American countries went through a severe sequence of crisis, stabilization, and adjustment beginning in the early 1980s. Their educational systems went through a rapid liberalization of higher education markets, including the emergence of a plethora of private universities and financial pressure on public universities pushing them toward meeting the requirements of the markets. This is happening at the same time that globalization is both offering the opportunities opened by the emerging knowledge society and threatening higher education with the increasing commodification and privatization of knowledge. In such a context—and given the functions that Latin American countries could and should expect from their higher education systems—the question is simple: can these functions be adequately performed by an increasingly private system of higher education? Or is there a strategic role for public universities? Or, to put it more bluntly: can higher education become a true commodity? In order to answer this question, we need to briefly examine several of the characteristics of knowledge and higher education, insofar as they are to be treated as private economic goods.

HIGHER EDUCATION IS NOT A LUXURY
While in some places the prevailing opinion may be that higher education is a luxury good, today it is increasingly recognized that, very much like basic education, higher education is an essential public good. Restricting access to knowledge remains, therefore, wasteful and inefficient—not to say immoral.

But higher education, as one of the most important institutional settings for the production and dissemination of knowledge, has a public character not just for this reason, but because of its long-term ability to produce a critical mass of technical, professional, and scientific personnel and to stimulate thought and research, irrespective of individual socioeconomic backgrounds, well beyond the short-term profitability of firms, the immediate return to individuals, and even the specific political interest of current governments. Even if sometimes it does produce almost immediate results, higher education is not, and should not be seen as, something that would generate results "for today," but, rather, as a long-term investment in our most basic capacities. Profit-based education and profit-based research will be biased both toward the logic of consumption and the logic of short-term and private returns. Public education is required if the longer-term and wider social scope of higher education—of knowledge—as a social investment is to prevail.

HIGHER EDUCATION IS NOT "JUST FOR YOU . . ."
One of the reasons private markets work so well—or are supposed to work so well—is because the cost of those goods and services produced and exchanged through those markets is paid by those who receive and enjoy the benefit from their consumption. In the jargon of economics, this is so in the absence of externalities, that is, if consumption or production activities do not have any effects on other people or institutions, beyond that effect perceived by those who sold and bought those

goods. There are no externalities if the only costs and benefits of each good are those that actually translate into that commodity's market price. What you buy, what you pay for, what you, and only you get, if you paid for it, then the pleasure or utility of consuming it is "just for you." No strings attached.

But education, higher education in particular, is anything but free from externalities. My learning can hardly be seen as something that has an impact only on me. As it has been argued again and again, education has, above all, an impact on society as a whole: it produces learning communities, not just learned individuals. Over and beyond private returns, education produces indispensable social returns. By producing both learned individuals and learning communities, education produces entrepreneurial individuals and entrepreneurial environments; it produces leaders, and it produces democratic environments where leadership can be positively exercised. In short, higher education is, as it must be, an externality laden activity and, consequently, an activity whose costs and benefits can only be poorly represented through private market prices. And this is true both in terms of the individual consumer—for whom a price reflecting the full cost of higher education would appear prohibitively expensive when compared with his or her expected private returns—and in terms of the institution supplying education, which could not charge individual consumers for the cost involved in producing education's external effects. (See Smith.)

HIGHER EDUCATION IS NOT YOUR EVERYDAY COMMODITY

Another reason for markets working well—when they do—is quite simple: individual consumers know what they are buying, what they are paying for, and both the costs and benefits of such goods and services as the ones they buy every day. Information is perfect and equally distributed: consumers know as much as producers, and vice versa. In such cases, confronted with both consumers' knowledge and other firms' competition, the only way for a firm to be profitable is to respond to the consumers' commands: this is the ideal world of consumer sovereignty, the world where the consumer is king.

But higher education is not your everyday commodity. With higher education, even if you know what you are paying for, you don't know whether the costs are inflated and, in particular, you don't know what you are getting until it is too late. In fact, to make things worse, in many cases you do not even know what it is that you want or need to get out of higher education. How could you know beforehand what you should know, for example, to be a good economist? Why pay for some knowledge if I am not sure that it is the knowledge I actually need, and if I don't know what knowledge I am actually getting? These problems have only gotten worse with the rapidly changing pace of the knowledge society, where today's most useful knowledge might easily be tomorrow's waste. This casts considerable doubt on the distinction between "just-in-case" and "just-in-time" knowledge.

In fact, markets might not work at all and some rather important goods and services could very well go unproduced. This could typically be the case with those aspects of higher education hardest to translate into verifiable and timely skills and information.

Higher Education Is Not a Piece of Cake

Individual decisions through market exchanges are also supposed to produce optimal results because consumers know their *true preferences and needs*. They know what they want better than anybody else. This is one of the most basic arguments for opposing any kind of public intervention in or "distortion" of market choices. It is an argument based—apparently—on freedom: the consumers' freedom to decide what they want by themselves. Based on their preferences, and only limited by their budget restrictions, consumers would freely choose what they want. The argument, however, is not as simple as it seems, as both preferences and budget restrictions are essentially social products. Let's deal, first, with preferences.

The debate on tastes and preferences is long and complex. First is the question of whether *my* preferences are *just my* preferences or how much they are the reflection of *other people's* preferences, and what the answer to this question would imply for consumer theory. An even more damaging question refers to the social construction of preferences not just by *others* but by those who supply the goods, raising the question suggested by Karelis that institutions of higher education might well shape preferences.

But it is not to these problems I want to refer here, but to a more difficult question raised, among others, by Amartya Sen: people do not have one and only one set of preferences hierarchically ordered. This is clearest when we feel badly about our own, free, voluntary decisions exactly because we have different sets of preferences, acting at different levels of our own selves. We can, in short, dislike some of our own preferences. Yes, we are complex. And that is why we look for help—in others, in government, in God—to make some decisions we feel we might not make well by ourselves.

Another unrelated reason regards the peculiar character of some goods, which are not a piece of cake, to be bought, then consumed and enjoyed. Some goods, however—and education is probably the best example—are anything but a piece of cake: their consumption demands hard work, it demands our time and effort before we can really enjoy them, and even while we are enjoying them. These are goods that, over and above their production cost, have a consumption cost.

This consumption cost can, in turn, be separated into two different components. On the one hand, our consumption of these goods—higher education, for example—requires an effort that, in turn, allows for our better enjoyment: we learn to learn, we acquire the taste, we get the knack of it. This component could be likened to our consumption investment, since it increases our ability to further consume, enjoy, and benefit from these goods. On the other hand, these goods do require effort each time we consume them; past investments are not enough. If my enjoyment depends on my performing this extra effort, but I do not know or understand that enjoyment until I do make the effort, then my preferences would be unable to tell me how much I really like that particular good. Should I read *Ulysses*? Should I spend a hundred dollars and four or five hours for a Wagnerian opera? For both reasons, education is a typical merit good: I don't know how good it is for me, or I only know after I make the effort. Then why would I make the effort in the first place? Prices do not reflect such costs, nor can they reflect the potential benefits.

According to economics literature, merit goods are those whose consumption cost detracts from the potential benefits. Therefore, we tend to subsidize these goods—like arts and culture—or even to make their consumption compulsory. Higher education fits perfectly in this category: it is certainly not a piece of cake. Without its public provision, without incentives, or without a subsidy, individual decisions would certainly mean that we would study less than what we would have wanted, had we known.

This problem might be further compounded if what the labor market asks for is signals rather than real education. Then, I will try to buy signals, without the cost of consuming real education: thus, this market failure creates markets for "fake" education.

HIGHER EDUCATION DOES NOT COME CHEAP

Finally, we come to the problem of the budget constraint confronted by individual consumers when trying to make those choices that would maximize their satisfaction, utility, or well-being. Aside from the many problems already mentioned, the fact is that markets do not react to what people actually need or want, but to what they *demand*, that is, to those needs or wants they are really willing and capable of paying for. But, of course, this means that market demand will be as much influenced by people's share of total wealth.

This might not be a problem—or, at least, not a dramatic problem —if the existing distribution of wealth were such that everybody were able to satisfy their most important needs and their most pressing desires and where income inequalities only allowed some people to satisfy some other, more trivial, or luxury, needs or wishes. That, however, is not the case in Latin America, which has the dubious merit of being the most unequal region in the world.

When income and wealth distribution are so unequal that large proportions of the population do not have access—they cannot demand— some of the basic elements for a decent quality of life, when they cannot have adequate sanitation and basic health services, when they cannot have access to a good and complete education, when they cannot live in a decent house and a safe neighborhood, then these inequalities result in a significantly unequal distribution of opportunities and, in turn, in an arrested development process. It is probably for this reason, the lack of access to basic social goods and services, that it has been fashionable to refer to higher education as some sort of luxury in Latin American countries, and to consider that spending public resources in subsidizing higher education was something that would further increase existing inequalities. This argument, however well intentioned, is wrong and damaging, as it loses sight of the dynamics of development.

Higher education is expensive. But if higher education is some sort of merit good with some of its benefits hidden behind its consumption costs; if these consumption costs are higher for those whose incomes and living conditions are lower; if many of higher education's benefits are social or collective, not just individual; and if private individual benefits from higher education tend to be rather long-term benefits, then there is every reason to believe that youngsters from middle- and lower-income families would be significantly discouraged from going from basic into tertiary or higher education. This is much more so since that decision would also carry a significant opportunity cost in terms of forgone short-term incomes, which, again, are more important the lower the present family income. If to all this we were to add the much higher cost or price of an increasingly private higher education, then we would be truly surrendering one of the most successful mechanisms for social mobility and, in so doing, we would also do a disservice to the consolidation of modern and effective democracies in Latin America.

Summing up, we can easily argue that knowledge—and higher education in particular—constitute what we could call *incommodious commodities*, or, as Karl Polanyi argued about labor, land, and capital, we could say that they constitute fictitious commodities. Even though they can be bought and sold as commodities in the market, they cannot be adequately produced or consumed like true commodities.

THE CHALLENGE AHEAD

Markets, competition, the profit motive, cannot fully, adequately, sufficiently, and efficiently deal with the allocation and utilization of resources required by society and its members with respect to such goods or activities as education and knowledge. Some aspects or parts of education and knowledge can be handled privately, through markets, even through profit-led firms, but others cannot. And even those partial aspects of higher education that sometimes can be separated and commodified, probably should remain inseparable from their public aspects.

Knowledge production and knowledge distribution and dissemination, for example, are two distinct and distinguishable functions of higher education, but it is not that clear that they can or should become fully separated. Knowledge distribution and dissemination subsidizes and stimulates knowledge production, but they also challenge the production of knowledge, by confronting it with other ideas and knowledge processes. The challenge, then, is how to balance these functions and perspectives, and that is a key challenge for universities. This is particularly problematic since knowledge does not and cannot exist in itself, but only embodied, bundled, or packaged in other social products:

things, institutions, and people. But these other social products, even if they act as vehicles of knowledge, are also, at the same time, many different things: they are not just objectified knowledge, but knowledge-laden objects or processes, institutions, or people.

Of course, there is space for the market and for private higher education. But only insofar as these do not substitute for higher public education, insofar as they do not steal resources from those aspects of higher education that, so far, have been packaged together with the more self-oriented, vocational, marketable aspects of it. The problem is how they coexist, how they interact so that they do not undercut each other and, especially, so that private education and the commodification of academic life do not absorb and undermine the essential public aspects of education. They can coexist, but they are not good substitutes: private education can very well crowd out public education. And this is a question of power. It is power that lurks behind market signals. The prices that globalization is increasingly transforming into the only right prices are the only acceptable measure of opportunity costs. But this is not just a question of efficiency, it is a question of democracy and a question of justice.

REFERENCES

David, Paul. (2002, February). "Economic Fundamentals of the Knowledge Society." SIEPR Discussion Paper No. 01-14. Stanford Institute for Economic Policy Research, 19.

Interamerican Development Bank. (1997). *Higher Education in Latin America and the Caribbean: Strategy Document.* Washington, D.C.: Interamerican Development Bank.

Sachs, Jeffrey, and Joaquín Vial. (2002). "Can Latin America Compete?" In *Latin American Competitiveness Report 2000–2002.* World Economic Forum.

Salmi, Jamil (2000). "Tertiary Education in the Twenty First Century: Challenges and Opportunities." LCSHD Paper Series No. 62. The World Bank, Latin America and the Caribbean Regional Office, Human Development Department, 4–6.

Task Force on Higher Education and Society. (2000). *Higher Education in Developing Countries: Peril and Promise.* Washington, D.C.: World Bank and UNESCO.

World Bank. (1989): *Costa Rica: Public Sector Expenditure Review,* Washington, D.C.: World Bank.

———. (1991). *World Development Report: 1990.* Washington, D.C.: World Bank.

———. (1999): *World Development Report 1998–1999: Knowledge for Development.* Washington, D.C.: World Bank.

CHAPTER 12

Corporate, Technological, Epistemic, and Democratic Challenges: Mapping the Political Economy of University Futures

Sohail Inayatullah

CHANGING STUDENT EXPECTATIONS (access to global systems of knowledge, including transparency and international accreditation), the Internet (virtual education; moving from campus-centered to person-centered, and far more customized, individually tailored education), global corporatization (reduced state funding for universities and the development of a market culture on campuses), and transformed content (multicultural education) are current trends that will dramatically influence all the world's universities. Indeed, the potential for dramatic transformation is so great that in the next fifteen to twenty years, it is far from certain that universities as currently constituted—campus-based, state-funded, and local student-oriented—will exist. Certainly, the current model for the university will cease to be the hegemonic one.

Of course, rich universities like Harvard will be able to continue without too much challenge, but the state-supported university will be challenged. Asian nations, where education is defined by the dictates of the Ministry of Education, will also face the efficiency-oriented, privatization forces of globalization. Their command and control structure will be challenged by globalization—market pressures, technological innovations, and the brain gain (that is, from graduates returning home from the United States and England).

CORPORATIZATION

Corporatization, the entrance of huge multinational players into the educational market, will create far more competition than traditional universities are prepared for. *The Economist* estimates that total spending on education in the United States in 2001 was $800 billion. By 2003, the private capital invested will total $10 billion, just for the virtual higher education market and $11 billion in the private sector serving the corporate market. Indeed, John Chambers, CEO of Cisco Systems, calls online education "the killer application of the internet." Jeanne Meister, president of Corporate University Xchange (CUX), expects that by 2010 there will be more corporate universities in the United States than traditional ones. They are and will continue to challenge the academy's monopolization of accreditation. Globalization thus provides the structure and the Net the vehicle. Pearson, a large British media group that owns 50 percent of *The Economist*, is betting its future on it, hoping that it can provide the online material for the two million people seeking a degree online annually. Motorola, Accenture, Cisco, and McDonald's as well as News Corporation all seek to become respectable universities. Cisco Networking Academies have trained 135,000 students in ninety-four countries. Motorola has a new division called Motorola Learning and Certification that resells educational programs. Accenture has purchased a former college campus and spends 6.5 percent of its revenues on educating employees.

Of course, much of this is not new. Corporate education has always been big. What is new is that corporate universities seek to enter markets traditionally monopolized by academics. And, given pressures on corporations to be more inclusive of minorities, to be more multicultural and more triple-bottom-line-oriented (prosperity, planet, people), it may be that corporate universities are embracing diversity at a quicker pace than traditional universities.

Clearly, when billion-dollar corporations want to enter the market —a rapidly growing market, especially with the aging of the population and with national barriers to education slowly breaking down—the challenge to the traditional university becomes dramatic—indeed, mission-, if not life-threatening. With an expanding market of hundreds of millions of learners, money will follow future money. Money will transform education, or, at the very least, dominate the discourse concerning which values are most important—the student, the academic, the administrator, the community, or corporate interests.

For community education and for communities traditionally tied to a local regional university and seeking economic vitality, the future will become far more daunting. As universities globalize, corporatize, and virtualize—moving services to low-cost areas—their place-bound identity will increasingly disappear. This is a far cry from the classical European, Islamic, or Indic university, concerned mostly with moral education.

In Bologna in the twelfth century, the university was student-run. If the professor was late, he was fined by students. Some teachers were even forced to leave the city. Paradoxically, corporatization with its customer-first ideology may return us to a student-run university. The Academy beware!

UNIVERSITY DIMENSIONS

At one time the university was student-run. We know that it is no longer so; if anything it is administration-run. Who will run it in the future? To understand this we need to explore the different dimensions of the university. The university is partly about social control, but it is also about baby-sitting. What to do with young people? How do we keep them out of trouble? The other dimension is national development. We have schools to convince everyone that we're a good people, that we have the best system. Each nation engages in social control. It uses education to give legitimacy to the nation-state, to make good patriots. We also have small community colleges, where the goal is to go to a small college to get practical education and then a real job after graduation.

Thus, the classical view of knowledge for the cultivation of the mind has been supplanted by the industrial model. And, as you might expect, the big growth in jobs in the university are in the area of the bureaucracy. Whereas tenure is being eliminated in favor of part-time employment throughout the world, the university administration continues to expand.

Of course, the nature of administration is changing as well: it is being forced to become far more student-friendly. Because government subsidies of education have been reduced, it is students who pay academic and administrative wages. Fees provide the backbone of the private university. Customer satisfaction and student retention become far more important than in the traditional state-subsidized university. As Flora Chang of Tamkang University notes, "Student satisfaction through customer surveys, student retention data, and alumni loyalty are crucial factors" for future success.

One key question will be: what can be automated? Who can be replaced by the Internet and web education? Perhaps both faculty and administration will be in trouble. This is the debate: too many administrators or too many professors? A third perspective is a market perspective: there are not enough students and thus each university believes it must globalize and attract students from all over the world to attend their physical campus as well as take courses from their virtual campuses. However, generally, most universities still think of students in narrow ways as young people or as students from one's own nation. But with the aging population and with the Internet (with bandwidth likely to keep on increasing), one's paying students can be from anywhere.

The other classical view of the university—as a shared culture focused on scholarship and science—is academic-led, but that too has been challenged. And of course the dot.com model even challenges what the university should look like. Should it be place-bound or virtual? Should it be based on a hierarchical model or a networked model?

For academics, the biggest challenge is the university as a corporation. And we know that in the United States corporate funding for the university increased from $850 million in 1985 to $4.25 billion in less than a decade. In the past twenty years it has increased by eight times. It is likely that East Asian nations will follow this pattern. So far it is the state that has exclusively engaged in education. However, globalization is opening up this space in East Asia, with foreign and local education suppliers seeking to reduce the control of the Ministry of Education.

Thus, the big money is coming from corporations and the funding from the government is gradually being reduced as per the dictates of the globalization model. While most presidents of the university would prefer a different model, they have no choice. Education is increasingly becoming an economic good. Humanities departments are being downsized throughout the world since their contribution to jobs is not direct. Unfortunately, forgotten is their indirect contribution, that of creating smart, multilingual, multicultural individuals—what some call social capital. In East Asia, however, language remains central to understanding other cultures, training civil servants, and opening up new markets.

Corporatization does have some quite insidious effects. First, information is no longer free, as corporations use it for profit making. A survey of 210 life-science companies in 1994 found that 58 percent of those sponsoring academic research required delays of more than six months before publication. The content of science itself changes as the funding increases. In a 1996 study published in the *Annals of Internal Medicine*, 98 percent of papers based on industry-sponsored research reflected favorably on the drugs being examined as compared with 79 percent based on research not funded by the industry. What accounts for that 19 percent variation? And how will the public then see the university? As with the medical system, once patients believe that doctors are beholden to certain drug companies or web sites they are less likely to trust them. This holds true for university research as well.

But there is another side to globalization. In 1989 in the United States, 364 new start-up companies were licensed on the basis of an academic invention. University technology transfer activities generated $34 billion in the United States, supporting 280,000 jobs.

The university is becoming more global and also producing incredible wealth. So there are two sides to globalization.

VIRTUALIZATION: THE DOT.COM REVOLUTION

The dot.com revolution has mixed reviews. For example, at one Australian university, overnight, the prefix for academic e-mails was changed from edu.au to .com. The academics asked why this occurred. While some were upset that this happened without consultation, others were concerned that the moral basis of the university was being transformed, and they were deeply troubled by this corporatization. The administration responded that the university could no longer compete globally as an @.edu.au institution and instead had to become a dot.com. Eventually the university went back to edu.au as the pressure from academics was too great. With the dot.com world having lost its shine, perhaps it was a wise move.

But the university administration could see the handwriting on the wall. The traditional model of the classical liberal arts state-subsidized university was ending, and a new model was emerging. The mistake they made was not engaging in dialogue with others, not living the dot.com network model but instead using the power-based secrecy model of the industrial era.

The other problem that administrations have not yet begun to see is that much of middle management can and is likely to be eliminated. The emerging knowledge economy—via the Net and future artificial intelligence systems—will lead to disintermediation. With a good information system, you don't need all the secretaries, the clerks, or those higher up the ladder. Of course, the politics of firing or retraining is a different matter and central to how the future university and overall world economy is to be organized.

Surveys at Tamkang University, Taiwan, found that professors and administrators were enthusiastic about virtualization. Professors believed it would free their time spent at the university, and increase interaction with colleagues and students, and administrators saw the cost savings. Deans, however, saw it eroding their power base—control of the faculty—and students saw it taking away from what they valued most: face-to-face (not face-to-blur, huge classes) education. They desired a degree of broadband but not virtual classes.

It appears that what constitutes education is changing from being academy-focused to being customer/student-focused, from being campus-focused to being virtual, from being state-subsidized to being corporate-funded. Over time, and certainly with fits and starts, the university may become a process; it may no longer be simply a place, with fixed 9–5 work patterns and fixed schedules for classes. It may become a network.

MULTICULTURAL REALITIES

But there is a deeper possibility of change with regard to the epistemic bases of knowledge, of content, of what is taught, of how it is taught and who teaches—essentially, this is the multicultural turn. In its tokenistic form, multiculturalism became a government fad of the past decade in postindustrial societies, its most controversial feature being its excesses of political correctness. In its deeper nature it is about inclusiveness. At heart, argues Ashis Nandy (2000), multiculturalism is about dissent, about contesting the categories of knowledge that modernity has given us. And even with multiculturalism, often criticized and co-opted, and used strategically to ensure representation, still the future is likely to be more and more about an ethics of inclusion instead of a politics of exclusion. Of course, the struggle will be long and hard, and more often than not, instead of new curriculum, there will be just more special departments of the Other.

Deep multiculturalism challenges what is taught, how it is taught, the knowledge categories used to teach, and the way departments enclose the Other. It provides a worldview in which to create new models of learning and new universities that better capture the many ways students know the world. As futures researcher Paul Wildman (1998) reminds us, this can extend to concepts such as "multiversities" and even "subversities" that encourage participation from scholars and students who dwell at the periphery of knowledge. In this form, multiculturalism goes beyond merely inclusion of "other" ethnicities, to a questioning of the whole paradigm of Western scientific rationalism on which centuries of university traditions are founded. In this perspective, multiple ways of knowing including spiritual or consciousness models of self, in which, as James Grant (2000) for the Maharishi University of Management and Marcus Bussey (2000) of the Ananda Marga Gurukul University assert, the main driver in transforming universities of the next century will be an explosion of inner enlightenment, a new age of higher consciousness is about to begin, at three levels. The first is inclusion of others, in terms of who gains admission into universities, and who teaches, ensuring that those on the periphery gain entrance. A second level is less concerned with quantifiable representation and more with inclusion of others' ways of knowing—expanding the canon of what constitutes knowledge as well as how knowledge is realized. A third level is what Indian philosopher P. R. Sarkar calls the liberation of the intellect, an education that transcends the limitation of geographical sentiments, religious sentiments, race-based sentiments, and even humanism, moving toward a planetary spiritual consciousness and touching upon the spiritual.

In terms of curriculum and disciplinary boundaries, multiculturalism challenges the notion that only one science exists. Western science, instead of being seen as a quest for truth, is considered to be one way of knowing among many. Alternative sciences include feminist science, Tantric science, and Islamic science. They are still engaged in empirical and verifiable research, but the questions asked and the ethical framework are different. Generally, this type of research is more concerned with indigenous problems and with local concerns. It is less violent to nature and "subjects" and more concerned with integrated self and other, mind and body, intellect and intuition.

What's happening throughout universities is that scholars are contesting the content of scholarship. How, for example, is history taught? Are all civilizations included, or are only Western thinkers? Are only Western notions of discovery and culture honored?

Many years ago, I gave a lecture at an Australian university and questioned how they were teaching their main course on world history. I noted that the grand thinkers from Islamic, Sinic, and Indian civilizations were not included. Why? And when other civilizations were briefly mentioned, they were written as threats to the West or as barbarians. Women and nature were absent. I argued that this creates a view of history that is not only inaccurate but violent since other cultures see themselves through these hegemonic eyes. Instead of creating an inclusive history of humanity's struggle, a history of one particular civilization becomes valorized.

While it is unlikely that the professor who teaches this course will change, students have changed. They want multiple global perspectives. They understand that they need to learn about other cultures from those cultures' perspectives. Globalization in the form of changing immigration patterns is moving the Organization for Economic Corporation and Development (OECD) nations by necessity toward better representation, irrespective of attacks on multiculturalism as "political correctness."

The multicultural challenge to the traditional university can be defined as below:

- challenge to the Western canon
- challenge to intellect as the only way of knowing
- challenge to the divorce of the academic from body and spirit—challenge to egghead vision of self/other
- challenge to the modernist classification of knowledge
- challenge to traditional science (feminist, Islamic, postnormal, Indian)
- challenges to pedagogy, curriculum as well as evaluation

We are already seeing the rise of multiculturalism in OECD nations. For example, at one conference in Boston, when participants were asked to list the five American authors they believed most necessary for a quality education, they placed Toni Morrison second and Maya Angelou third. Others on the top ten list included Malcolm X and James Baldwin. The first was Mark Twain.

The multicultural perspective challenges the foundation of knowledge as well. Multicultural education is about creating structures and processes that allow for the expression of the many civilizations, communities, and individuals that we are. Multicultural education contests the value neutrality of current institutions such as the library. For example, merely including texts from other civilizations does not constitute a multicultural library. Ensuring that the contents of texts are not ethnocentric is an important step, but this does not begin to problematize the definitional categories used in conventional libraries. For example, in the multicultural perspective, we need to ask what a library would look like if it used the knowledge paradigms of other civilizations. How would knowledge be rearranged? What would the library floors look like? In Hawaiian culture, for example, there might be floors for the gods, for the *aina* and genealogy. In Tantra, empirical science would exist alongside intuitional science. Floor and shelf space would privilege the superconscious and unconscious layers of reality instead of focusing only on empirical levels of the real. In Islam, since knowledge is considered *tawhidic* (based on the unity of God), philosophy, science, and religion would no longer occupy the discrete spaces they currently do. Of course, the spatiality of "floors" must also be deconstructed. Information systems from other civilizations might not privilege bookknowledge, focusing instead on storytelling and dreamtime as well as wisdom received from elders/ancestors (as in Australian Aboriginal) and perhaps even "angels" (either metaphorically or ontologically).

A multicultural library might look like the World Wide Web but include other alternative ways of knowing and being. Most certainly knowledge from different civilizations in this alternative vision of the "library" would not be relegated to a minor site or constituted as an exotic field of inquiry such as Asian, ethnic, or feminist studies, as are the practices of current libraries. The homogeneity of the library as an organizing information system must be reconstructed if we are to begin to develop the conceptual framework of multicultural education.

Thus, not only is the structure of the university changing, that is, virtualization, but the content is being transformed as well. Now what does this mean in terms of policy prescriptions? If you want your university to have a bright future, you have to understand the changing nature of the student—changing demographics (older, more females) and changing expectations (more multicultural). Generally, while getting a job will always be important, the equation has changed to planet, prosperity, and people, with a strong concern for the environment, for wealth creation, and for engaging with others and other cultures. For academics, the multicultural is also about the changing role of the professor. The university becomes not just a site of gaining knowledge, but a place for experiencing other dimensions of reality, at the very least, for balancing body, mind, and spirit.

DEMOCRATIZING THE FEUDAL MIND

The role of academics is changing as well. Generally, the hardest notion for senior professors to swallow is the democratization of the university. We want democracy for government, but we don't want democracy for universities.

The university remains feudal. For example, while the economy in East Asian nations is transformed, the feudal mind has not changed. This is the grand question for East Asian nations: how to create a culture of innovation; how to go to the next level of economic development; instead of copying, how to create. To create an innovative learning organization, you can't have a culture of fear. This means real democracy in details like what type of seating arrangement should be allowed in the classroom. Can students challenge professors? Can junior professors challenge senior academics without fear of reprisal? Innovation comes from questioning. Along with a learning organization, however, is the notion of a healing organization. By merely focusing on learning we forget that much of our life is spent focused on relationships—with our inner self, with colleagues, with nature, with the cosmos, and with the university itself.

In British systems, the university structure is profoundly feudal. A strong distinction is made between the professor and the lecturer. Indeed, the professor is high on top of the pyramid with others way below (and the president of the university residing on the mountaintop).

Can we democratize the university? Of course, it is difficult to do this, as few of us like being challenged. We all have our view of reality, our favorite models, and we believe we are correct. But creating a learning organization means challenging basic structures and finding new ways to create knowledge and wealth. It doesn't mean always going to the president for solutions. Transforming the feudal university is very difficult. However, I am not discounting the importance of respect for leadership, discipline, and hard work—challenging authority doesn't mean being rude, it means contesting the foundations of how we go about creating a good society.

As universities change their nature—reducing tenured positions and increasing teaching loads—the health of the institution becomes an issue. Sick institutions can emerge quite quickly, unless there is a focus on creating ways to learn and heal, to develop sustainable and transformative relationships.

However, democratization will not be easy, given the trends mentioned above. For the Asian academic, for example, the choices shrink daily. He or she can choose between the four big M's. The first M is the Ministry of Education. Choosing this career means funded research focused only on the Ministry's needs, and it means being dependent on government. When states go wrong, or punish dissent, as in Malaysia or Indonesia, or Pakistan and India, losing one's job and getting sent to prison are real possibilities. Textbooks are written with the other nation described as the enemy, as in India and Pakistan. The professor must teach these texts or lose his or her position. One Pakistani academic, for example, was jailed for giving a lecture on alternative futures that contested the notion of Pakistan as an eternal state.

The second choice is the Mullah, or the cleric. This is money not from the corporation or state but the Islamic worldview competing with the modern. In real terms this has meant soft and strong versions of Wahibism—the creation of International Islamic Universities with Saudi funds, as in Kuala Lumpur, Malaysia. Freedom of inquiry is problematic here as well, as boundaries of inquiry are legislated by the university's charter. Instead of spiritual pluralism what results is uncritical traditionalism.

If we combine the first two choices we get a mixture of religious hierarchy with feudal and national hierarchy, creating very little space for the academic. In the Indian context, this would be the Brahmin who goes to Oxford to study economics, joins the World Bank, and returns to Delhi to work with the Ministry of Economic Development.

The third M is Microsoft, focusing one's career on developing content for the new emerging universities. This is the quickly developing area of Net education. The costs for the academic here, too, are high— it is contract work, often involving a loss of face-to-face interaction, of collegial relationships, and of the academy with a moral mission. Volume and speed are likely to become more important than integrity and the inner life.

The final M is McDonaldization. This is the move to the convenience 7/11 university, the Australian model, with large student volume, in and out, with academics having heavy teaching loads. A professorship essentially becomes focused on gaining grants.

Leaving these M's is a possibility, depending on the nature of the state one lives in. However, the traditional imagination of the university is not a possibility. The route in the past fifty years was the escape to the Western university, but with these universities in trouble as well, this route seems blocked.

So far I have touched upon four trends—corporatization, virtualization, multiculturalism, and democratization—as well as the basic mission of the university. Given these trends and the mission, what are the possibilities for the university, and what are the possible structures?

POSSIBLE STRUCTURES

I see three possible structures. One is being a leading university, joining the world's elite, Harvard, Stanford, Oxford. The focus then is: "We are only going to get the best and the brightest students from around the world." But the challenge to this model comes from the dot.com world. The big money is unlikely to be in teaching but in content design. The issue is that once you put your name on CD ROMs and on Internet content, does that diminish your brand name and your exclusivity? If anyone can take an elite university's web course, is the university still elite? This is the issue of franchising. Should you focus on a small customer base that can pay a lot, or become like the University of Phoenix (the largest university in the United States, which offers no tenure and uses short courses as well as flexible delivery—a kind of just-in-time education)?

Large universities have two clear choices—to become an elite university or a low-cost producer with hundreds of millions of new students all over the world as potential purchasers. A third choice for the smaller university is the niche university, focused in a particular area of excellence (regional concerns, for example).

The challenge for the traditional university is new competition from global players: multimedia corporations, elite universities that are expanding and branding, and low-cost producers. These issues are already of concern in the United States, and soon they will be crucial in Asia as well. I see this in East Asian nations (and those colonized by England) since the state plays such a strong role in education. But eventually in five or ten years the competition will come here as well. All universities will find themselves in a global market.

However, a university can find ways to be all these structures, developing different campuses. One could be focused on lifelong learning. A second could be research-focused, linked to government and industry. A third could be elite-based, having student-friendly teacher-student faculty ratios. The Internet could link them all, or there could be a fourth virtual campus, an online university. In these worlds, what stands out is the loss of community building found in place-bound universities. However, as universities homogenize through globalization, communities may find niches.

SCENARIOS FOR THE FUTURE

The next question involves the probable scenarios for the future of the university. We use scenarios to reduce uncertainty. Scenarios are also important in that they also help us rethink the present—they give us a distance from today.

Earlier futures studies focused entirely on single point prediction. The field then moved to scenario planning, to alternative futures. But now it is moving to capacity development, with creating learning organizations where foresight is a continuous part of what the organization does.

Studies that examine corporations that have survived over a hundred years have found that the one key factor in explaining longevity was the capacity to tolerate ideas from the margins. Even for corporate universities, the capacity to tolerate dissent, indeed, to nurture different ideas or new ideas from the margins is crucial.

In terms of scenarios, the first one is the Star Alliance model. I borrow this term from the airlines, where the passenger is always taken care of; there is easy movement from one airline to the other. Everything is smooth. For the university, this would mean easy movement of student credits, faculty, and programs. A student could take one semester at Stanford, a second semester in Tamkang, and a third semester at Singapore National University. Professors could also change every semester. So it means a similar web of movement. Star Alliance works because customers are happy. The airlines are happy because they get brand loyalty. The student might say, "I know if I join this university, my credits are transferable. I could access the best professor. I could access the best knowledge in the world."

The weakness in this scenario is the proportioning of funds as well as the costs of movement to the local community, to community building, and to place itself.

The second scenario is what I call Virtual Touch. This vision of the future of the university combines the best of face-to-face pedagogy (human warmth, mentoring) with virtual pedagogy (instant, anywhere in the world, at your own time and speed). If it is just technology, then you get bored students, staring at a distant professor. But if it is just face-to-face, you don't get enough information. The universities who can combine both will do very well. Ultimately, that will mean wearable wireless computers. We already know that in Japan they use the wireless phone to dial up a web site to find out the latest movie, or weather forecast, or stock quote.

In ten years, it is going to be an age of wearable computers, so we can have a computer with us all the time. I can find out everything. I can test the minerals in the water, for example, to see if it is clean or not. This technology is almost developed now. Based on where my microphone was made (China, Taiwan, or the United Kingdom), I can just dial up to get product information. And this information will be linked to my values, and what type of world I want to see. Thus, I'll purchase products that are environmentally friendly, and from corporations that treat women well. And students can shop for a university course in the same way: is it well taught, what is the professor like, how much democracy is in the class, and what are the values of the university?

The third scenario: a university without walls—the entire world becomes a university. As Majid Tehranian (1996) writes: "If all goes well, the entire human society will become a university without walls and national boundaries." We don't need specific universities anymore since the university is everywhere, a true knowledge economy where humans constantly learn and use their knowledge to create processes that will lead to a better, fairer, richer, and happier world.

THE FUTURE OF THE PROFESSION

What is the role of the academic in this dramatically changing world? The first possibility is the traditional professor—this is the agent of authority, great in one field but not very knowledgeable about other fields. They may know physics but not complexity theory. They are useful in that they are brilliant in one area, but not so useful since they have a hard time adapting to change.

The second role is the professor as web content designer. While the current faculty is unlikely to engage in these activities, younger people, the so-called digital natives, will. For example, my children, eight and six, clearly see their future in the design of new digital technologies. Other young people as well see knowledge as quite different than we do. They see knowledge as interactive, multidisciplinary, and always changing. They want to be web designers and information designers. Whereas the old role of academics was to write books, the new role is that of creating new types of interactive content. And the content will likely be far more global and multicultural than we have so far seen. It appears that an entirely different world is being created.

If you design and teach a web-based course, then you need to focus on students and use action learning methods. Action learning means that the content of the course is developed with the students' learning needs in mind. While professors may have certain authoritative knowledge, their role is more of a mentor and the knowledge navigator to help students develop their potential based on the categories they believe are important.

This is good news for academics who retain their positions. Most of the professors I speak with would prefer less teaching—information transmission—and more communication. The mentoring role is far more rewarding personally. The old method has been to give a long lecture. The new way of thinking is to tell the students to access the web and find out. Afterward there can be a discussion. The professor then has to learn how to listen to students' needs and not just to lecture to them. What is unique about our era is that we now have the technology to do this. Do we have the political will and the wisdom?

COMMUNITY AND THE UNIVERSITY

What do these trends mean for the university's relationship with community? Clearly it is under threat. It is global corporatization or spaceless time that is far more important than local and immediate time. Community, however, can be an antidote to many of the threats. It could unite academics, making them fall back on each other to question the future of the university. On a more instrumental note, regional universities, or universities specifically designed and developed for a locale, are likely to become more, not less, important as the trends of globalization, virtualization, multiculturalism, and democratization continue. Certainly, democracy needs the notion of community, and multiculturalism is essentially about increasing community building and levels of inclusion.

Possibilities for community spaces include:

1. Alliance with other communities—like-minded learning communities. This is a novel challenge, and means moving outside the national arena to define and search for other communities in similar situations. Sister cities is a dimension of this, but far more important is the real contact, and not photo opportunities.
2. Alliance with the corporate world—attract businesses to survive.
3. Communities aligning with social movements, that is, creating moral spaces. Prosperity is an issue here. However, a strong local community can ensure that basic needs are met, even if globalized wealth does not raise everyone's wealth (at least local strength will ensure that globalization does not reduce local wealth).
4. Communities themselves transforming. Their only hope is to create global-local spaces since academics are now becoming virtual and global. Only a program that has place-bound local dimensions with that of global mobility can prosper.

DISSENTING FUTURES

What makes the role of the academic unique is that he or she can challenge authority. When the system becomes too capitalistic, this can be questioned. If it is too religious, this too can be countered. All the excesses of the system can be challenged. And who can do this? Those who work for the government can't since they fear losing their jobs. Those belonging to the church, temple, or mosque can't since they are ideologically bound. And the problem with globalization lies in making efficiency the only criterion, so that moral space is lost. As academics we should never lose sight of our responsibility to create new futures, to inspire students, to ask what-if questions, to think the unthinkable, to go outside current parameters of knowledge. This is our responsibility to current and future generations.

REFERENCES

Bussey, Marcus. (2000). "Homo Tantricus: Tantra as an Episteme for Future Generations." In Inayatullah and Gidley, *The University in Transformation*. (Westport, Conn.: Bergin and Garvey.

The Economist. (2001, February 17). "Online Education: Lessons of a Virtual Timetable," 71–75.

Glazer, Nathan. (1997). *We Are All Multiculturalists Now*. Cambridge, Mass.: Harvard University Press.

Grant, James. (2000). "Consciousness-based Education: A Future of Higher Education in the New Millennium." In Inayatullah and Gidley, *The University in Transition*.

Inayatullah, Sohail. (1996). "The Multicultural Challenge to the Future of Knowledge." *Periodica Islamica*, *6*(1), 35–40.

Inayatullah, Sohail, and Jennifer Gidley (eds.). (2000). *The University in Transformation: Global Perspectives on the Futures of the University*. Westport, Conn.: Bergin and Garvey.

Nandy, Ashis. (2000). "Recovery of Indigenous Knowledge and Dissenting Futures of the University." In Inayatullah and Gidley, *The University in Transition*.

Press, Eyal, and Jennifer Washburn. (2000). "The Kept University." *The Atlantic Monthly*, 39–54.

Tehranian, Majid. (1996). "The End of the University." *Information Society*, *12*(4), 444–446.

Wildman, P. (1998). "From the Monophonic University to Polyphonic Multiversities." *Futures*, *30*(7), 625–635.

Wiseman, L. (1991). "The University President: Academic Leadership in an Era of Fund Raising and Legislative Affairs." In *Managing Institutions of Higher Education into the Twenty-First Century*, ed. R. Sims and S. Sims. Westport, Conn.: Greenwood.

PART V

THE FUTURE OF
HIGHER EDUCATION

INTRODUCTION

THE TWO ESSAYS that conclude our volume offer comprehensive and thoughtful overviews of our present situation, globally, nationally, and locally, and each makes arguments regarding possible futures for higher education in a globalizing world. But as we have noted before, the understanding of globalization powerfully influences how they see the various pieces fitting together.

Tom Abeles is surely the most enthusiastic of the contributors to this volume regarding the role of the new technologies in what he sees as the emergence of "a transformed university that has been struggling to become visible for over a half century." He begins with a brief "history," and while it is clear that he believes in the values of a "liberal education" both morally and practically, he also suggests that the *practices* of institutions of higher education, especially the modularization of the curriculum (as lamented by Karelis), have made even "just-in-case" knowledge amenable to delivery via the Internet. "Complete course packages" providing didactic materials, visuals, faculty support materials, and even online discussion and independent support represent but the beginnings of this technological transformation. As part of this, "specialized research efforts and narrowly focused academic journals" promote "extended webs" made easy with current and rapidly developing new technologies. With "cyber natives" who must be lifelong learners seeking the requisite short-term "knowledge," "time-based learning" and the inherited modes of assessment and credentialing are also put in question. Abeles suggests that what will emerge is now only vaguely in place, but he shows no signs of despair, suggesting also that there is no place for faculty nostalgia. On the other hand, Abeles would seem to be in considerable disagreement with the several prognoses of Delanty.

Delanty challenges both the nostalgic defense of the "traditional" conception of the university and the prediction of its imminent demise, propelled by the "allegedly global age of informational capitalism." For him, "globalization in fact offers the university the possibility of fulfilling what is perhaps its key role, namely, to provide institutional spaces where cognitive models for society to learn can emerge." He roots his analysis in terms of "kinds" of knowledge and in a historical understanding of the university as "a key institution of modernity" and "the site where knowledge, culture, and society interconnect." He argues that "from the 1960s on, the political project of modernity entered the university at about the same time that modernity entered a new phase" and "with this came a more critical and transformative kind of knowledge that could not be contained in either the practical or theoretical structures." Thus, while he affirms that the university is in transition as a result of global forces adumbrated in the essays of this volume, he also notes (agreeing with Wagner) that these processes are not unilinear and the university is both many-sided and "resilient." Hence, there is the chance for the university to evolve a new identity in the global age. He concludes, "The university cannot enlighten society as the Humboldtian and Kantian model of the university assumed nor can it reflect the power and prestige of the nation-state and the aspirations of the professions," but "in the knowledge society," it can provide the structures for public debate between expert and lay cultures." Whether indeed the opportunity will be grasped remains to be seen.

CHAPTER 13

THE CHANGING CRAFT NATURE OF HIGHER EDUCATION: A STORY OF THE SELF-REORGANIZING UNIVERSITY

Tom P. Abeles

EVER SINCE the first scholars sat on the steps of the libraries in Alexandria selling their services as guides to the knowledge locked in the stacks, education has been a craft "business," often subsidized by the scholars themselves in order to pursue higher learning. Even the Greek schools had to operate on a cash flow model; each scholar had to market his unique skills to the larger public.

In just this manner, individuals and schools developed their own reputations for both the content and the quality of the work that they provided for their students and followers. As time progressed, individuals and communities found that they had certain intellectual needs that drove them to underwrite the creation of institutions and the hiring of scholars with specific skills and knowledge for both the founders' own needs and the needs of the community at large. This led to the creation of a number of different institutions, underwritten by both private parties and public monies.

Scholars often participated in the larger deliberations surrounding the purpose and direction of these institutions and the roles and responsibilities of the faculty. During this deliberation, several transformations occurred. First, the scholars gained more control over the direction of activities at the institutions. Like the priests in the temple, the faculty became interpreters of what was to be learned; those who underwrote the costs deferred control over what might be deemed worthy of extracting from an academic experience.

The second shift came when it was seen as important to establish standards for institutions and the individual faculty as postsecondary education became ubiquitous. At this point the faculty at various institutions became bodies that certified within and across institutions. This became even more ingrained once the idea of research became a critical part of the academic institution and the results were published in peer-reviewed journals.

Regardless of the reasons, postsecondary institutions were seen to be gateways to participation in that part of society that made decisions and provided the individuals who would enter political office; more important, they appeared to create the gateway to economic success. While there were differing agendas among public and private institutions, the bottom line to aspirants was deemed to be the fiscal bottom line. Those who graduated from certain institutions had opportunities, often unique to those institutions, with regards to political, social, or religious influence, and economic power. And, by having established its hegemony as the center for public intellectuals, the university maintained its right and claimed the privilege of determining what constituted critical core knowledge in order to obtain an academic degree.

But slowly the system began to develop some fatal cracks. The success of science and technology forced society to recognize the need for continuing education. No longer was or is a high school diploma sufficient to participate fully in the wealth of society. The extension of study into a specialized postsecondary institution becomes, almost, the base standard, whether this is a vocational institution or a traditional four-year college or university. The success also seems to require that this path provide a graduate with some definable skill, often in a science or technology arena.

Also, as society demands a postsecondary experience for gaining economic status, more individuals are becoming sensitive to the costs, whether borne totally or in part by those seeking the experience or whether borne by the public at large. With increasing concern about the cost recovery of such an investment, the short-lived hegemony of the faculty lies broken.

Like the early visitors at the gates to the libraries of Alexandria, seekers are again asking for knowledge that they deem important; but they are also questioning the costs that are being incurred in the acquisition of this experience. With research playing an increasing role in The Academy and where this knowledge does not always come friction free, serious questions are also arising about both extant and evolving knowledge and how this impacts on the institution as well as those seeking access to knowledge.

Here it is worth emphasizing two points. First, K–12 education in general is considered, like food, clothing, and shelter, to be a commodity, part of a balanced economic armamentarium. Thus, as the system requires a rise in intellectual nutrients, the postsecondary experience is being perceived in the same light. Thus, cost becomes an issue. Second, the intangibles of a college experience, while recognized, are weighted more like the choices made when purchasing an automobile—a standard model, which is reliable transportation, or one with luxury accessories. Like the car in the United States, postsecondary education is becoming essential; the decision on how or what to acquire is being made in almost the same manner. In fact, the choice of an institution, by a potential student, can be swayed more by the amenities, such as prestige or campus features, than by the basics of the educational curriculum.

Just-in-Case Knowledge

Liberal studies is the area that was once emphasized in the postsecondary arena. Most who went to a university would enter into a professional life and into a society that demanded broad intellectual knowledge and social skills that allowed them to participate in the world of wealth and influence. In studying the disenfranchised in the United States, Earl Shorris determined that these selfsame skills were, perhaps, more necessary for the "jobless" to function effectively in today's society than a more applied curriculum. Robert Bates Graber (1995) has noted in his *Valuing Useless Knowledge* that liberal studies was an area that parents did not want as a major for their children. Yet, in the end, he suggests that liberal studies may be the last hope for a humanity trying to save itself in a dissipative world.

In "more gentle times" universities were seen as fulfilling several functions within society. Among these were the training for professions and providing sets of knowledge that would allow an individual to function within the larger society, or within a segment of the larger society. Much of this latter knowledge appeared under the rubric of liberal studies or liberal arts and sciences. These were perceived to be knowledge sets that would be available to the individual under a variety of situations either in a professional position or within a particular social setting. This knowledge was expected of an "educated" individual.

In order to provide some balance, universities created options where students did not have to master all of these liberal studies skills but could pick an appropriate number of courses from selected areas. Thus, individuals would be certified as having attained a liberal education, though not all students would have picked the same combination of courses from each area. Similarly, English skills were considered a core requirement for all students. Disciplines such as engineering would focus courses specifically on the needs of their students, but the same courses would meet institutional graduation requirements.

While these restructurings were happening within The Academy, the world outside of the ivy-covered walls was also changing. Employers started raising the bar so that a basic entry-level degree started moving from K–12 to K–16. College became a prerequisite as opposed to an optional path for those who would enter what once was an almost hereditary segment of society. The professions became open to all who graduated from college. Additionally, the professions started adding more requirements for their undergraduate certification, forcing shrinkage of the portion of a degree that could be required or could be optioned for liberal studies.

Liberal studies requirements became more difficult to rationalize in the face of increasing demands being made by more technical programs, including the preprofessional programs such as medicine and law as well as those programs focused on sending students on toward Ph.D.'s and other advanced degrees. A college degree became commodified. Students expected that their investment in an advanced degree would allow them to acquire a skill set that gave them access to that segment of society that was separated by both wealth and social status. The latter could be "acquired."

The other factor that has not been fully assessed is that most students, directly or indirectly, paid for grades 13–16 while the state paid for K–12. Thus, real concerns arose about the value received for the money invested, whether it involved the choice of institutions or the particular curriculum. For those who were focused on the professions, liberal studies became, not a set of value-added courses, but requirements that had to be fulfilled, potentially limiting options more directly devoted to the particular arena of the degree focus.

Practical-minded students, particularly as information age technologies became prevalent in the university, began to notice an interesting set of facts. First, the modularization of courses often decoupled the courses from each other. Not only was the previous course not necessary for subsequent courses, but also the connection with the larger academic program often seemed to be missing. In other words, the courses existed in isolation and thus the knowledge that was supposed to be mastered moved from a status of being required in the general scheme to just being required to obtain certification in that singular module. The knowledge became "just-in-case."

In fact, this realization sat well with all the lessons that The Academy taught about using the library and other resources. If, indeed, such knowledge were needed in the future, then it could easily be accessed through the card catalogue, or, today, through one of the many powerful search and meta-search engines on the Internet. Technical knowledge could be accessed when needed and liberal knowledge lost its imperative.

Second, with modularization, course content needing to be mastered could also be compartmentalized, stored in short-term memory, and discarded, to be recovered when needed, if ever needed. In other words, course credits could be obtained like trading stamps. Once acquired, they could be accumulated for the certification needed for the degree. Content stored in short-term memory could be purged and new materials stored so that the next module could be acquired.

Finally, as the professions and job qualifications rose in the minds of the students, materials not directly focused on the particular program lost their hegemony, a fact we see in the recent shrinking of liberal studies programs in many academic institutions. It also became clear in many of the professional programs once students understood what was needed on a consistent basis and what became "just-in-case" knowledge.

Core knowledge is cumulative. Fail to get the basics in a foreign language, mathematics, and the sciences such as biology and chemistry and the foundation is hard-pressed to sustain what must be added to the intellectual structure. Most humanities courses, though, have fewer cumulative needs, particularly in a modular approach to obtaining a degree.

Few students expect to be on a quiz program where miscellaneous knowledge becomes critical. And once courses are passed, few expect to have to draw upon such knowledge beyond the class in which it was required for a grade. Interestingly enough, the corporate world seems to support this as they move to peer-to-peer community networking, where it becomes critical to build knowledge ecologies and shared personal networks to complement the powerful search strategies within the content realm.

Just-in-Time Knowledge

The cost per bit of information is getting cheaper; the cost for a useful bit of information is becoming more expensive. Students learn this very quickly when they try to figure out what information is critical to solve a particular problem or to pass a particular test or course. While academics believe in a systems approach to knowledge in general and their discipline in particular, students realize, quickly, that each compartmentalized unit called a class has packaged certain knowledge and, of that knowledge, only certain bits are needed to solve the puzzle to obtain the grade to pass the course.

What students understand, and what the faculty and institution are in denial regarding, is that students need courses or units to obtain a degree. Time and money often do not offer the luxury of straying much beyond the path toward the diploma. And thus the correct knowledge, in the right sequence in time and space, is the critical coin of the realm. Of course, industry also works on the same premise. The job has to be accomplished in an expedient, timely, and fiscally responsible manner.

Unfortunately, the current unit/credit model that provides for a degree encourages just-in-time knowledge rather than the broad, interdisciplinary approach that might serve as a better set of tools for solving problems down the line. The Oxbridge (Oxford/Cambridge) model, where courses were not dominant, offered a better path to what academics supposedly treasure. Yet, even in ritual-dominated England, the past is giving way to the course-based measure of student achievement. It works better for administrative needs.

While academics may wish for a broader-based curriculum for students, they feel the same pressure within their own specialized research. The need to "publish/perish" demands ever increasing specialization and narrowing of focus. This is true not only for the areas under study but also for the depth of knowledge that is discovered prior to dissemination of the findings. One starts to see the rapidly increasing amount of material in the intellectual literature.

Interestingly, most faculty will readily admit that they would not do very well in the examinations students applying to graduate schools are required to take. And, surprisingly, they also find that the specialized examinations for admission to candidacy for the doctorate within the discipline present more than a challenge.

Of even greater concern, and the subject of a future discussion, is that, in spite of these professional difficulties within disciplines, there appears little hesitancy on the part of some academics to cross the broad boundaries between the sciences and the humanities. The perceived gap between the Two Cultures as defined by C. P. Snow in the 1950s has given rise to more than intellectual skirmishes between these two communities. These intellectual altercations have often been looked at rather askance by members of The Academy and have done little to enhance the credibility of academics on the outside of the Ivory Tower.

THE DEMISE OF THE CRAFT INDUSTRY

At one time the university served as the repository of knowledge. The library housed collections that were unique or difficult to duplicate. Academics needed to assemble around scarce intellectual resources and students needed to travel to these campuses to learn from the scholars and to access these resources. Modern reproductive techniques, starting with movable type and evolving to electronic storage/delivery systems, have obviated the need for storage while the Internet has connected ever more specialized faculty with their peers, globally.

As faculty continue to create more specialized research efforts and narrowly focused academic journals, their collegial networks tend to extend across campuses and continents rather than developing locally with associates in the same department or on the same campus. Such extended webs are made easier with the growing sophistication of powerful search engines and the increasing availability of peer-to-peer software.

Today many departments have their fiscal resources spread thin as they carefully pick and choose among these specialized scholars to try to offer a spectrum of expertise while maintaining a critical cohort in selected areas. Some have chosen to create "visiting scholar" positions as an option for expanding knowledge presence in the form of a faculty position.

Broadband communication reduces the need of faculty movement to bring these experts to multiple campuses. Additionally, one might see the rise of the "independent scholar," one who wanders between campuses via cyberspace while not having a traditional campus home. The existence of "virtual universities" with only an administrative campus clearly shows the potential that can only expand as bandwidth increases and connectivity becomes ubiquitous.

The ubiquity of knowledge raises two major issues. The first, and most obvious, is the question of the purpose of an academic campus. With the exception of the need for specialized laboratories and studios, some of which are now becoming virtual, what is the purpose of a university campus? Or does the purpose become inverted where community, for example, is primary and academics become only one of many factors that drive the creation of a campus experience? Many institutions were created with more than basic scholarly pursuits in mind. Public universities also had larger purposes than the obtaining of intellectual knowledge useful in employment.

Such observations are causing changes in campus designs, such as apartments instead of dormitories and computer stations and coffeehouses in redesigned libraries. Yet, planners have been reluctant to rethink the design of a campus from the ground up. The preferred path is one that backs into the future and denies the transformative changes under way.

The second major issue arises because of the fact that nowhere is denial greater than among the faculty. In the United States the average percentage of adjuncts exceeds 40 percent. At the same time, some universities, often with the encouragement and participation of the private sector, are packaging their best courses so that they can be offered to other institutions as bandwidth and tools allow.

Most of these are faint simulacra of what can and will be done as the bandwidth increases and the "New Media" starts to approach the "holodeck" on the *Enterprise*. In fact, glimpses can be seen in the work of the British Open University (BOU), which produces broadcast quality courses, and the materials of such media producers as TV's Discovery Channel and the efforts of Disney studios, or some of the programs for K–12 students now available in a variety of packages. As the BOU has discovered, academic materials, prepared with a commercial eye, can be amortized over a number of venues. Additionally, as has been pointed out by several authors, the emerging generation of cyber savvy students will demand such quality when available over handcrafted, didactic presentations of potentially lesser intellectual value.

World-class experts are few and far between. Those who are scholars as well as classroom performers are scarce commodities. Producers of documentary films regularly use scholars as experts and, often, actors to portray scholars in order to create the most effective materials. Learning experiences, and life itself, can be considered to be those stories. And the "tweed jacketed scholar" may not communicate even his or her own ideas as effectively as those crafted by a skilled teller of stories. In a world that is broadband wired, educational experiences for large public markets are going to be packaged in the same manner as automobiles, from the Geo Metro to the Lexus. Academics, scholars, will not have to handcraft each experience like a Lamborghini or a Rolls Royce. Rather, as skilled and knowledgeable individuals, they will fulfill many of the roles now occupied by adjuncts, teaching assistants, and graduate students. In the end, the students will receive a higher-quality experience, whether in brick or click space.

Grades 13–16 will become more like K–12 as college seamlessly extends the secondary experience. Today one can obtain complete course packages in many disciplines, including the sciences. These provide didactic materials, visuals, faculty support materials, and even online discussion and independent support. For sciences, there are even virtual laboratories. And in the future, there will be laboratories where students can actually perform experiments from their desktops.

What this effectively does is to commodify the didactic portion of an academic experience. Of course, each of these experiences will vary in sophistication and thus there will be a spread in the pricing, similar to those we see in academia today, but more similar to the spread we find in other commodities, from clothing to automobiles. Thus, the role of the academic, like that of the campus, must be reinvented. Academia in virtual space will be different from what happens on a physical campus. One will then have to determine not only the value of various virtual experiences but also the cost/benefit ratio of an on-campus education.

It is clear, though, that some will wish to have a more traditional campus experience, one that could be re-created with the same skill that is seen on a visit to the hyper-reality of Disney World. An academic campus could be an experience, but one where there would be an infinite number of choices. And some of these could even be virtual, given technology's potential. The academic then becomes a "cast member" in the Disney sense of the world. Today the academic plays many roles on the campus stage and many more can be crafted by well-trained educators.

In industry, a large percentage of the training budget may be allocated to training the trainers. Teachers in K–12 are required to take methods classes, as are professional actors. Up to the present day, post-secondary faculty are not so required because of their subject matter expertise. With the need to master the presentation of course materials subsumed by professional producers, the scholar returns to the role of an actor in either brick or click space. The scholarly craft guild has been deconstructed and reformed around a new stage with a new set of roles to perform.

THE DECONSTRUCTION OF RESEARCH

Advanced training beyond K–16 has been the domain of the graduate schools. In major institutions, these are often separately administered and only certain academics are endorsed so that they can direct research and offer courses suitable for postgraduate study. As more faculty obtained advanced degrees, each had to define an academic niche to establish intellectual hegemony over an increasingly smaller body of knowledge.

Today, advanced search engines and an increasingly "semantic" web is reweaving these areas, allowing bridges to be built and scholars to draw from previously inaccessible materials separated by specialized journals, meta-data, and distance. The sword cuts both ways. It breaks down barriers to communication and community but also destroys the walls around intellectual specializations that allowed an academic to establish a unique and unassailable area of expertise.

Open source publishing today is also making materials, once obscured by cost of access, available to a larger public and more readily translated into materials for use in the K–16 learning arena, increasing access to "just-in-time" knowledge in the classroom and the larger community outside of The Academy. This open access coupled with reduced funding for basic research in all arenas puts considerable pressure on the academic community to selectively choose areas of research that will be of import to a wider audience. It will also force the community into carefully weighing how it represents its areas of specialization.

With the ability to communicate and to collaborate at great distance, research groups are no longer limited by the need to be in the same physical space, with exceptions. This opportunity coupled with the restrictions discussed above will force a consolidation of groups but not necessarily a loss of specialization. Rather, it drives toward a collaborative complex intellectual ecosystem rather than islands of academic monocultures. In industry, the knowledge management arena is pushing rapidly to build peer-to-peer collaborative networks so that individuals in a multinational corporation can collaborate with each other regardless of specialization or physical location. Academia, in its conservative mode, will continue to be a lagging indicator as it also moves in the direction of group collaboration rather than the establishment of individual islands of knowledge. This consolidation will filter into the 13–16 teaching arena as faculties have reduced pressure to play the role of the solitary researcher and are driven more toward the traditional role of scholar/educator.

The natural course of action is to concentrate research under a few key scholars, creating major research groups and subgroups that may be spread across numerous institutions. Internal information sharing coupled with open source publications will reduce the transient scholarly literature, raise its quality, and increase its availability across a larger community both inside and outside academia. Interestingly, this should reduce the overhead and free up more resources for carrying out research. With the pressure to generate income from outside sources through licensing, the ability, through larger collaborations, to carry an idea to commercialization will be enhanced. This will hold across disciplines from the humanities to the hard sciences and applications engineering.

Of course, this concentration could have a countervailing effect by making it harder for individuals, whose ideas may be orthogonal to the mainstreams of intellectual thought, to find a voice. But, in many ways, such creative ideas have always found it difficult to obtain an audience within the established orthodoxy. Ease of publishing ideas on the Internet may increase the exposure to such radical innovation. Only time will provide us with a perspective as to the problems or opportunities afforded by electronic distribution to the intellectually disenfranchised.

THE SELF-REORGANIZING UNIVERSITY

In 1973 George Land wrote a small text, *Grow or Die*, in which he described the traditional sigmoid growth curve familiar to those in biology and the social sciences. His seminal idea, though, was that growth must continue beyond the upper plateau. For this to occur there must be a transformation, a change in the type of growth, in order to see a new sigmoid curve start to generate. His idea lagged behind the mathematics of Poincaré but presaged what is known today as chaos theory. The key is that the transformational change required a leap across a gap, one that is not easily bridged. If that leap cannot be made, then the pattern is to slip back to a point on the rapidly rising slope of the old curve and begin the climb again, creating the hysteresis loop familiar in physics. For many, such behavior leads to collapse or death.

The saving grace in these situations is to look at this growth curve at two levels. The first is the macro, which describes the system behavior, the pattern of all individuals averaged over time. The second, the micro, describes the pattern of an individual. At the macro decision point there will be some early adopters, or risk takers who bridge the gap. As more see the possibility, we get the familiar growth curve for group change, innovators, early adopters, and others who are transforming. We see two curves, the macro-curve of transformational change and the curve depicting how fast the transition progresses. In complex systems, this reorganization and transformation moves inexorably forward. Ants within colonies may be destroyed by catastrophic events, but the colony reorganizes and emerges changed, yet the same. Communities experience catastrophic events; yet, after a suitable time one arises in the morning to find the paper at the door, milk on the shelf of the corner grocer's, and the traffic light functioning at the intersection. Yet in these changes, lives may be lost, buildings replaced by new edifices, and life's patterns changed.

After 500 years has The University of Humboldt, Kant, and Newman reached a plateau in its evolution? In a global society, one striving for pluralism and open access, has the digital revolution and the Internet not only precipitated changes and new opportunities, but also laid bare the problems within The Academy at all levels? Perhaps one of the most profound changes is the acceptance of the fact that, globally, the university is seen to be providing the terminal degree for an individual to enter the workforce. The bar has been raised from secondary degrees to two- and four-year degrees from a postsecondary institution. In fact, many two-year institutions are seriously examining being able to provide their students with the equivalent of a four-year certification. Of course, there are expectations, particularly now that most who attend must pay all or part of the costs. Will this expense yield a return on investment? Thus students arrive, not as supplicants seeking enlightenment, but as consumers looking at a value proposition, within both the academic and larger campus experiences.

In addition to facing a consumer society, the academy is now facing competition, not only from other institutions, once separated by geography, but also from a variety of new, for-profit institutions, spawned by entrepreneurs as well as offshoots from traditional universities. The Internet allows access to a global audience who can select from individual courses, credit and noncredit programs, and a variety of certification routes. The advent of "bulk buyers" such as the U.S. Army, also levels the costs and will force interchangeability of courses, potentially further reducing the basic academic experience to a commodity—a seamless extension of the K–12 experience.

The Internet and the advent of the microprocessor-driven technologies has created a new and emerging generation of cyber natives who are approaching an aging faculty, composed primarily of cyber immigrants. The natives approach learning differently. Attention spans, use of information, values, and needs differ from those of previous students, whether they enter the traditional campus or participate in virtual space.

The academy, like the disturbed ant colony, has reached a transition point. This is true for institutions as well as faculty who, currently, provide the academic experience. While one knows that the system is disturbed, globally, the sun will rise, students will enroll, and the academy will provide. Today, there is a very large hysteresis effect. Institutions are trying to, essentially, put Humpty Dumpty back together again rather than seeing what could, should, or ought to be the direction that must be taken. The current effort has a high-energy input factor to try to reverse the entropic effects of the disturbance.

One of the fundamentals that has been shattered is time-based learning, where students' competency in a particular area is defined by semesters, quarters, or other units of time. We all know that it takes a certain length of time for a pregnancy, to bake a cake, or to travel from point A to point B. And we all know that these times are always approximate. But learning is a different story. The measure of a person's mastery of a particular body of knowledge with a time "yard stick" can be equivalent to measuring a volume of water in a lake with an atomic clock.

The Internet with its "just-in-time" access to knowledge shows the principal fallacies both in the amount of time an individual needs to master that knowledge as well as the use of a time span to validate that the student has such mastery. Additionally, it questions the arbitrary fractioning of the academic experience into time modules, including the familiar four years to achieve a degree. More important, the Internet questions whether the knowledge that has been packaged in the past is still appropriate for inclusion in an educational experience. Part of the rationale for creation of time-based programs started with pre-school and runs through the K–12 curriculum. School is seen not only as a vehicle for providing content skills but also as an institution that provides socialization and serves as the equivalent of "day care." One of the issues is the connection of education to the world outside of the schoolhouse, where life was once tied to the seasons in a largely agrarian economy. Habits are hard to break.

Time was also an artificial method of creating peer groups and keeping them together. The United States has seen the failure of this process when peers reach high school graduation with a lack of basic competency in such skills as reading, writing, and mathematics, having been passed regardless of academic competency. The Myth lies shattered at the level of the university where, as in life, there is a spread of ages in all levels.

Additionally, the "social life" and the life of a scholar have been decoupled, though some simulacrum of integration is still being attempted. College residences are becoming apartment complexes with students often leading dual lives as wage earners and students, much like the previous world of K–12/home; educational experiences are becoming commodified as faculty lead a schizophrenic existence between educational commitments and the world of publish/perish; and the function of the institution has become balkanized into separate operations from admissions to student advising and inter/intramural athletics. In other words, particularly in the larger research institutions, the "community" is held together primarily by the thin thread of tradition.

The ability to access didactic information from electronic sources, coupled with the issue of time, indicates that the entire concept of what is taught needs rethinking. For example, the Internet, through a variety of parties, provides, very easily, the familiar "just-in-time" knowledge. Furthermore, just-in-case knowledge can and is being delivered through the use of "learning objects," modules that can be packaged and reused or accessed on an as needed basis. In the latter case, the idea was to be able to assemble these objects into familiar lessons or courses. Yet, many individuals access these on the web on a "need-to-know" basis. These could be as simple as how to carry out an operation in a spreadsheet to problems as complex as how to handle personnel issues. Included are a plethora of conversations on the larger social and philosophical issues traditionally offered in liberal studies programs.

The business community and students understand this. Pragmatically, they know that the real is in an application. Thus, many see familiar seat time, in both brick and click space, devoted to university mandated/validated acquisition as less than productive. Furthermore, experience in the knowledge management area clearly shows that evaluation out of context may be less than meaningful. This holds for both "just-in-time" and "just-in-case" knowledge.

Moreover, the turning inward to their peers for validation has opened up the role of public intellectual to independent scholars and professionals, many of whom are not affiliated with The Academy. Thus, the intellectual hegemony, the arbitration of values, traditionally inculcated by the university, has been broken.

As we have learned, all textbooks are not equal. The same will hold for didactic knowledge packaged as learning objects. Institutions and faculty approach this understanding with either elation at the thought of markets or fear. What both sides fail to realize is that the very possibility of creating these objects and even full sets of objects points to a changing role of the institution and the faculty. This becomes increasingly clear once one steps outside of the box that defines the "degree" and "classes" in terms of time. Uniform certification, such as a "bachelor's degree," increasingly can be called into question since all institutions are also not created equal. Studies show that while college graduates may have greater potential for earning than non-college graduates, when the cross-institution data are analyzed, these potentials follow a curve that tails at the low end below other, noncollege opportunities. Thus, certification via institutional degrees may be called into question. This becomes increasingly clear as the pressure increases for absolute interchangeability of courses between institutions. In one state in the United States all community college credits transfer fully and equivalently to the more prestigious state university. Professionals such as doctors, lawyers, and nurses have also recognized this for some time and have established external agencies for validating the proficiency of the graduates. Of course, the original institution's imprimatur adds value.

The "open" universities, the mega-institutions exemplified by the British Open University, have, from inception, decoupled the evaluations from the acquisition of knowledge, as have institutions such as Oxford and Cambridge. This deconstruction starts to define the self-organizing university, the catastrophic transformation and recovery from reorganization.

University faculty have obtained their Ph.D.'s, which, today, de facto, implies that they have done original research and will continue on this path. Rapidly being accepted is a variance, termed a "doctorate" with an area of specialization. These degrees imply research was carried out but the person intends, primarily, to be a practitioner of the art rather than a researcher on the intellectual frontiers.

In the K–12 system, many faculty, as part of their continuing education, obtain their doctorates, so that the differences between K–12 and 13–16 faculty start to diminish in the same manner that the split between secondary and postsecondary education loses its catastrophic separation. This implies that the high school student does not transform over the summer from an academic caterpillar into a college "butterfly," and that also the role and function of the university academic and the K–12 faculty may become almost congruent.

What the doctorate or the Ph.D. should define is both the knowledge and the skill set to provide the foundation, or long half-life knowledge, both across and within disciplines. Furthermore, if the university experience is to be reconstructed, the faculty roles must transcend the content arena and must restore the academic community, albeit transformed. Research is neither neglected nor divorced from the university, but it too is reconstructed. As José Ortega y Gasset (1944) has suggested in his *Mission of the University*, centers of excellence will provide core research facilities where academics can concentrate on specific projects when away from their principal duties, working with students. Other faculty not requiring such facilities are also given opportunities for speculative work as may be appropriate. Students will also have opportunities to participate at levels that are appropriate to their needs and skills.

SELF-ORGANIZED UNIVERSITY REPRISED

The rise of the Internet and the larger e-infrastructure has acted as midwife for a transformed university that has been struggling to become visible for over a half century. And it may take close to this time period for institutions to change, in part because of the high sunk capital costs and in part due to the conservative nature of those who compose the academy. But the pins have been knocked out from the barriers holding back the tides of change. The libraries and archives, the sinecures of sacred knowledge, are now ubiquitous in the bits and bytes of cyberspace. Specific content expertise can be found on the emerging semantic web with the click of a mouse; and self-organizing bands of cybernauts surf the web, scavenging and redistributing knowledge in their travels.

But knowledge, not even common knowledge, is not friction free. One of the principal functions of the reorganized university is to provide the long half-life knowledge and the skill sets that will allow students to participate in the emerging knowledge age. To accomplish this, the structure of the institutions must change so that competency is evaluated by measures other than "seat time"; faculty must provide skill sets that do not necessarily encompass the traditional functions of research or preparation of didactic materials. Evaluations may also be separated from the role of the faculty, as we are starting to see in K–12 systems with independently developed testing.

The relationship with students and the larger community will change as lifelong learning becomes standard. Students may receive more than the traditional diploma, cap tassel, and plea from the alumni association; rather, students may see such points as transitions as they continue to remain academically involved. In fact, this lifelong relationship might begin before the end of high school and terminate only with death.

Research remains an enigma. Academics may never see a student except in the context of a research project. Other faculty may never become involved in research or only carry out research on sabbaticals or breaks in teaching. Certain academics and institutions will constitute the core of research and development programs, possibly with other public- and private-sector organizations, shifting the entire publish/perish model, raising productivity, eliminating "noise," and raising the value or reducing the cost for useful bits of research information.

The Academy, which has been composed of traditional public and private institutions, will participate in a global marketplace of ideas, products, and services. Didactic materials may be developed, sold, delivered, and supported by a variety of parties in the competitive markets. Similarly, new relationships will be developed between the institutions and public- and private-sector clients, globally. Faculty may find themselves attached to one or more of these institutions and at a variety of levels from adjunct to chaired faculty. Students will become lifelong learners with the ability to draw from global resources.

What we see is not yet fully manifest. The road is under construction, and the visibility is clouded by the dust created by the rapid evolution. What seems certain in all this haze is that there will be many fatalities, not just of the new entrants on the highway of change, but also existing institutions, both public and private, traveling on the global throughway.

REFERENCES

Ainsworth-Land, George T. (1973). *Grow or Die*. New York: Random House.

Graber, Robert Bates. (1995). *Valuing Useless Knowledge*. Kirksville, Mo.: Truman State University Press.

Gross, Paul, and Norman Levitt. (1998). *Higher Superstition*. Baltimore: Johns Hopkins University Press.

Levitt, Norman. (1998). *Prometheus Bedeviled*. New Brunswick, N.J.: Rutgers University Press.

Ortega y Gasset, José. (1944). *Mission of the University*. Princeton: Princeton University Press.

Prensky, Marc. (2001). *Digital Game-Based Learning*. New York: McGraw Hill. Note that Prensky has a series of articles on this subject in *On the Horizon*, http://www.emeraldinsight.com/oth.htm>. One can also search the Stanford University web site for their new project entitled MediaX, which is predicated on the emerging cyber natives.

Prigogine, Ilya, and Isabelle Stengers. (1984). *Order Out of Chaos*. New York: Bantam.

Rushkoff, Douglass. (1995). *Playing the Future*. New York: HarperCollins.

Shorris, Earl. (1997, September). "In the Hands of the Restless Poor." *Harper's Magazine*, 50–58. For a more extensive discussion, see Earl Shorris (1997). *New American Blues*. New York: W.W. Norton.

Snow, C. P. (1964). *The Two Cultures and a Second Look*. Cambridge: Cambridge University Press.

CHAPTER 14

DOES THE UNIVERSITY HAVE A FUTURE?

Gerard Delanty

THE DEBATE ABOUT THE UNIVERSITY today is very different from some of the major debates on the university over the past century and a half. The grandiose and programmatic visions of the modern university in the seminal works of Cardinal John Henry Newman, Karl Jaspers, Talcott Parsons, Jürgen Habermas, Alvin Gouldner, and Pierre Bourdieu reflected the self-confidence of the university as an institution with a moral and cultural mission. Today the debate has shifted to a defensive stance on the one side and on the other to a largely negative view of the university as an anachronistic institution clinging to a modernity in ruins. On the whole the current debate is dominated by the liberal view of the university as a bastion of high modernity and the postmodern thesis of the obsolescence of the university along with the institutions of modernity in the allegedly global age of informational capitalism. It is the aim of this chapter to offer an alternative view to these positions that look either to culture or to technology.

The liberal conception of the university goes back to the mid-nineteenth century, having its roots in the idea of the university proposed in Cardinal John Henry Newman's famous book, *The Idea of the University* (1852). More of a conservative idea than a liberal one, the aim of a liberal education, according to Newman and many who were to follow him, is to transmit the received wisdom of the past into the minds of youth in order to secure the passing on of tradition. The liberal view of the university thus held to a conception of the university that was essentially reproductive rather than creative of new knowledge. In this view,

242 · *Globalization and Higher Education*

with its origins in English pastoral care and liberal Irish Catholicism, science and the world of research was subordinated to teaching. This vision of the university was resurrected in the 1980s culture wars by conservative and radical liberals alike. Traditional liberals such as Allan Bloom in his *The Closing of the American Mind* (1987) saw the high and universalistic culture of the university under attack by the low and relativistic culture coming from politics and popular cultures. Others, such as Russell Jacoby, saw the universalistic intellectual being overshadowed by the expert, leading to intellectual paralysis of the university. Despite the defensive and varied nature of the liberal response, there was never any doubt that the university could withstand the intrusion of the low culture. As exemplified in the classic work of Pierre Bourdieu, the university houses "state nobility," in which forms of cultural capital are perpetuated.

In the 1990s, as the culture wars abated, another and more potent debate took place that was less defensive than offensive in tone. This has generally been part of the postmodern attack on modernity. The postmodern critique—as in Bill Readings' well-known book, *The University in Ruins* (1996), which was reiterated in Lyotard's *Postmodern Condition* (1997)—argued that as an institution of modernity the university would suffer the same fate as the nation-state. Globalization, it was argued, is eroding the presuppositions of the university as an institution that serves the state. The result is the end of knowledge along with the end of modernity and the end of the nation-state.

Typically some of the arguments that were given were that the university is becoming dominated by market values instead of academic values; partnerships with industry are replacing the pact with the state that was forged in the modern period; science is fleeing the university and being conducted more and more outside the university in laboratories in major corporations. The assumptions behind these positions were that globalization was bringing about the end of the nation-state and that the university always rested on a universal form as defined by a particular understanding of modernity. Even in those accounts that did not use postmodern theories—such as the argument about "mode 2 knowledge production" and the rise of academic capitalism in general—a wide spectrum of writers announced the marginalization of the university.

Against these two scenarios my contention is that a sober look at the university in the longer perspective of history reveals a slightly different picture. The university today is indeed in transition but not in a terminal phase. The assessment in this chapter will be neither one of modernist self-confidence nor one of postmodern crisis. Globalization in fact offers the university the possibility of fulfilling what is perhaps its key role, namely, to provide institutional spaces where cognitive models for society to learn can emerge. In this respect the role of the university cannot be reduced to the specific forms that knowledge takes. Rather, it is the role of the university to connect these cognitive forms.

The chapter is organized into four parts. In the first part I present three concepts of knowledge, arguing that a definition of the university must address each of these. In the second part I describe how a historical and philosophical approach to the question of the university in transition reveals that the university is in a constant process of evolution and that this reflects some of the major epistemic shifts in modern society. In the third part I examine critically some of the assumptions of the globalization thesis that the university is being fundamentally challenged. In the final part I argue that the current shift is one in which new possibilities for the university are emerging.

KNOWLEDGE AND THE UNIVERSITY

What is a university? The Latin *universitas* simply designated a defined group of people pursuing a collective goal and in that sense it suggested something communal. The term was not exclusively applied to universities and indeed many of the ancient universities—Plato's Academy or Aristotle's Lyceum—did not use the term. Universities emerged around the idea of governance, and the many forms of the university from the early middle ages on reflected the diversity of forms of governance, ranging from craft guilds to municipal corporations to state schools. In any case, underlying the university was the attempt to govern something called knowledge. But like the university, there is a diversity of forms of knowledge, making its governance increasingly elusive.

It is useful to begin by defining three kinds of knowledge. We can speak of knowledge as science, knowledge as action, and knowledge as cognition or reflection. Knowledge as science is the most obvious kind of knowledge. It refers to academic knowledge, the creation of new knowledge by scientific inquiry. In contrast to knowledge as science we also have knowledge as action, which might be more broadly called knowledge as doing or praxis. The history of Western thought has been deeply divided on whether this constitutes knowledge. Plato drew a sharp distinction between the high culture of knowledge and the low culture of opinion and banished all forms of opinion from the world of the *logos*. This was the basis of all of the main forms of modernity. However, many of the oppositional currents in modernity drew on *doxa*, ranging from Aristotle's and Marx's *Homo faber*, that humanity makes itself in its own image by action, to contemporary views of the validity of common-sense, everyday, tacit, and local forms of knowledge. Thus, practical knowledge could be a form of pragmatic knowing, that is, knowing by doing. Today the demarcation of science from nonscience is becoming more and more difficult as a result of the growing availability and hence contestability of knowledge, the delegitimation of expertise, and the uncertainty of knowledge.

This suggests a third kind of knowledge, namely, knowledge as cognition. Knowledge is more than knowing in the theoretical and practical modes but is an essentially reflective process. This notion of knowledge is best captured by Hegel's idea of phenomenological knowledge, or in more contemporary terms, by the idea of reflexivity. Knowledge is a transformative and critical endeavor. Cognition pertains to a broader category of knowledge and consists of the capacity to create new things, ways of action, structures from the existing forms and ways of doing things. In this sense it is neither purely theoretical nor practical.

The argument made in this chapter is that it is the third kind of knowledge that the university is to develop. Clearly the first kind of knowledge, knowledge as science, is a central task of the university, but it is not the only one. The growing salience of knowledge as action does not exhaust the forms of knowledge. With this differentiated view of knowledge, some further distinctions can also be made with a view to a provisional definition of the university. In the university, four functions —research, teaching, training, and cultural transformation—are combined. These functions broadly correspond to the roles of researcher/ scientist, teacher, trainer, and intellectual. The diversity of universities is a reflection of the numerous ways these functions are combined.

Looking at the extraordinary diversity of universities that have existed in history—from the ancient, medieval, and modern forms—we can say that the university is an institution that expresses these four functions in a variety of ways. In this respect, what is particularly interesting is how different cultures of knowledge are realized in the university. My thesis is that universities can be seen as a site of cognitive struggle whereby different cultures of knowledge have been formed and have entered into conflict with each other. In the brief sketch that follows I argue that there has been a progressive realization of knowledge as science, knowledge as praxis, and knowledge as cognition. In my view, virtuality, the current technological revolution, does not amount to something fundamentally new but is simply a new space in which old forms of knowledge can be expressed in new ways.

THE UNIVERSITY AND THE TRANSFORMATION OF MODERNITY

Rather than tell the story of the university as one of simple continuity or discontinuity, a more adequate narrative would see it in terms of the transformation of modernity. The university in a very specific sense is a key institution of modernity, and some of the major shifts in modernity have been mirrored in the changing nature of the university. The university and parliament emerged at much the same time, and while the modern state attempted to draw them into its sphere of influence, a certain resistance was always exercised by both parliament and the university to the modern state project. I would like to suggest that what underlies both the university and parliament is a certain discursivity. Parliaments were discursively constituted spaces that set limits to state power and rendered political rule discursive. Universities, too, were essentially discursive spaces in which knowledge was generated, reproduced, and transmitted by public forms of communication. Viewed in this way, the alleged crisis of the nation-state does not herald the end of parliaments and universities and all other forms of communication. As the social theory of Habermas argues, modernity can be viewed in terms of the progressive extension of communication into all spheres of society. Parliaments and other institutions of democracy are today seeking new roles for themselves. This is the case too of universities. But first a few remarks on how universities might be seen in the context of epistemic shifts in modernity.

Four major epistemic shifts occurred with modernity, to which correspond its four main societal forms. In the context of the present debate on the university, each of these corresponds too to the four main forms of the university. The first epistemic shift occurred with the emergence of the cultural project of modernity in the eighteenth century. Articulated around progressive secularization, cultural nationalism, and the institutionalization of science, modernity initially took a pronounced cultural form. The modern university, as symbolized by the Humboldt University and the ideas of Immanuel Kant in his work *The Conflict of the Faculties* (1798), encapsulated this development. The Humboldt University was based on the unity of teaching and research, a unity that reflected the unity of the German nation and the view that teaching is the communication of research. The autonomy of the university, based on the autonomy of knowledge as organized into faculties of reason, was a reflection of the autonomy of the state. It was a reflection of the modern discourse of the self as a creative process, as the idea of *Bildung* indicates.

The Humboldt University stressed research, the autonomy of the professoriate, and the shaping of the self in the encounter with knowledge. It was very influential and the main alternative to the Oxbridge conservative model of the university that emphasized teaching. Within England itself the German model opened up a huge discussion on secularization, as the debate around the foundation of University College in the early nineteenth century attests. However, in time the Enlightenment model became an anachronism and no different from the idea of liberal education. In any case in Germany from the last quarter of the nineteenth century the university was not solely a cultural agent but also an agent of social and economic modernization. By the end of the nineteenth century, modernity was to move into a new phase with the consolidation of the nation-state and industrial capitalism. From the mid-nineteenth to the middle of the twentieth centuries capitalist or "organized" modernity took over from liberal modernity and the university was inevitably drawn into the programmatic and centralizing tendencies in accelerated modernization. This was the age of disciplinary specialization in which university departments replaced faculties, teaching and research were separated, vocational training was introduced, basic and applied research were distinguished, and professional associations were formed. As the social project of modernity took off around the formation of a class society and nation-state, the university inevitably became drawn into its project. In Britain, civic universities were created to serve the needs of the new professional society, and in the United States the Land Grant Act provided for the creation of new state universities that would be alternatives to the liberal education colleges. The kind of knowledge produced by the university was no longer exclusively theoretical but was also practical. However, this practical knowledge was largely concerned with the accreditation of professional competence.

In the first two models modernity was self-consciously outside the great political events of the modern age (bourgeois emancipation movements, the workers movement, the antislavery movement, the suffragette movement, for example). But it was inevitable that the ivory tower would collapse. From an elite institution with the rise of mass society it opened its doors to the nascent professional middle classes and became more and more implicated in the political struggles of what Alvin Gouldner called the "new class." From the 1960s on, the political project of modernity entered the university at about the same time that modernity entered a new phase. In the later decades of the twentieth century, cultural and social projects of its earlier phases reached certain limits. New political currents emerged—feminism, nationalist liberation movements, environmental and human rights movements—eroding the old boundaries of state and society. Politics increasingly entered the university. With this came a more critical and transformative kind of knowledge that could not be contained in either the practical or theoretical structures. The mass university in Europe, America, and the developing world was one of the critical spaces in modern society where new cognitive models emerged, challenging the institutions of modernity in much the same way that the modern university challenged the institutions of the middle ages. Although highly resistant to change, the university by virtue of its mass nature nurtured many new discourses, such as feminism, human rights, environmentalism, and participatory democracy. The form of knowledge that typifies these developments is less theoretical and practical knowledge than cognitive knowledge. New forms of critique and reflexivity were shaped in these movements occurring within universities that were becoming more and more part of the wider public sphere.

In the past ten years or so it has become apparent that another major shift is occurring in modernity, although the full implications of it are hard to measure. While the three earlier shifts were cultural, social, and political, the fourth shift is essentially economic and techno-logical. It is evident in the increased scale of globalization as measured by financial markets, information and communication technologies, the mobility of goods and people, and new transnational processes such as European integration and enlargement. The degree and scale of what might be summed up as globalization will be debated, but for present purposes it can be described as a major shift in the nature of modernity. The central feature of this shift is not the emergence of a single world or Americanization but the increasing intensity of forms of communi-cation unconstrained by time and space. The epistemic shift that this has ushered in is one of virtual knowledge, uncertainty, and diversity. The university has come to reflect this major shift in modernity and like many other parts of society has become fragile. Economic and techno-logical forces have impacted on the university, undermining some of its modernist assumptions based on the idea of autonomy and underpinned by academic self-governance. The question that needs to be answered is whether this fourth shift is undermining the progressive achieve-ments of the first three or is a new model altogether. I am of the view that the rupture is less severe than might appear to be the case.

MYTHS OF GLOBALIZATION

The university today is being restructured. The decline of academic self-governance due to the casualization of academic labor and the loss of intellectual ownership over teaching (although this is not true of much of research) cannot be doubted. External regimes of governance responding to new stakeholders (taxpayers, parents, alumni, investors) have led to greater financial accountability (such as formal audit rank-ings for research, teaching quality). Rather than the traditional academic governance, corporate governance is more the norm, with performance indicators, efficiency, quality, and transparency the order of the day. Internal forms of governance mirror the external ones, with audits of all kinds, ranging from internal reviews to appraisal schemes and self-assessment. There has been a clear move from teacher- to learner-based forms of instruction, with legal accountability becoming part of the everyday life of the academic. New ideologies of governance have emerged, challenging the older ones' accountability, flexibility, and transparency. Just as the department replaced the faculty, the department today is being replaced by programs and disciplinarity and inter-disciplinarity are being displaced by multidisciplinarity. The module reflects the market trend to a prepackaged unit of consumption that can be delivered online by any instructor. Universities are now run by managers not by students or teachers, except what is required for ceremonial adequacy. We can agree too that there is a growing presence of market values in research as well as in teaching, as several contributors to this volume have pointed out.

However, despite these obvious developments, which can be adumbrated at great length, the argument advanced here is that when viewed in the longer perspective of history and in light of the three cultures of knowledge discussed earlier, the current developments can be viewed much differently. The university is a highly resilient institution that has easily adapted to change. It has taken many diverse forms both historically and in the contemporary context. It is unlikely that the technological revolution in communication and information will bring about the end of the university or the end of the other logics of the university. The technological revolution is occurring at the end of a long period of institutional formation and we have little evidence to indicate that the university is unable to respond. As Michael Margolis argues, a shift has occurred from the collegial to the corporate university. However, I would argue this shift is a multidirectional one, not a unilinear one with the corporate university replacing the traditional university. The latter will continue to exist, albeit it will also change and the corporate university will have not an entirely novel form. In this context I would also make the claim that we are not just moving from academic freedom to market freedom, but both coexist.

One question that arises from this, and from other chapters in this volume, is why widening participation must be an overriding normative value. Higher education is good and its greater availability can only be good—even if it will be compromised—but in my view it is an over-valued public good. Participation takes different forms. Thus, higher education need not be reducible to formal accreditation but can have purposes other than serving the legitimating requirement of professional competence. In any case, whatever one's view of this is, my argument has been that the debate on the university must address questions beyond the fiscal crisis of the university, a crisis that has come with widening participation.

250 · *Globalization and Higher Education*

Many of the exaggerated scenarios typically refer to mass teaching providers rather than to research universities. Undoubtedly there will be more of these kinds of institutions. The research function of the university and its graduate programs will not simply fade away with the rise of the corporate virtual university industry.

Those who have responded to the globalization challenge can be divided into those who think globalization is happening on an epochal scale and those who think it is less of a historical shift. Within these groups a further divide is between those who see globalization as a good thing and those who see it as a bad thing. A measured response will be to see it in all these ways. We need to be more broad-minded in assessing its impact and to be more critical in evaluating it. In this respect Jaishree Odin's chapter in this volume is interesting in that it avoids polemics and shows very well how virtual education can be a positive and empowering form of learning. It demonstrates that the traditionalist opposition to virtual instruction is unwarranted. The argument, again, must be that higher education needs to co-opt the new educational technologies, and not simply relegate them to low-grade teaching institutions.

But to the central question as to whether information and communication technologies can save the university, or rather equip it to survive the funding crisis it has entered into with massified mass education, or to use the new term, *widening participation*, my argument is that rather than jump to an affirmative conclusion we need to avoid simple technological determinism. We need to think about the many basic questions relating to the values on which the university is based and we need to scrutinize critically the new values. Academics are not good capitalists and they might be advised to note that some of the euphoria about e-commerce is fading as one dot.com after the other goes bust.

A recent survey in the United Kingdom reveals that many universities are already realizing the false promises of the virtual economy. In December 2001 the U.S. publishing giant McGraw-Hill closed the U.K. arm of its lifelong learning operation, which was devoted to supplying and designing e-learning. This led to a survey that has attracted some attention in the media. The general point emerging from it is that new technologies are not in demand in the United Kingdom for virtual education and are overhyped vendors. A sobering fact as reported in some newspaper articles is that many American institutions are also withdrawing from distance online delivery (e.g., DePaul University in Chicago, which has suffered a drop in enrollments; others were also mentioned). Aside from declining enrollments, sustaining interactive learning is expensive. Online enrollment needs forty students to make it profitable, but on average in the United States these programs get twenty-five and many are not viable at that number. Another newspaper report relating to the report of the Observatory on Borderless Higher Education, set up by the U.K. vice-chancellors last year, warns that many of these virtual programs are not commercially sustainable. Indeed, it is true that virtual universities like Phoenix and UMUC (University of Maryland University College) have large numbers of distance students, but these are mostly U.S. forces personnel. The case of Phoenix is also interesting in that it was unable to sustain interactivity with large classes and had to restrict classes, thus increasing costs to a point that its online courses became more expensive than its on-campus programs.

To what degree generalizations can be made is of course debatable, but it is at least interesting to see that in the media there is a debate about the viability of new technologies for widening participation. What I think these arguments are saying is that higher education is moving to more mixed forms of delivery, with the more positive aspects of online instruction absorbed into traditional teaching; aside from the lower end of the provision and in certain key areas such as professional training (MBA, business), the virtual university is largely a myth. Perhaps a distinction needs to be made between its commercial uses and its pedagogical value. This is also in line with much recent research on the social impact of communication and information technologies, which suggests that these technologies rather than creating new social realities are in fact simply allowing people to do what they always did.

In sum, the debate as I see it is whether the problem of the expansion of higher education can be solved by technology. Obviously, a key question is whether the problem is of widening participation or of outreaching the financial resources to provide for it. I do not think the question of higher education can be posed in fiscal terms for which there are technological solutions. It is wrong in my view to see the university as simply resisting change where it has been allegedly embraced elsewhere. As Peter Wagner has argued in this volume, the European university cannot simply be compared to the American university, where the market is more central.

252 · Globalization and Higher Education

In the final section of the chapter I suggest a different view of the current situation. This will entail looking at higher education in the context of the wider question of the university.

THE UNIVERSITY AND CITIZENSHIP

I see the university as a zone of mediation between knowledge as science (academic or theoretical knowledge) and knowledge as praxis (practical or everyday knowledge). This conception of knowledge suggests a communicative concept of the university as a site of interconnectivity. The university cannot enlighten society as the Humboldtian and Kantian model of the university assumed, nor can it reflect the power and prestige of the nation-state and the aspirations of the professions, but it can provide the structures for public debate between expert and lay cultures. I believe this is how the university can evolve a new identity in the global age.

I argued that the university is a key institution of modernity and is the site where knowledge, culture, and society interconnect. The university is a producer and transformer of knowledge as science and knowledge as culture. It cannot be reduced to either science or culture, for it is an institution that mediates, or interconnects, several discourses in society, in particular, the encounter between knowledge as academic discourse and culturally articulated cognitive structures. Such a cautiously "universalistic" view of the university suggests that its key role is linked to reflexive communication and citizenship.

The identity of the university is thus determined neither by technocratic-managerial strategies nor by purely academic pursuits: in the "knowledge society" knowledge cannot be reduced to its "uses" or to itself because it is embedded in the deeper cognitive complexes of society, in conceptual structures, and in the epistemic structures of power and interests. Rather than being a passive actor, drawn helplessly into the market, it can be a transformer of such value systems. Thus, rather than speak of the demise of the university as a result of the postmodern scenarios of the fragmentation of knowledge, the retreat of the state, and the embracing of market values, the university must find ways to expand reflexively the discursive capacity of society and by doing so to enhance citizenship in the knowledge society.

While recent developments clearly do undermine many of the traditional functions of the university, it is important to see that the university is a resilient institution that has been formed in a continuous process of change. Moreover, there have been many historical as well as national models of the university, which as an institution that is based on universalistic values—such as science and the world scientific community—is also, and necessarily so, very flexible and can accommodate different demands. The limited universalism that is preserved in the university, and which justifies the continued use of the term *university*, despite pluralization and ever greater differentiation, is one of interconnectivity.

The university is one of the few sites in society where several societal functions coincide, albeit within the context of highly specialized domains. The most important of these cognitive functions of the university are the functions of research, teaching, training, and critique. These functions correspond, I have argued, to the roles of the academic as expert, as teacher, as trainer, and as intellectual. To interconnect these functions is a central function of the university and perhaps might be said to constitute a new kind of communicative governance.

Despite specialization within the university, it can hardly be denied that multidisciplinarity and dedifferentiation have become more salient in recent times. As a result there are more opportunities for common interests to emerge. The university is forced to live in a world that has been transformed by knowledge. Due to the scientization of the public, there is a greater consciousness of science and also a growing distrust of expert systems. This means a new role of the university will have to be found as a result of new kinds of communication between expert systems and public discourse. In the knowledge society the university is more reflexively connected with society. This kind of interconnectivity is reflexive, with multiple and reciprocal links. As a result of the new links between the university and society that have arisen due to the scientization of politics, the new technologies and mass education as well as new links between the sciences, the university finds itself drawn more and more into issues of the governance of science.

In recent years in many countries, especially in the Anglo-American world, the university has come under increased scrutiny. Questions are being asked about its role in the emerging knowledge-based economies. No longer isolated from the profane world of the marketplace in which it is increasingly forced to operate, the university must also compete with other institutions for diminishing subsidies and at the same time perform more and more functions. Its existing epistemic structures are also being questioned, as new demands for accountability arise. And as the politics of the risk society penetrate into the academy, the crisis in the legitimacy of science and expertise has inevitable consequences for the university. So far the response of the university has been defensive when it has not been fatalistic. The alternative view put forward here is that the university can take greater responsibility for society than is currently the case. It can become more pivotal to knowledge policies and to citizenship in the emerging technological society. In this kind of society the university is necessary to orient society in coping with societal learning. This communicative function of the university is one of the most crucial tasks it can perform for the wider democratic governance of knowledge.

Central to this project is the challenge of learning to live with choice in a global world of uncertainty. As Zygmunt Bauman has argued, the current period is characterized by seemingly endless choice. Politics is unable to offer solutions to all the problems it is presented with. Many of these problems relate to technology and to culture, perhaps the two most potent forces challenging the nation-state. On the one side, the new technologies (in communications, biotechnology, genetics, financial markets, medicine, and defense) are undermining the older forms of system integration based on the state and, on the other side, the wars over cultural identity and belonging (nationalism, ethnicity and race, religion, communitarian populism) are undermining the older forms of social integration based on the autonomy of the social. The project of modernity as it has traditionally been conceived is poorly equipped to unite these domains and reestablish a principle of unity and purpose, for knowledge has ceased to offer the prospect of emancipation. In the knowledge society everything is knowledge. In the global crisis of the risk society, the Enlightenment's "republic of science" has suffered the same fate as the modern republic. Perhaps it is the role of the university to enable society to live with choice and uncertainty. Taming the new technologies and providing a cultural orientation for society is central to that challenge. It is for this reason that we can speak of the continued relevance of the university.

SELECTED BIBLIOGRAPHY

Aronowitz, Stanley. *The Knowledge Factory: Dismantling the Corporate University and Creating True Higher Learning.* Boston: Beacon, 2000. A political "radical" and academic conservative, Aronowitz connects labor market issues with education in a useful way, but would seem to be a bit nostalgic regarding City College (in the 1930s), his personal experiences as a blue-collar worker who made it, and unions. Perhaps paradoxically, while he rejects Dewey's "largely ignored concept of education for democracy and democracy in education" as "beyond possibility" given the present situation, he offers us a more democratic, integrated version of the old Chicago core: history, literature, science, and philosophy (177). Unfortunately, he seems to lack understanding of the institutional obstacles to his reconstruction. He finds no justification for employing the new technologies (even while he thinks of CD-ROMs and e-mail as the core of this).

Bérubé, Michael, and Cary Nelson (eds.). *Higher Education Under Fire: Politics, Economics and the Crisis of the Humanities.* New York: Routledge, 1995. This volume does not succeed in its promise to "orchestrate" perspectives on the "discourses of fiscal policy, politics and the production of knowledge" (5). Most of the contributors are in English Departments and related fields. Despite the title, there is very little economics (Michael Apple's quasi-Marxist account is an exception), but as the subtitle also suggests, the main concern is the recent cultural wars. Barry Gross's right-wing polemic may be the most interesting.

Clark, Burton R. *Creating Entrepreneurial Universities: Organizational Pathways of Transformation.* Oxford: Pergamon, 2001. Sheldon Rothblatt, an informed historian of higher education, writes (on Amazon): "Here is an exploration, at once empirical and conceptual, in language that is sharp and effective, of the way we live now. Clark looks for and finds pathways out of current difficulties that address that old dilemma in the history of universities: how to escape from the vexations of the present without losing sight of the qualities that made universities so very special in the first place." (Clark has a very good essay in Rothblatt and Wittrock, below).

Cole, Jonathan R., Elinor G. Barber, and Stephen R. Graubard (eds.). *The Research University in a Time of Discontent.* Baltimore: Johns Hopkins University Press, 1993. This volume is mainly a defense of current practices in higher education: not surprising given that the contributors include five presidents (two emeriti), one VP (of Rockefeller), two provosts, the CEO of the Academy of Sciences, the president emeritus of the Association of American Universities, the editor of *Daedalus*, and three well-known neo-conservative social scientists.

Currie, Jan, and Janice Angela Newson (eds.). *Universities and Globalization: Critical Perspectives*. Thousand Oaks, Calif.: Sage, 1998. This volume is excellent for comparative work on higher education, including Currie on Australia and America, Sheila Slaughter on Canadian universities, Donald Fisher and Kjell Rubenson on Norway, Arild Tjeldvoll on higher education reform in Australia and France, and Robert Lingard and Fazal Rizvi on the impact of NAFTA on Mexican universities.

Delanty, Gerard. *Challenging Knowledge: The University in the Knowledge Society*. Buckingham, England: Open University Press, 2001. If we had to pick one book, this would be it. Delanty offers a very well-informed account of the modern university in transition, from its beginnings to today. He seems to have read everyone that is pertinent (including participants at the conference behind this book) and has put it together in a convincing way. He argues that the late 1960s and 1970s were critical, both as regards "organized modernity," a dramatic shift in the production and legitimation of knowledge, and then as regards the self-understanding of the university. But unlike those who hold to grim scenarios (either postmodern or instrumentalist), he offers that the role of the university could be enhanced in a direction that would contribute to more democratic and cosmopolitan forms of citizenship.

Duderstadt, James J. *A University for the 21st Century*. Ann Arbor: University of Michigan Press, 2000. Duderstadt writes as a former president of the University of Michigan. The book is disappointing, partly because of the neatly bulleted style and because some of the ground is familiar. He has, however, a deep appreciation of governance issues ("the history of higher education in America suggests that, in reality, the faculty has had relatively little influence over the evolution of the university" [247]), the causes and consequences of "privatization," and the challenge of the new technologies that could promote "the growth of entirely new learning organizations" (304). This book could be read in conjunction with Ruch and Delanty.

Inayatullah, Sohail, and Jennifer Gidley (eds.). *The University in Transformation: Global Perspectives on the Futures of the University*. Westport, Conn.: Greenwood, 2000. This volume contains a range of essays (some by the participants of the conference behind this book) on pertinent topics. Very good comparative materials.

Jarvis, Peter. *Universities and Corporate Universities: The Higher Learning Industry in Global Society*. London: Kegan Paul, 2001. A professor of continuing education, Jarvis argues that globalization forces "a learning market" in which established institutions no longer have a monopoly, given the increasing importance of "corporate universities." Corporate universities are understood not as universities as corporations, but as institutions like McDonald's Hamburger University, which includes a twenty-two-language simultaneous facility and has trained 65,000 managers. By 1995, there were over 1,000 corporate universities with budgets totaling over $52 billion (113). Distance education, led by the British Open University, is "one of the easiest ways of marketing education" and developing technologies will extend this. Quoting Kenny-Wallace, "traditional universities are no longer the dominant players in the creation and communication of knowledge, especially in cyberspace. Just-in-case education has moved to just-in-time and just-for-you . . . Plato.com has arrived" (113). Jarvis concludes that since the traditional university does not know what it is, it is easy for a wholly instrumental discourse to dominate.

Lucas, Christopher J. *Crisis in the Academy: Rethinking Higher Education in America.* New York: St. Martin's, 1996. A historical account that demystifies some prevailing beliefs, for example, about general education, tenure, open admission, the culture of faculties, and governance. Lucas offers some very positive ideas for reform, including, for example, abandoning the idea of a disciplinary department as an autonomous unit for resource allocations and redesigning administrative configurations that would enable realizing clearly articulated goals, which include the development of skills, general education, vocational training, and then assessing the outcomes: an effort at "truth-in-advertising." The volume is weak on new technologies and their potential.

Readings, Bill. *University in Ruins.* Cambridge, Mass.: Harvard University Press, 1996. Completed just prior to his death in the crash of American Eagle flight 4184, Readings' book is provocative, but too often obscure and intemperate. The basic argument is that the modern university came into existence as an embodiment of German idealist thought, mediated by Humboldt and Newman, and had as its goal the transmission of "culture." But since "the nation-state is no longer the primary instance of the reproduction of global capitals, 'culture'—as the symbolic and political counterpart of the project of integration pursued by the nation-state—has lost its purchase" (12). Readings concludes that "we should try to replace the empty idea of excellence with the empty name of Thought." Unlike "excellence," Thought "does not masquerade as an idea" (160). "Thought demands that we ask what it means, because its status as mere name—radically detached from truth—enforces that question" (160). "Cultural Studies," for him, is not a possible answer since "culture no longer matters as an *idea* for the institution" (91). The history is dubious, and the analysis, both abstract and overgeneralized, would seem to be distorted by Readings' disciplinary and theoretical perspective.

Rothblatt, Sheldon, and Bjorn Wittrock (eds.). *The European and American University Since 1800: Historical and Sociological Essays.* Cambridge: Cambridge University Press, 1993. This volume contains the most useful set of historical and comparative overviews. See especially essays by Clark and Wittrock.

Ruch, Richard S. *Higher Ed, Inc.: The Rise of the For-Profit University.* Baltimore: Johns Hopkins University Press, 2001. Ruch's book is an extremely helpful account of the rise of the for-profit educational institutions and the consequences for the non-profits. For him, "the question and the challenge is not whether to become more responsive, but how to do so in the face of a tradition of resistance, a history of inertia, and a system of decision making that inhibits quick decisions and rapid response to change" (151).

Slaughter, Sheila, and Larry L. Leslie. *Academic Capitalism: Politics, Policies, and the Entrepreneurial University.* Baltimore: Johns Hopkins University Press, 1999. This volume is a generally conventional social scientific examination of critical aspects of higher education, including in the argument self-conscious "theory" and a good deal of quantitative information and survey research materials. The authors conclude: "We see academic capitalism in general, and science and technology in particular, as bringing about broad change in higher education to the point where the center of the academy has shifted from a liberal arts core to an entrepreneurial periphery" (207). Two "scenarios," a worst case and a best case (242–245), are very persuasive, and neither is encouraging.

Smith, Charles W. *Market Values in American Higher Education: The Pitfalls and Promises.* Lanham: Rowman and Littlefield, 2000. Smith finds a number of "false diagnoses and faulty cures," for example, serious misreading of the fiscal and organizational realities, which have resulted in a "paste and mix response" to growth in higher education. He argues that we need to decide what we want and determine clearly what we have, and concludes with some "guiding principles" and specific recommendations.

Solomon, Robert and John. *Up the University: Recreating Higher Education.* Reading, Mass.: Addison Wesley, 1993. A professor of philosophy and his brother, a professor of classics, offer an energetic look at the university from "the inside." The book is fun reading. They have one very powerful thesis: universities exist to teach undergraduates, but indeed, they are currently structured so as to make this nearly impossible. The obstacles begin with corporate administration, and extend to distortion regarding "research," the Ph.D. dissertation, the institutionalization of departments, and the reward system of faculty, including cynical "teaching awards" and the tenure system. The Solomons reject nailing the faculty as "easy targets" (e.g., as with Sykes's *Profscam*) and argue for strong faculty governance; but they are not clear whether many (or most) faculty are clear themselves about what they should be doing and just cannot, or whether the typical faculty's warm endorsement of "liberal education" suggests that they are serious victims of ideologies that sustain all those practices that they rightly condemn.

Spring, Joel. *Education and the Rise of Global Economy.* Mahwah, N.J.: Erlbaum, 1998. Spring had argued (in *Education and the Rise of the Corporate State*, 1972) that "only elimination of government-operated schools could produce the freedom of thought required for the exercise of democratic power" (xi). He now sees this to be naïve "in the face of the uncontrolled power of global corporations." Accordingly, he thinks that "the right to an education should include an education in human rights and democratic power." Some useful data, but the analysis is thin.

Sykes, Charles J. *Profscam: Professors and the Demise of Higher Education.* New York: St. Martin's, 1990. Sykes holds the professoriate singularly responsible for most of the problems in higher education. The Solomons (above) quote one illustrative piece from Sykes's text: "The story of the collapse of American higher education is the story of the rise of the professoriat. No understanding of the academic disease is possible without an understanding of the Academic Man, this strange mutation of 20th-century academia who has the pretensions of an ecclesiastic, the artfulness of witch doctor, and the soul of a bureaucrat. Almost single-handedly, the professors have destroyed the university as a center of learning and have desolated higher education" (see Solomon and Solomon, 204f).

White, Geoffrey D. (ed.). *Campus, Inc.: Corporate Power in the Ivory Tower.* Amherst: Prometheus, 2000. The volume is a collection of essays by "leftish" critics, including David Noble, Michael Parenti, Leonard Minsky, Sheila Slaughter, Howard Zinn, Michael Zweig, and Ralph Nader. Some are too brief, some offer critiques of specific aspects of the problem, and some provide small case studies.

LIST OF CONTRIBUTORS

Tom P. Abeles is president of Sagacity, Inc., a member of the Global Alliance for Transnational Education, and the editor of *Horizon*. He is currently developing a virtual campus for the graduate school at Hamline University. Dr. Abeles has been active in discussions, in print and online, of the implications of the digital revolution.

Alan Bowen-James is CEO of NextEd, an Asia-based provider of online learning solutions for the corporate, professional, and higher education markets. Founded in Hong Kong in 1998, NextEd has eight offices in Australia, China, Hong Kong, Malaysia, the United Kingdom, and the United States.

Jan Currie is associate professor of education at Murdock University, Australia. She is co-editor of *Universities and Globalization: Critical Perspectives* (Sage, 1998).

Gerard Delanty is professor of sociology at the University of Liverpool, United Kingdom. He was visiting professor at York University, Toronto, in 1998, and visiting professor at Doshisha University, Kyoto, Japan, in 2000. He is author of *Inventing Europe: Idea, Identity, Reality* (Macmillan, 1995), *Social Theory in a Changing World* (Polity, 1999), *Modernity and Postmodernity: Knowledge, Power, the Self* (Sage, 2000), *Citizenship in a Global Age* (Open University Press, 2000), and *Challenging Knowledge: The University in the Knowledge Society* (Open University Press, 2001). Professor Delanty is editor of the *European Journal of Social Theory*.

Leonardo Garnier is a political economist at the University of Costa Rica. His writings have focused on the problems of globalization and human rights. He has had extensive experience with UN agencies, Programa de las Naciones Unidas para el Des (PNUD), and Economic Commission for Latin America and the Caribbean (ECLAC), and most recently with UNICEF in Ecuador.

Su Hao is chair of the Department of Diplomacy of the College of Foreign Affairs at Beijing University, China, and recently a Fulbright Fellow at Columbia University. He has had a continuing interest in the consequences of globalization on higher education in China.

Sohail Inayatullah does extensive work in Australian and East Asian universities, especially on corporatization, the Internet, multiculturalism, democratization, and organizational transformation. He is co-editor of *The University in Transformation: Global Perspectives on the Futures of the University* (Greenwood, 2000).

Charles Karelis is former president of Colgate University and, for many years, was program director of the Fund for the Improvement of Postsecondary Education

(FIPSE), the U.S. Department of Education. In the latter capacity he was involved with a host of innovative programs.

Peter T. Manicas is professor of sociology and director of the liberal studies program at the University of Hawai'i at Mānoa. He has authored many books and articles, and has only recently turned his attention to problems in higher education.

Michael Margolis is professor of political science, University of Cincinnati, and the author of the widely read essay, "Brave New Universities," and with David Resnick, *Politics as Usual: The "Cyberspace Revolution"* (Sage, 2000).

John J. McDermott is Distinguished Professor of Philosophy and Humanities, Texas A&M University. He was a Danforth Fellow and is the author of many books and articles on American culture and philosophy, including philosophy of education.

Jaishree K. Odin is an associate professor in the liberal studies program at the University of Hawai'i at Mānoa. She has published extensively on online pedagogy and the implications of the new technologies. More recently, she served as assistant dean for Outreach College, responsible for developing various entirely new online programs for UH Mānoa.

Richard S. Ruch is author of *Higher Ed, Inc.: The Rise of the For-Profit University* (Johns Hopkins University Press, 2001). He has served as chief academic officer at DeVry College of Technology, and as dean of the College of Business Administration at Rider University. He is currently studying theology at Princeton Theological Seminary.

Charles W. Smith is professor of sociology at Queens College, CUNY, New York, and a former dean, provost, and assistant to the president at Queens College. He is author of *Market Values in American Higher Education: The Pitfalls and the Promises* (Rowman and Littlefield, 2000), *Understanding the Mind of the Market* (Rowman and Littlefield, 1999), and *Auctions: The Social Construction of Value* (The Free Press, 1989). Professor Smith is the editor of *Journal for the Theory of Social Behavior.*

Scott L. Thomas, Institute of Higher Education at the University of Georgia, has authored (and co-authored) a number of important studies of student attitudes and the income effects of higher education, including differences in outcomes for graduates of types of institutions.

Peter Wagner, University of Warwick, is currently based at the European University Institute in Florence. His publications include *The Scholar's Space: A Topography of Academic Practices* (with Heidrun Friese, in German, Berlin, 1993); *A Sociology of Modernity* (London, 1994); *The Social Sciences and the State: France, Italy, Germany, 1870–1980* (in German, Campus, 1990). Wagner was with the *Wissenschaftszentrum Berlin für Sozialforschung* and the Free University of Berlin, and has conducted research at the *Centre National de la Recherche Scientifique*, Paris, the Institute for Advanced Study, Princeton, the Swedish Collegium for Advanced Study in the Social Sciences, Upsala, and the Center for Studies in Higher Education at the University of California, Berkeley.

Index

Abeles, Tom, xix, 22, 221
academic decision making, 13, 37, 51, 60, 69, 76–77, 95. *See also* governance
academic freedom, 27, 37, 51, 53; and market freedom, 249; study of, in Australia, 56–57
academic standards, 57, 88, 128; declining, 149
access: to education, 5, 17, 25–26, 106, 142, 143, 149, 250; the Internet and, 45, 148, 250; to student services, 149
accountability, 51, 57, 60, 78, 90
accreditation, 31, 85, 88, 122, 249; process of, 86; standards for, 87
Adelman, Clifford, 113
Adler, Mortimer, 100
administration, 51, 80; cost of hierarchical, 80; student-friendly, 98, 204
administrator(s), 26, 27, 74, 81
Allport, C., 48
Annan, Kofi, 47
Appadurai, A., 43
Arendt, Hannah, 21
Argosy Education Group, 84, 91–92
Aristotle, 21, 135, 243, 244

Bauman, Zygmunt, 254
Bayh-Dole Act, 26
Bildung, xviii, 246
Birnbaum, R., 49
Bloom, Allan, 242
Boesky, Ivan, 109
Bok, Derek, 27
Bordo, Michael, D., 169
Bourdieu, Pierre, 115, 241, 242
Bowen, Howard, 113
Bowen-James, Alan, xix, 3–5
Boyer, Ernest, 142
Brabazon, T., 52
Brainard, Jeffrey, 27
Breneman, David, 36

Brint, Stephen, 116
British Open University, 33, 230, 237
Bromwell, Nick, 28
Brown, P., 44
Bull, Hedley, 170
Bussey, Marcus, 208

capitalism, xvii, 42, 142; varieties of, 19, 43. *See also* neo-liberalism
Carnegie Foundation Study, 51
Chambers, John, 203
Chang, Flora, 205
Chipman, Lauchlan, 59
Chun, Marc, 95
Cicero, 99
Clark, Ian, 171
Coady, Tony, 55
Cole, M., 153
collaborative learning, 145, 155–156
college degree and earning power, 82, 89, 116–120; *Chart 1*, 108, *Chart 3*, 117
collegiality: democratic, 53, 54, 60, 87; loss of, 52–53, 56, 249; networks of, 229
Collier, R., 53
commodification: college degree and, 226; of education, 69, 194–200, 225, 236; of knowledge, 21, 47, 53, 69, 191–193, 225, 231
community: balkanization of, 52, 217, 236; business, 237; colleges, 113; distance-independent, of learning, 145, 148, 149, 223; learning and research, 87, 129, 145; networking, 227; as regulative, 11–13, 232; of scholars, 52; service, 35
Considine, M., 55, 58
constructivist: pedagogy, 155–156; theorists, 154
consumer society, 150, 235
corporatization of the university, 26, 36–38, 45, 69, 78, 128, 149, 166, 249; criticism of, 36–38

correspondence schools, 85
cost-effectiveness, 20, 69, 83, 93
costs, 35, 48, 66, 74, 77, 79; and benefits of college, 85–86, 117–120, 224; and debt burden, *Chart 4*, 119; of going to college, 110, 224; of growing administration, 80; instructional, 32; tuition, 79, 109
course(s) 37, 79, 91, 236; content, 88, 89; hybrid, 149; interchangeability of, 237; modularization of, 226–227; online, 149; postgraduate, 54, 55, 57; value-added, 226. *See also* curriculum
Cowen, Scott, 95
cultural: capital, 115, 120; citizenship, 152; identity, 194
culture(s), 70; diversity of, 58, 59; dominant, 74; goals, 69, 73; interconnections between, 152; plurality of, 43, 46, 152; unity of, 152. *See also* multiculturalism
curriculum: development of, 91, 92, 97; faculty control over, 51, 88, 89; frag- mented (modularization of), 145, 236, 249; instrumentalism in, 47, 190; inter- nationalizing of, 46, 173–174; issues, 77, 127; K–12, 236; multiculturalism and, 208–209; rethinking, 150–153; shift in, 94, 107, 144
Currie, Jan, xv, xvi, xviii, 5, 17, 149

Danforth, Samuel, 131
David, Paul, 192
de Alva, Jorge, 92
Delanty, Gerard, xv, xvi, xviii, xix, 14, 128, 221–222
democratization, in Asia, 211–213; of the university, 60
De Vry, 88, 91, 92, 97
Dewey, John, 34, 35, 100–101, 128, 133, 135, 151, 154
digital: growing, divide, 48; "natives" and "immigrants," 153–154, 235
Dillenbourg, P., 155
diploma mills, xv, 66
distance education/learning, xvii, 48, 87, 121, 133, 141, 174; assumed rationale of, 28–34, 45–46; cost of, 29, 32, 52, 250–251; criticism of, 34–35; and face- to-face teaching, 127, 134–138; impact on on-campus students, 149; and partici- pation, 250–251; and pedagogy, 153–159, 236, 250. *See also* digital; online educa- tion; technologies, new
Duderstadt, James, xv, xvi, 154

Eaten, Judith, 87–88
economic: advantages, 115; investment in college, 111; returns, 107; value of college degree, 85–86, 104, 109, 115, 117–120, *Charts* 1 & 2, 108
economy, 7, 14, 44, 94; agrarian, 100; global, 42, 47; globalized, 104, 105; globalizing, 66; knowledge, 46, 66, 105
education. *See* higher education
Educational Management Corporation, 84, 88, 91, 92
efficiency: and electronic technologies, 137; goal of, 142; luxury of inefficiency as opposed to, 89–90; organizational, 18, 20; of support services, 149
Eichengreen, Barry, 169
Eisenstein, Elizabeth, 148
enrollment, xvi, 25, 26, 34, 45, 55, 88, 94, 95, 106–107, 109

faculty: adjunct/part-time, 27, 74, 90, 92, 230; as agents, 28, 35, 38, 81, 127, 144, 211, 258; as corporate employees, 26–27; credentials, 87; full-time, 48, 89, 90, 91, 92, 230; meetings, 95; roles: teaching, research, governance, 27, 51, 56, 60, 91–93, 216, 232–233, 236, 238; shifting from tenure-track to adjunct, 141; spe- cialization, 228; unions, 73; untenured, 27; use of technology, 58, 129, 158, 205
for-profits, xv, 31, 45, 48, 66, 101; faculty and, 89–93; growth of, xviii, 106; lessons from, 93–98; and market, 85–86; missional diversity of, 66; nonprofits' relationship with, 32, 66, 83–85, 96, 101; quality and, 86–87; transformation of traditional model and, 93; values and, 88–89
Freud, Sigmund, 135
funding higher education, xv, 10, 25–26, 44, 55, 59, 77, 79, 202, 205; in Asia, 212–213; fees, tuition and, 15, 57, 66, 109; in Latin America, 182. *See also* market

Gardner, Howard, 100
Garnier, Leonardo, xv, xvi, xviii, xix, 17, 19, 20, 21, 165, 166
Gilbert, Alan, 59
Giroux, Henry A., 152
globalization, xiv, 3, 14, 69, 138, 139, 165, 167, 173, 222; as Americanization, 8; contested meanings of, xvi, 7–8, 42; and knowledge, 191; microprocesses of, 49;

modernity and, 242, 248; as multidimensional process, 10–11; myths of, 18–21, 248–251; neo-liberal, 44–45; new cognitive models and, 243; privatizing forces of, 202; three dimensions of, 7–12

globalized political elites and higher education, 171–173; China and, 176–178

Gouldner, Alvin, 241

governance: academic self-, 248; communicative, 253; declining faculty, 128, 149; in for-profits, 88, 97–98; hierarchical vs. non-hierarchical, 51, 73, 76–77, 80, 87, 97; redefining, 94, 97. *See also* academic decision making

Graber, Robert Bates, 225

Graff, Gerald, 145

Grant, James, 208

Guan-you, Lee, 175

Gumport, Patricia, 95

Habermas, Jurgen, 241, 245

Hall, Peter, 19, 43

Hamilton, Clive, 59

Hao, Su, xv, xvi, xviii, xix, 17, 165

Hegel, G. W. F., 244

Henderson, I., 47

higher education: diversity of, xv, 15, 93; and globalization, xiv, 4–5, 9–11, 16–18, 44–45, 69, 104, 190–193, 202, 248–250; goals of, 25, 29, 70, 85, 98–101, 144–145, 204, 225–228; growth of, 106; history of, 13–15, 204, 223–225, 241–243; massification of, 29, 45, 247, 249; mission of, 15, 74, 75, 86, 89, 93, 94, 97, 150, 152; new organizational models in, 96, 148, 238–240; as public good, 21–22, 195; varieties of, xv–xvi, 15–16. *See also* university

Higher Education Research Institute at UCLA, student survey, 85–86, 109

Hiltz, Roxanne, 155

Humboldt, Wilhelm von, 12, 13, 152, 222, 234, 252; University, 246

Inayatullah, Sohail, xv, xvi, xix, 10, 166

intellectual: center in traditional and for-profit institutions, 89–93; property, 47, 57; standards, 49

interdisciplinary programs, 128, 145, 150, 249, 253. *See also* curriculum

Internet, 42, 174, 205, 214, 236; course materials and, 159; cyber natives and, 235; distance education/learning and,

xvii, 31, 32, 33, 45, 48, 221; global communities and, 229; information access and, 148, 227; the university and, 238. *See also* distance education/learning; online education; technologies, new

Irvin, Douglas, A., 169

Isocrates, 99

Jacoby, Russell, 242

James, William, 136

Jaspers, Karl, 241

Jonassen, D. H., 153

Jones International University, 36

Joy, Bill, 131, 132

Julius, Daniel, 97

Kaczynski, T. J., 131–132

Kant, Immanuel, 13, 222, 234, 246, 252

Karabel, Jerome, 114, 116

Karabell, Zachary, 90, 93

Karelis, Charles, xvii, xviii, xix, 127, 128, 150, 152, 197, 221

Kayrooz, C., 56

Kemshal-Bell, Guy, 157

Kimball, Bruce, 98, 99, 100

knowledge, xix, 70, 74, 98; advancement of, 92; commodification of, 190–200; decoupling production and dissemination of, 121; democratization of, 148; dissemination of, 74, 115, 200; ecologies, 227; instrumentalizing of, 150, 192, 195; -intensive society, 153; "just-in-case," xix, 225–228, 236, 237; "just-in-time," xix, 228–229, 232, 235, 236–237; kinds of, 243–245; knowing and sharing of, 101; meaning and function of, 128; production of, 14, 49, 159; representation of, 155; technology-mediated model, 156; traditional model, 154, 204

Krugman, Paul, 47

Land, George, 233

Land Grant Act, 85, 247; Morrill, 100

leadership, 97; hierarchical, 76, 77; top-down, 77; universities providing, 194

Leslie, Larry, xv

liberal: education, 94, 98–100, 107, 113, 127, 143–144, 226, 241; studies, 225, 226, 237; values, 145, 221

library, 29, 87, 134, 135, 223, 224, 227; access and, 74; archives and, 239; electronic, 174; multiculturalism and, 210; services, 149

Lucas, Christopher, 151
Lyotard, Jean-François, 150, 242

managerialism: and Anglo-American universities, 58, 80, 81; in higher education, 47, 49, 50, 52, 54, 56, 58, 60. *See also* academic decision making
Marginson, S., 55, 58
Margolis, Michael, xvii, xviii, 5, 17, 149, 249
market: efficiency, 17, 28, 46, 141, 195–196; elite university and, 35, 197, 202; forces, 42, 47, 59, 94, 95, 150, 189; free, 59, 78; functioning in higher education, viii, 9, 11–15, 21, 31, 66, 73–81, 88, 140–144, 200–201, 252; labor, 107, 109, 111; misunderstanding of, 47, 71–73; -place, 46, 85, 88, 89, 145, 150, 239; processes, 73, 74; as sense of freedom, 59; standard, 49; stock, 72, 81; the university and, values, 141–142, 242. *See also* commodification; globalization; neo-liberalism
Marx, Karl, 244
Mayne, Alan, 171
McDermott, John J., xix, 127, 128
McGrew, Anthony, 167, 168
McGuire, Patricia, 89
McInnis, 56
McLoughlin, C., 156
McLuhan, Marshall, 168
Meikeljohn, Alexander, 145
Merton, Robert, 12
meritocracy, 114
Milken, Michael, 109
Modelski, George, 169
multiculturalism: Americanization and, 8; commodification of knowledge and, 166; knowledge and, 165; neo-liberal, 42; politically neutral, 42; processes of, 165; skepticism about, 46–47; the university and, 207–211; world politics and, 167–171

Nandy, Ashis, 207
National Bureau of Economic Research study (1999), 86
National Center for Education Statistics (NCES), 82–83, 106
neo-classical economic theory assessed, 73, 166, 194–199
neo-liberalism, vii, 3, 5, 45, 165, 188; characterized, 42; consequences of, 55. *See also* market; globalization
Newman, John Henry, 25, 34, 35, 234, 241

Noble, David, 32

Odin, Jaishree K., xviii, xix, 22, 33, 128, 250
O'Kane, M., 49–50
Oliver, R., 156
online: education, 33, 36, 46, 52, 128, 148–149; instructor and student survey of, education, 157–158; learning, xvii, 48, 155–158; learning and traditional institutions, 149; partnerships, 149; providers and recipients of, education, 34, 48. *See also* distance education/learning; Internet; technologies, new
Organization for Economic Cooperation and Development (OECD): countries, 45, 185, 209; report, 179
Ortega y Gasset, José, 238

Parsons, Talcott, 241
Patten, James van, 173
Peck, K. L., 153
Pierson, C., 44
Plato, 98, 99, 132, 243, 244
Poincaré, Henri, 234
Polanyi, Karl, 71, 200
postsecondary education 104, 224, 225; in the US, 105, 106, 107; value of, 116. *See also* higher education
Prensky, Marc, 153
price, 85, 71, 72, 76, 86. *See also* commodification; market
privatization, xvi–xvii, 59; in Australia, 47

Quintilian, 99

Readings, Bill, 152, 242
reform(s), 20, 55; in the curriculum, 147, 150–153; Dawkins, in Australia, 55; of pedagogy, 153–159
research, 27, 35, 127, 250; as assumed task, 128, 143; criteria in tenure, 27; deconstruction of, 232–233; duplication of, 90–91; funding of, 26–27, 48, 56–57, 141
Royce, Josiah, 138
Ruch, Richard S., xv, xvi, xvii, xviii, 19, 66, 67

Salais, Robert, 19
Sarkar, P. R., 208
Schneider, D., 155
Schwartz, Steven, 59
Sen, Amartya, 197
Shorris, Earl, 225

Singh, M., 53
Slaughter, Sheila, xv
Smith, Charles W., xvii, xviii, xix, 17, 19, 65, 66, 67, 71, 78, 142, 189, 196
Snow, C. P., 229
Socrates, 98, 127, 132
Sophists, 99
Soros, George, 46–47
Soskice, David, 19, 43
Southwick, Ron, 27
Sperber, Murray, 25
Sperling, John, 92
Storper, Michael, 19
students: attitudes: xvi, 85–86, 109, 202, 205, 234; as consumers, 20, 107, 111, 142–144, 196–199; global potential of, xiv; traditional, 32, 82, 107
Sullivan, William M., 25
Summers, Lawrence, 172

Task Force on Higher Education and Society, 181, 182, 190–191
Taylor, Kit Sims, 28
teaching: face-to-face, 139; as performance, 231–233; rethinking, 153–159, 215; vs training, 25, 47, 84
technologies, new: consequences of using, 132, 133; and efficiency, 137; instructional, 158; investment in, 76, 140, 141; and pedagogy 105, 128, 134, 153–159; students and, 226–228; uses of, xviii, 94, 127, 128, 221. *See also* distance education/learning; Internet; online education
Tehranian, Majid, 215
tenure, 27, 28, 37, 51, 78, 84. *See also* faculty
tertiary education, 45
Thomas, Scott L., xv, xvi, xviii, xix, 17, 20, 66
Tierney, William, 94
Trow, Martin, 29
tuition, 31, 66, 79, 110; as fee in Australia, 54–55
Twigg, Carol A., 37

United Nations Economic Commission for Latin American and the Caribbean (ECLAC), 184
United Nations Educational, Scientific and Cultural Organization (UNESCO), 175, 181
United States Bureau of Labor Statistics, 105

university, the: American, xvi, 25–28, 111–114; Asian, 207, 208, 211, 212; Australian, 54–59; borderless, 45; Canadian 50, 54; Chinese, 173, 176, 177; commercialization of, 47; corporate, 24, 203–204; culture, 60; European, 15, 16; as a firm, 18; the future of, 54, 159–161, 214–218, 238–240, 252–254; governance of, from historical perspective 13–15; internationalization of, 46; Latin American, 181–186; legitimating function of, 53; management of, 49–51, 60; market rationality and, 18; mission of, 25; modernity and, 245; neo-liberal globalization and, 44; organizational efficiency and, 18; as a place of dissensus, 152, 217; privatized, 48, 59; research and corporate funding for, 26, 206; restructuring of, 51, 93–96, 104, 238–240; self cultivation and, 142; site of interconnectivity and, 252–254; transformation of, 54; the western model and, 245–247. *See also* corporatization of the university; higher education
University of Phoenix, xvii, 36, 66, 88, 90, 92, 93

Values, 47, 60, 71, 72, 76, 77, 83, 94, 115; classical, 100; cultural and civic, 69; educational, 101, 140, 141, 142; and liberal education, 221; loss of traditional, 53–54
virtual university, xvii, xviii, 206–207, 215, 229–232, 250, 251
vocational training, 19, 47, 48, 67, 73, 100
Vygotsky, Lev, 154

Wagner, Peter, xv, xviii, 3, 5, 222, 251
Weber, Max, xvii, 115
Whitehead, Alfred North, 135
Wildman, Paul, 208
Wilson, B. J., 153
Wilson, Woodrow, 144, 145
Winston, Gordon, 140, 141
Woody, Todd, 3
World Bank Public Sector Expenditure Report, 182
World Development Report, 182–183, 191

Young, Michael, 114
Yudoff, Mark, 27